I'd like to commend Tim for putting together a very courageous book. Not only does *The Mystery Experience* go further than any other book I've come across in trying to clarify what is meant by enlightenment or the awakened state, but it also exceeds all expectations in its ability to pull together the seemingly disparate views of science and spirituality to form a coherent whole that embraces both.
Stephen Gawtry, editor of *The Watkins Review*

Tim Freke's work is an open door inviting one and all into the Mystery.
Ram Dass, author of *Be Here Now*

All I can say is WOW! I was totally absorbed, stunned and knocked out by the sheer beauty of the book. It's not a word I use very often, but this is a work of genius. A real tour de force.
Peter Gandy, author of *The Jesus Mysteries*

In this remarkably erudite, yet delightfully easy-to-read book, my esteemed friend Tim addresses the very heart of the imponderable mystery of existence, kits you up with all the equipment you need for the journey to reach it, along with one of the clearest maps available, wraps it all up neatly and gives it you as a present you'll cherish forever.
Barefoot Doctor, author of *The Message*

Tim Freke is a unique voice in contemporary spiritual teaching. He is a hugely entertaining twenty-first century street-wise commentator. At the same time he has a deep understanding of human spirituality and is one of the most well-versed scholars of the world's religions.
William Bloom, author of *The Power of Modern Spirituality*

Thank you Tim, for being a pioneer, a guide, and a teacher par excellence. Read this book and travel the journey into yourself to find the mysterious in every moment of ordinariness.
Ed and Deb Shapiro, authors of *Be the Change*

Tim Freke has an honours degree in philosophy and is the author of many groundbreaking books, including co-authoring *The Jesus Mysteries*, which was a *Daily Telegraph* 'Book of the Year' and top-10 bestseller in the UK and USA. His cutting-edge work on Gnosticism and pioneering spiritual philosophy have established his reputation as a scholar and free-thinker. He is often featured in documentaries and interviewed by the global media, such as the BBC and the History Channel.

Tim runs 'mystery experience retreats' internationally, in which he guides others directly to a spiritually awakened state. He also performs as a 'stand-up philosopher' – a concept he developed from the ancient idea of a philosopher as a travelling 'spiritual entertainer' who transforms people's consciousness. Tim lives with his wife and two children in Glastonbury, England. For more information see **www.timothyfreke.com**.

A SELECTION OF BOOKS BY TIM FREKE

How Long Is Now?
Lucid Living

Co-authored with Peter Gandy

The Gospel Of The Second Coming
The Jesus Mysteries
Jesus And The Lost Goddess
The Laughing Jesus
The Hermetica

THE MYSTERY EXPERIENCE

A REVOLUTIONARY APPROACH
TO SPIRITUAL AWAKENING

WATKINS PUBLISHING

LONDON

Distributed in the USA and Canada by Sterling Publishing Co., Inc.
387Park Avenue South, New York, NY 10016-8810

This edition first published in the UK and USA 2012 by
Watkins Publishing, Sixth Floor, Castle House,
75–76 Wells Street, London W1T 3QH

1 3 5 7 9 10 8 6 4 2

Designed and typeset by Mark Bracey

Printed and bound by Imago in China

Library of Congress Cataloging-in-Publication Data Available

ISBN: 978-1-78028-149-0

www.watkinspublishing.co.uk

For information about custom editions, special sales, premium and
corporate purchases, please contact Sterling Special Sales
Department at 800-805-5489 or specialsales@sterlingpub.com

CONTENTS

This book is dedicated
to my daughter Aya

ACKNOWLEDGEMENTS

This book would not exist without the support of a large number of people to who I am extremely grateful.

I particularly want to thank Peter Gandy for all his deep insights, warm friendship and constant encouragement. This book is the product of four decades of exploring the mystery together.

I want to express my gratitude to my publisher Michael Mann for believing in this project throughout the creative process, and his enthusiasm for the book I have finally authored.

Finally, I want to thank my wonderful family... my wife Debbie, my mum Ellen, and my children... for putting up with me being away in the world of ideas for such a long period, and loving me through all the ups and downs of the adventure of life.

PREPARING FOR THE JOURNEY

CHAPTER 1

THE MYSTERY EXPERIENCE

Welcome to this book. I want to invite you on a life-transforming journey of awakening. In this chapter I'm going to begin by introducing you to the 'mystery experience'.

This is the mystery experience. It's happening now. Something wonderfully mysterious is going on. We're conscious of being alive, but we don't know what life is. How astonishing! We inhabit a vast universe, but we don't know what the universe is. How amazing! We're experiencing this moment, but we don't know what this moment is. How intriguing!

If I examine this moment I see that I'm experiencing a tapestry of shapes and colours that I call the 'world'. But what is the world? I'm experiencing thoughts and feelings arising in my mind. But where do they come from? I feel certain that I exist. But I don't know why I exist. How bewildering!

Life is so utterly mysterious it takes my breath away. Yet normally most of us go about our business as if being alive was nothing remarkable. We pretend we know what's going on, when really we don't. We act as if we understand what it is to be a human being, when actually it is an enormous enigma of mind-boggling proportions.

In this book I want to explore with you the 'mystery experience' that spontaneously arises when we become profoundly conscious of the mystery of life. You can taste the mystery experience by simply focusing your attention on the mystery. Then your state of consciousness will immediately start to change.

You'll become acutely aware that you exist and how amazing that is. You'll see the familiar world with curious eyes. Your mind will own up to how little it really understands reality. Your heart will start to race with the excitement of being alive. But this is a superficial taste of the mystery experience. The deeper we go into the mystery, the deeper the mystery experience becomes.

In this book we're going to make a journey into the depths of the mystery experience, because this leads to what is often called 'spiritual awakening'. When we spiritually awaken we find ourselves entering an altered state of consciousness that is hard to describe. But there's no missing how wonderful it *feels*.

Recently I dreamt I was standing on a stage about to talk to a large audience about the mystery experience, as I often do in my waking life during one of my stand-up philosophy shows. Before I started to talk I paused, because I couldn't find the words to express how amazing the experience is. Then suddenly I knew what to do, because I remembered that I could fly! So I simply said 'The mystery experience feels like this'... and I soared up into the air... dancing ecstatically in the emptiness of space... swooping up and down in effortless abandon.

I wish I could swoop and dive for you right now, to convey how it feels to be awake to the mystery. But I haven't worked out how to fly in waking life. And this is a book so you wouldn't see me anyway. That means I'll have to describe the mystery experience in words for you as best I can. I'm going to give it a go!

When I dive deeply into the mystery experience it feels as if I'm dissolving in an ocean of love. There's an awe-inspiring sense of oneness with the universe. My sensual body comes alive. The search for meaning is resolved into a wordless 'understanding', which is so deep it must be felt not thought. There's the silent certainty that all is well; and such a feeling of relief... like coming home.

THE WOW OF AWAKENING

I've been exploring the mystery experience ever since a spontaneous awakening when I was a 12-year-old boy. Over the decades I've had the privilege of being with many people when they've found themselves in the awakened state for the first time. And the most common thing that people say is simply 'WOW'.

In recent years I've been running mystery experience retreats in which I guide people directly to the awakened state. Afterwards I receive a large number of moving emails from participants. By far the most used word is 'WOW', which is usually in capital letters followed by a string of exclamation marks!!!

I like the word 'wow'. I think of the word as modern American slang, but my dictionary tells me it's a natural expression that originated in 16th-century Scotland. 'Wow' is a way of expressing astonishment and wonder. It's a great word to describe how it feels when we awaken, because the mystery experience is a very big WOW. It's better than the best surprise you've ever had.

There are many ways of being wowed. There's the aesthetic wow of listening to beautiful music. The scientific wow of understanding the grandeur of the universe. The wow of pleasure when eating gourmet food. The wow of sport when witnessing extraordinary physical skill. The wow of learning when you surprise yourself with your own competence.

This book is about the WOW of awakening. The deep WOW of appreciating the mystery of existence. The ecstatic WOW of realizing how amazing life is. The simple WOW of being alive. The inexpressible WOW of seeing what-is beyond words.

At the end of a mystery experience retreat I ran in Las Vegas, whilst we luxuriated together in the wonder of the WOW, people attempted to describe what they were experiencing in various ways. Then a lovely woman called Kate said:

> This is what everyone wants to feel.

I love this description of the awakened state, because it's so simple and so true. The mystery experience is the WOW that everyone is searching for. We all long to feel alive and when we awaken we feel totally alive. We all long for freedom and when we awaken we know that we're completely free. We all long for love and when we awaken we become immersed in limitless love.

I've spent my life exploring the world's spiritual traditions, because at their mystical heart they all offer us ways to awaken to the WOW. Spirituality is often misunderstood as a way of thinking about life, but first and foremost it's a guide to transforming consciousness and *experiencing* something beyond words.

Zen Master Daie put it perfectly, nearly a thousand years ago, when he wrote:

> All the teachings the sages have expounded are no more than commentaries on the sudden cry… Ah, This!

So let me plagiarize old man Daie and say right now:

> I'm no sage and all the ideas in this book are just
> commentaries on the joyous whoop… WOW! This is it!

I remember many years ago, at one of my very first weekend seminars, a young woman arrived dressed all in black and feeling very withdrawn. At the end, beaming and brimming with love, she announced: 'I feel like a convert to… *something*.' Yeah! That's it. I'm also a convert to… *something*. In this book I want to invite you to experience the WOW and become a convert to… *something*!

THE WAY OF WONDER

The experience of awakening is notoriously hard to put into words. But actually all experiences are hard to describe, unless the person we're talking to is familiar with the experience we're talking about. Could we tell a blind person what it's like to see a sunset? Could we tell a deaf person what it's like to be moved by music?

You know what I mean when I say 'I feel angry', because you've also experienced anger. You know what I mean when I say 'I feel happy', because you've also experienced happiness. Communication relies on shared experience. So I'm going to introduce you to the awakened state by focusing on an experience you're already familiar with.

I want to share with you a way of waking up to the WOW that begins with the simple experience of wonder. If you wonder deeply enough you'll start to awaken. You'll become conscious of the breathtaking mystery of existence and the mystery experience will spontaneously arise.

Our journey starts with wondering, which leads to the mystery, and at the heart of the mystery is the WOW. The Gnostic 'Gospel of Matthias' explains:

> Wondering at the things that are before you is the first step
> to the deeper knowledge.

Zen Master Sengstan asserts:

> It is because I wondered deeply that I attained a
> penetrating realization. If you do not reflect and examine
> your whole life will be buried away.

Being willing to wonder is a prerequisite for awakening because, in
the face of the breathtaking mystery of life, if we don't feel curious
we simply aren't very conscious. When being alive doesn't fill us
with wonder we're already half-dead.

The Art of Wondering

I'm a philosopher and this book is a celebration of philosophy as
the art of wondering. Socrates, one of my philosophical heroes,
tells us:

> The feeling of wonder is the touchstone of the
> philosopher. Wonder is the only beginning of philosophy.

This is an old-school view of philosophy. These days philosophy
tends to be seen as dry conceptual inquiry. I studied this modern
form of philosophy at university many years ago. It was fascinating
and great training for the mind. But ultimately I could see that I
was becoming lost in a maze of words. I was much more interested
in spiritual philosophy, which I found could lead me out of the
maze of words to the mystery experience.

Spiritual philosophy doesn't seek to obscure the mystery with
ideas, but to reveal the mystery *through* ideas. It recognizes the
obvious fact that concepts are no more than concepts, which can
never contain the mystery. It doesn't propose ultimate answers,
rather a new way of seeing that makes the experience of life even
more wondrous.

The Neo-Platonic philosopher Plotinus is a spokesperson for
this approach to philosophy when he declares:

The job of the philosopher is to awaken us to the vision.

I resonate deeply with this. For me the job of the philosopher is to help us wonder so deeply that we go beyond words to the WOW. And then the philosopher's 'um?' is transformed into the yogi's '*om*'.

A WONDERFUL LIFE

In this chapter I've been bigging up how good it feels to be immersed in the mystery experience, because I want to whet your appetite for the meal ahead. But it's important that you understand that the WOW is not just some passing peak experience or ultimately irrelevant high. Spiritual awakening affects how we think, feel and act. It gives rise to a new way of living our everyday lives.

Socrates famously declared:

The unexamined life is not worth living.

The modern philosopher Alphonso Lingis added:

The unlived life is not worth examining.

Both are true. If we never dare to examine life we subsist in a semi-conscious stupor. But life is only worth examining because this can help us to live more fully.

In this book I'm going to share with you a profound philosophical story about life, which can wake you up to the WOW *and* transform your experience of living. But I want you to remember that it's only a story. The mystery of existence can never be explained away. Life is always more than we think. As the philosopher Alfred North Whitehead explained:

Philosophy begins in wonder. And, at the end, when philosophic thought has done its best, the wonder remains.

CHAPTER 2

FROM ME TO YOU

In this chapter I want to introduce myself, so you can get a sense of where I'm coming from. I also want to prepare you for the variety of content in this book, which is going to include spiritual philosophy, scientific insights, criticisms of other ways of thinking, experiential exercises, and practical ways of transforming our everyday lives.

I'm writing this book to share the mystery experience with you. A book is inevitably a one-way conversation, but I don't want this to be a lecture. I'd much prefer it to feel like a 'tête à tête' or better still a 'heart to heart'. I want to connect with you in the most authentic way I can, because when we're real with each other magic happens.

As I write this book I want to reach through the page to touch you. And, as you read this book, I want you to never forget that these are more than simply words on a page. As the American poet Walt Whitman says so directly in one of his poems:

> Camerado, this is no book,
> Who touches this touches a man,
> (Is it night? are we here together alone?)
> It is I you hold and who holds you.

We're in different places in the web of space–time, but we're together here and now nevertheless. So let me tell you a bit about myself. I want to be up front about something important right from the start. Just because I'm a teacher of spiritual awakening, that doesn't mean I see myself as some sort of enlightened master. I'm simply a human being with a passion for the mystery experience.

During my life I've spent a great deal of time wondering, so I've inevitably become pretty good at it. If I wonder deeply it wakes me up to the WOW, so I've come to know the mystery experience well, which means I can guide others directly to it. What we focus on becomes our area of expertise. I've focused on spiritual awakening.

My journey of awakening hasn't led me to arrive at some 'fully realized' enlightened state. Indeed, these days I neither expect nor aspire to be enlightened. And that isn't an admission of spiritual failure, because I've come to feel the whole idea of special enlightened people is completely misconceived.

I've written more than 30 books on spiritual philosophy, but I still feel like a child taking my first teetering steps. How else could I feel in the face of the infinite mystery? I'm not claiming I have privileged knowledge of the way things are. I simply like to wonder.

I wonder if it might be like this? I wonder if it would be helpful to approach things in this way? And this wondering keeps waking me up to the WOW.

But this doesn't mean my life is always perfect and I'm continually content. My life is full of highs and lows, just as I suspect your life is. I'm writing these words to connect with you, precisely because we share the same dilemmas of life. We're all in the mystery of life together, and I want to offer to you what I've found of value, in gratitude for all that I've been given by others.

I'm not special in any way. At least I'm no more special than you or anyone else. I'm a family man in his early 50s, with all of the pressures and pleasures that come with being a responsible father and husband. I possess many admirable qualities, but I also have my faults… just ask my wife! If you met me, I hope you'd like me. But if you lived with me you'd eventually see another side, which you may not enjoy so much. And I have come to feel OK about that, because in my experience we're all capable of being both great souls and assholes. Right?

THE BIG QUESTION AND THE BIG ANSWER

If you're intrigued to know about my personal journey of awakening, then check out my last book *How Long Is Now?*, which is full of anecdotes and stories. There's no time for all that now, because we've got a very big adventure ahead of us. But before we set off I feel it may be helpful to at least share with you how my personal journey began and where it has led me.

As a boy it seemed very strange to me that all the grown-ups were preoccupied with trivia and never seemed to mention how profoundly mysterious life is. Life seemed like one big question and I felt intuitively sure there must be a big answer. I would often sit quietly wondering about life, because I figured that if I could work out what life is, then I'd know what I should be doing with it.

My favourite place to wonder was on Summerhouse Hill overlooking my busy little home-town. This is where I sat and wondered with my lovely mongrel dog Scrag beside me. I know it sounds like a Disney movie, but life's like that sometimes!

One day while I was wondering on Summerhouse Hill, something magical happened. I became so consumed by wonder that my state of consciousness spontaneously transformed. I tasted the mystery experience for the first time and it was WOW!

It's a long time ago but I can still vividly recall the feeling of being immersed in overwhelming, exquisite, ecstatic love. It felt as if the whole universe was pulsating with limitless love. It felt as if I was dissolving into this love and becoming one with the universe. It felt as if the world had become a wonderland. It felt like I'd been given the most amazing surprise. And yet it also felt as if I'd remembered something I'd always secretly known.

I had no way of understanding what was happening to me, but I knew that I'd found the big answer to the big question of life. And the answer was not a clever theory. It was a mysterious experience in which the big question dissolved into an ocean of love. This discovery changed my life.

Ever since that moment I've been exploring the mystery experience. I've continually experimented with ways to transform consciousness and to integrate the awakened state with my everyday life. But my spiritual journey hasn't brought me to a permanently awake state, as I once hoped and imagined it would. Something even more amazing has happened. I've become a lover of life.

A LOVE AFFAIR WITH LIFE

My unexpected awakening as a boy was the beginning of a love affair with life that in many ways resembles any other love affair. When we first fall in love something special happens. It's what we've been waiting to feel all our lives. But that's only the start of the journey of love, which is full of endless delights and challenges.

At some point during a love affair we may realize something that changes everything. We know that we're not engaged in a temporary romance, because we're deeply in love. This magic moment could happen in the ecstasy of making love or when doing the washing up. It could be when things are going well or when things are falling apart. Whenever it happens our world is never the same again.

It's hard to say how we know we're deeply in love. We just do. And when we fall deeply in love, we become unconditionally committed to our love affair. We understand that loving involves much more than just feeling great together. It means remembering we still love each other, even when we can't stand each other. It's being there for each other through the good times and the bad.

My love affair with life has been very similar to this. When I dissolved into the mystery experience as a boy it was love at first sight. This was the beginning of a romance, full of exquisite moments that came and went, often leaving me feeling bereft and alone. At a certain point I realized something that changed everything. I'd fallen deeply in love with life, completely and unconditionally. I knew I was committed to our love affair through the good times and the bad, in sickness and health, in joy and sorrow.

The ancients imagined life as a great Goddess. Sometimes I see myself as a lover of the Goddess. And my love affair with her is both rewarding and challenging. It's a profoundly transformative adventure of getting to know each other in all our various states. It's a dance in which we become one yet remain two.

Sometimes we're so happy together it's perfect. Sometimes we argue and fall out. Sometimes we make love and nothing really matters but the mystery of the moment. Sometimes we need to get down to the practical business of being together in time. Sometimes I can't stop enthusing about how beautiful she is. Sometimes I badmouth her because she's not behaving as I want her to. Sometimes I trust her totally, despite her capricious ways. Sometimes I doubt her love and become demanding of her affection. But through it all I never stop finding her mysteriously beguiling. I never forget that I truly love her.

The WOW is like passionate sex or tender intimacy. Such special moments can't be forced. They just happen when we're both in the mood. These magical experiences set our affair on fire, but it's sustained by a quieter love that is always present; a love of simply being together.

This love of simply *being* sustains me through the ups and downs of my relationship with life. It allows me to love life, even when I don't like what's happening. It makes me feel committed to life for better and worse, so that I endure the storms and dance in the rain.

My exploration of the mystery experience has transformed my life into a love affair. And this has changed how I see the spiritual adventure. I no longer aspire to arrive at some permanent enlightenment, which seems forever out of reach. I aspire to become a lover worthy of life.

THE MAGICAL MYSTERY TOUR

In this book I'm going to share with you a revolutionary new approach to awakening that can lead you deep into the WOW, so that you can become a lover of life. In this introductory part of the book I want to prepare you for our journey. In Part I we'll set off to explore the deep mystery of life. In Part II our journey will lead us to the astonishing discovery of the deep self. In Part III we'll arrive at the wonderful experience of deep love, which is at the heart of the mystery experience. Then in Part IV we'll make our way back to our everyday lives to see the human adventure in a wonderful new way.

Many books start with simple ideas, but may gradually become more complex. However, the way of awakening takes us in the opposite direction. The first half of our journey will involve seeing life in a radically new way, and when we need to think in unfamiliar ways it can seem difficult at first. But we're heading towards an understanding of life that is extremely simple, so much of the second half of our journey will be plain sailing.

I don't want to say too much about the journey that lies ahead, because I want it to be a magical mystery tour. But I do want you to feel safe to make the journey with me. In my experience when we feel safe we open up, so that the naturalness of the awakened state becomes apparent.

Every heart assured of safety opens instantly. This is a realization I've arrived at after sharing the mystery experience with people for so many years. During my retreats I do all I can to make people feel safe, so that they can dare to dive into the mystery. I want everyone to relax and be themselves, so that waking up becomes an effortless delight. It's harder to do that in a book, but I'm going to give it a go.

We all approach life with our own unique collection of ideas that we've picked up along the way. How the ideas in this book harmonize or conflict with your own present view of life is crucial to how comfortable you'll feel on our journey together. So I want to take a moment to reassure you about some things.

First I want to assure you that, although we'll begin our journey focusing on the wonder of life, I fully acknowledge that life is often not very wonderful at all. If you're going through a tough patch in your life, which we all inevitably do, I want you to know that this book isn't just going to be some irritating rant about how great life is… coming from someone who is clearly having a better time of things than you are.

I want us to be real about how life is. To make the journey of awakening we need to be willing to enter those dark corners of life, where we feel sad and lost, angry and bitter, trapped and alone. If we can't go there, we won't be free.

If you're new to the possibility of awakening, I want to assure you that entering the depths of the WOW doesn't require you to be spiritually experienced. In fact this can be an advantage, because you won't be burdened with the baggage of too many preconceptions.

If you're a long-time spiritual seeker, then I hope you'll find the ideas in this book help you make sense of your experience of awakening in an exciting new way. But I want to warn you that I'm going to challenge some common spiritual ideas. I'll need to be critical sometimes in order to articulate a new approach to spirituality.

Perhaps you feel that you understand the teachings of awakening intellectually, but haven't had the experience of awakening? Many people who attend my mystery experience retreats find themselves in this predicament. An intellectual understanding of awakening is very helpful, but we need to go beyond our ideas to experience the WOW.

I want to help you actually experience the WOW. So throughout this book I'm going to suggest some practical experiments that will lead you progressively deeper into the mystery experience. I encourage you to pause to do these experiments, because if you don't you may end up at the end of the book with just a pile of words.

Perhaps you're someone who's sceptical about awakening? You may fear you've embarked on a book full of mystical mumbo jumbo? If so… good for you! I like questioning people. In my opinion you can't be too sceptical, because if you become sceptical of everything you'll find your brain goes pop and you're dancing in the mystery.

A lot of spiritual books are full of irrational nonsense, so I completely understand why you may be sceptical about awakening. I want to assure you that I have great respect for rationality, which is simply the requirement that we have good reasons to adopt a particular way of seeing things. I'm a big fan of clear thinking. As long as the thoughts are interesting!

If you're coming from a scientific understanding of the world I want you to know that I'm fascinated by science. In our scientific age I feel it's imperative that we develop a form of spirituality that is compatible with the awesome discoveries of empirical science. So the relationship between spirituality and science is going to be one of the themes of this book.

If you're a *feeling* person I want to assure you that I am too. I may call myself a philosopher, but essentially for me the spiritual journey is about love. On our journey together there will be times when we need to traverse some tricky philosophical terrain, but this is only so we can travel deeper into the heart of life. We need to clarify the mind so that we can open the heart.

Wherever you are coming from I hope you find our journey together rewarding. The only real requirement is that you're willing to wonder about life... to be curious and open... to be an explorer. My dictionary tells me that the word 'explorer' means 'somebody who travels to places that were previously unknown or unnavigated'. That's where we're going. This is a book for explorers. If that sounds like you, I'm glad you've made it to base camp, because we're about to set off on a grand adventure.

CHAPTER 3

A NEW LANGUAGE
OF AWAKENING

In this chapter I'm going to explore the new language I'll be using throughout this book, to help you understand spiritual awakening in a fresh way. Like an overture before an opera, which plays some of the major musical themes that will be developed later, I'm sharing these ideas with you now to give you a glimpse of where we're going. I'm not expecting you to get all that I'm saying straight away. I simply want to plant some seeds.

Over the last four decades I've studied and written many books about the major spiritual traditions of the world. These different approaches to awakening have all influenced me profoundly, and I feel immense gratitude to those great spiritual explorers who've cleared a way for me through the bewilderment of life.

I love the simple naturalness of Taoism, the searing immediacy of Zen, the ecstatic devotion of Sufism, the philosophical depth of Advaita Vedanta, the expansive love of Christianity, the esoteric wisdom of Kabala, the magical earthiness of Shamanism. All these traditions and many others have touched me in different ways. But I've never seen myself as part of any particular spiritual tradition, because I've preferred to draw on all of the wisdom of the world.

In recent years I've been attempting to articulate a new philosophy of awakening. In my view spirituality, like everything else, needs to keep evolving if it is to stay alive. So I've felt inspired to create a new approach to spirituality, which has all the depth of the traditions I've studied, yet avoids some of the dead ends I've been down on my own journey of awakening.

To create this new way to the WOW I've developed a new language of awakening. The concepts we use matter, because the way we think conditions what we experience. The WOW is beyond words, but the words we use have a huge effect on how we approach the journey of awakening.

I've loved studying the spiritual traditions of the world and have immense respect for the wisdom they've bequeathed us as our heritage. But I've come to the conclusion that much of our traditional spiritual vocabulary is well past its sell-by date and starting to smell funny. So I've set out to develop new concepts that can help us explore a new way to the WOW. Lucid concepts that cast the perennial insights of spirituality in a fresh light. Living concepts that speak the language of today. Truthful concepts that authentically capture my own experience of the awakened state.

DIFFERENT WAYS OF SAYING 'WOW'!

In this chapter I want to share with you some of this new language of awakening. I've already introduced you to my concepts of the 'mystery experience' and the 'WOW', which I hope are working for you. Now I want to introduce you to more concepts that I use to describe the awakened state. These concepts are like signposts that point to the wordless awakening from different directions. Read the signs and then look where they're pointing.

The Deep Mystery

I find it helpful to imagine life as a great ocean. When I'm only conscious of the surface of life I seem to know what life is, which allows me to get on with my everyday existence. But when I reach below the surface of things, right down to the depths of life, I find myself immersed in the 'deep mystery'.

The deep mystery isn't a mystery that we could one day solve, such as 'is there life on Mars?' The deep mystery is the ultimate mystery of existence. The deep mystery is the primal mystery that the universe exists and we are here to think about it. It's the great mystery in which we live and breathe and have our being. And when we become conscious of the deep mystery… the mystery experience spontaneously arises.

Deep Awake

When I bob along on the surface of things my experience of life is shallow. But when I plumb the mysterious depths my appreciation of what it is to be alive deepens. I become 'deep awake'… which is like being awake… only more so.

Normally we're only superficially awake, but when we become conscious of the deep mystery we become deep awake. In the spiritual literature this awakened state is sometimes described as 'enlightenment', because it's like being lit up from within.

I avoid the term 'enlightenment', however, because it's become associated with the idea of an ultimate spiritual goal, only achievable by special people who give up everything and live in caves.

And this is very misleading, because the deep awake state can be experienced by anyone... even you and me.

Deep Knowing

Paradoxically, when I'm deep awake and immersed in the deep mystery, I find myself *knowing* something. But this isn't 'knowing' in the normal sense in which I know certain information about the world. It's a much deeper knowing than that. So I call it 'deep knowing'.

In the Western spiritual tradition this 'deep knowing' is called 'gnosis'. Gnosis is directly knowing the essence of things. It's the big answer to the big question of life. But this answer is not in the form of a collection of words. It's an immediate realization, unmediated by concepts. It's like having the most profound thought you've ever had... only without the thought.

Deep knowing transforms my experience of living, because it gives rise to a quiet confidence that, despite appearances, life is good. When I become deep awake, I have an unshakeable faith that fundamentally all is well. Even when things are rough on the surface, at the depths of life I experience a primal joy of being.

The Deep Self

When I become deep awake I see that I am much more than the person I appear to be on the surface of life. There's a deeper level to my identity, which I call the 'deep self'. When I bob along on the surface of life I don't notice the deep self, but it's always there. It's a permanent presence, which is always present, witnessing the ever-changing dramas of my superficial self.

The superficial self is what I appear to be. I appear to be 'Tim'. But the deep self is what *I am*... my mysterious essence... my ineffable spirit... my naked *being*. And when I become conscious of my deepest *being* I discover I am one with all *beings*. I see that as separate individuals you and I are like different waves on one great ocean of being.

The Universe Vision

When I'm conscious of the depths as well as the surface of life, I experience the 'universe vision'. The word 'universe' comes from *universus* meaning 'all together' or 'turned into one'. The universe vision is the profound recognition that essentially all is one.

This is not a bland experience of some monolithic 'oneness'. It's a profound experience of the 'uni-variety' of the universe. It's seeing that on the surface of life everything is separate, like waves on an ocean, but at the depths all is one.

When I experience the universe vision I find myself appreciating the multifarious variety of life as an expression of one mysterious essence. I understand that I am both separate and not separate from life. On the surface I appear to be a separate individual, but at the depths of my identity I am one with all that is.

Deep Love

When I know I'm essentially one with all, there is a profound sense of connectedness to life that I experience as all-encompassing love. Christians call this love 'Agape' and Buddhists call it 'compassion'. I call it 'deep love' because it spontaneously arises when I deep-know the deep self. In my previous books I've also called it 'big love', because this love is so very big.

I like the word 'love' because it's a *feeling* word. And deep love is an exquisite feeling that reaches right down into my body. It's the feeling that arises when I am conscious of *both* the surface separateness *and* the deep oneness.

Love is always an experience of communing as one through the separateness that divides us. When we love someone we share in their joy and suffering. We feel separate and not-separate from each other. We become conscious of the intimate depths of our connectedness. And that feels good.

In the same way, when I become conscious of the intimate depths of my connectedness to all of life, I find myself in love with life. When I know that I'm separate and not-separate from everything and everyone, I find myself in love with everything and everyone. And that feels very good indeed.

Sensual Aliveness

Awakening is intensely pleasurable. This is an important fact that traditional spirituality is often strangely silent about. Indeed, many spiritual traditions disapprove of pleasure, which seems crazy given how great it feels. I'm a big fan of pleasure. But when I'm only superficially awake I only partially feel the enjoyment available to me, because I'm partly numb.

When I am deep awake, however, I find myself really savouring the pleasures of life. I'm astonished by all I see and hear and touch in this world of wonders. My body wakes up to how sweet it is to be alive. To simply breathe feels delicious. To sense my feet on the ground is an unspeakable delight. And I want to dance because life is WOW!

Awakening is not an experience of disembodied enlightenment. It's an experience of 'sensual aliveness'. When I'm deep awake there is a visceral love of being, which permeates this wonderful skin-bag of nerves, meat and bones I call my body. Hurray for the body! Everybody should have one!

Enlivenment

Some spiritual traditions suggest that we awaken by retreating from life into passive equanimity and the absence of desire. But it's not like that for me. When I'm deep awake I enter a passionate state I call 'enlivenment', in which I feel intensely present and in love with the moment.

When I'm enlivened I'm filled with enthusiasm for life and I want to actively engage with the challenges before me. There's a spontaneous flow to my life that makes living magical. I'm inspired and creative. I'm at my best. My mundane life seems marvellous. The familiar world becomes a wonderland.

A Lover of Life

The WOW is an amazing experience, but it's much more than that. It leads to a new way of living as a 'lover of life'. I introduced you to this idea in the last chapter, and now I'd like to say more of what it means to be a lover of life, because it'll give you a better idea of where we're ultimately heading.

Being a lover of life doesn't mean always feeling that life's wonderful. It means loving life as it is. It means embracing both the good and bad of life. It means passionately enjoying and tenderly enduring the tumultuous adventure of life through which we learn how to love. Waking up to the WOW feels good, but it's not just a good feeling. To love deeply is sometimes to suffer deeply.

Last year my father died of a stroke. For the previous eight months he could move only one arm and he would lie in his bed plaintively muttering 'help me, help me'. It broke my heart because I love him. Being deep awake didn't stop me suffering and I didn't want it to. I wanted to suffer with my dad. I wanted to be right with him in the awfulness of the situation.

For me, awakening isn't about transcending suffering, as some spiritual traditions teach. Rather, awakening allows me to suffer willingly because of love. And then my heartbreak becomes poignant... meaningful... even beautiful. When I suffered with my dying dad there were precious moments of deep connection. The bitterness was also sweet. The deep pain plunged me down to the depths of life. It broke my heart and what poured out was a deeper love.

When I listen closely I hear the WOW of life expressing itself in many different tones of voice. There is the ecstatic WOW of joy and the subdued WOW of sadness. The intoxicating WOW of hope and the sobering WOW of disappointment. The warm WOW of intimacy and the piercing WOW of loss. The great song of life passes between the major and the minor modes... and I am stirred by both.

HAVE YOU BEEN WOWED?

Perhaps there have been moments in your life when you tasted the WOW in some of the ways I've been describing? Most of us, at some time or other, have found ourselves suddenly seeing through the superficialities of life and diving into the mysterious depths. This can happen when we embrace a newborn child...

or listen to beautiful music… or enjoy a deep conversation. It can happen when we confront death… or feel defeated by failure… or wrestle with a mental breakdown. It can happen at any time. It can happen now.

WONDERING
- WOW Experiment -

Our journey into the mystery experience is going to be an experiential adventure. So in this chapter I want you to taste the WOW for yourself by experimenting with 'wondering'. As the book progresses there will be more WOW experiments that will lead you deeper into the mystery experience.

I've introduced you to the approach to awakening we're going to be exploring and the new language we're going to be using. Now I want to invite you to experiment with an easy way of allowing the deep awake state to spontaneously arise. This is the first step on our journey into the depths of the mystery experience and what I want you to do is extremely simple.

I want you to wonder and then to notice what happens to your state of consciousness.

I want you to experience a moment of wonder right now.

I want you to see things as they really are… utterly mysterious and miraculous.

A Moment of Wonder

Shortly before he died of cancer the British playwright Dennis Potter did a moving interview, in which he shared the wonder that arises in the face of imminent death. Have a look at this and *get* what he is trying to tell us.

> … at this season, the blossom is out in full now, there in the west early. It's a plum tree, it looks like apple blossom but it's white, and looking at it, instead of saying 'Oh that's nice blossom'… last week looking at it through the window when I'm writing, I see it is the whitest, frothiest, blossomest blossom that there ever could be, and I can see it.
>
> Things are both more trivial than they ever were, and more important than they ever were, and the difference between the trivial and the important doesn't seem to matter.
>
> But the nowness of everything is absolutely wondrous, and if people could see that, you know. There's no way of telling you; you have to experience it, but the glory of it, if you like, the comfort of it, the reassurance… not that I'm interested in reassuring people – bugger that. The fact is, if you see the present tense, boy do you see it! And boy can you celebrate it.

Life is WOW and Dennis Potter could see that as he was dying. But why wait until you're dying? Now is WOW if you open up to it. Just take a moment to really wonder. As the American author Ray Bradbury says:

> Stuff your eyes with wonder… live as if you'd drop dead in ten seconds. See the world. It's more fantastic than any dream made or paid for in factories.

THE WOW OF NOW

Open yourself up to the wonder of life right now.

Be conscious of this moment with that deep part of you that appreciates music and art… that feels the beat and dances to its rhythm… that finds truth in poetry as well as theory.

Dive deeply into wonder and the world will start to sparkle.

There will be an experience of intense gratitude that arises when you see how glorious life really is.

There will be an experience of immense humility that arises when you see how impossible it is to comprehend such a mystery.

It Wonders Me…

There's a great phrase used colloquially in some areas of Pennsylvania. They say 'it wonders me'. I really like that because life wonders me deeply. Wonder with me.

It wonders me that the world is so rich and vivid.

It wonders me that the universe is so vast, yet full of exquisite detail.

It wonders me that I am alive and experiencing this precious moment.

It wonders me that I can think and feel and sense and imagine.

It wonders me that you are you, yet I am me.

It wonders me how good it feels to simply be.

It wonders me that I could ever forget how much I love being.

Does it wonder you?

The Miracle of Life

Take a look at this powerful poem by Walt Whitman, who's one of the great high priests of wonder. It's called 'Miracles' and is so full of wonder it points straight to the WOW. If you want to really *get* the vision Uncle Walt wants to share with you, read it aloud then look at the world through new eyes. Go on… as an experiment.

What shall I give? and which are my miracles?
Realism is mine – my miracles – Take freely,
Take without end – I offer them to you wherever your feet
    can carry you or your eyes reach.
Why! who makes much of a miracle?
As to me, I know of nothing else but miracles,
Whether I walk the streets of Manhattan,
Or dart my sight over the roofs of houses toward the sky,
Or wade with naked feet along the beach, just in the edge
    of the water,
Or stand under trees in the woods,
Or talk by day with any one I love – or sleep in the bed at
    night with any one I love,
Or sit at table at dinner with my mother,
Or look at strangers opposite me riding in the car,
Or watch honey-bees busy around the hive, of a summer
    forenoon,
Or animals feeding in the fields,
Or birds – or the wonderfulness of insects in the air,
Or the wonderfulness of the sun-down – or of stars
    shining so quiet and bright,

Or the exquisite, delicate, thin curve of the new moon in
    spring;
Or whether I go among those I like best, and that like me
    best – mechanics, boatmen, farmers,
Or among the savans – or to the soiree – or to the opera,
Or stand a long while looking at the movements of
    machinery,
Or behold children at their sports,
Or the admirable sight of the perfect old man, or the
    perfect old woman,
Or the sick in hospitals, or the dead carried to burial,
Or my own eyes and figure in the glass;
These, with the rest, one and all, are to me miracles,
The whole referring – yet each distinct, and in its place.
To me, every hour of the light and dark is a miracle,
Every cubic inch of space is a miracle,
Every square yard of the surface of the earth is spread
    with the same,
Every foot of the interior swarms with the same;
Every spear of grass – the frames, limbs, organs, of men
    and women, and all that concerns them,
All these to me are unspeakably perfect miracles.
To me the sea is a continual miracle;
The fishes that swim – the rocks – the motion of the waves
    – the ships, with men in them,
What stranger miracles are there?

PARALOGICAL THINKING

This book isn't just about wondering in the sense of being awed by life. It is also about wondering in the philosophical sense of exploring new insights into what it is to be alive.

This chapter is going to be more intellectually challenging than our previous introductory chapters, because I want to describe a new way of thinking that forms the foundation of my spiritual philosophy.

Having introduced some of my new language of awakening, I now want to pop one more new idea into our conceptual goody-bag. But this isn't a description of the WOW. It's a way of thinking about life that I call 'paralogical thinking'.

The idea of paralogical thinking may seem abstract at first, but it has far-reaching practical applications. It opens up an understanding of the depths of life and clears away the confusion that can prevent us awakening to the mystery experience. I want to introduce paralogical thinking to you now, because we're going to be using this way of thinking throughout this book.

The need for paralogical thinking arises from an important insight. *Life is profoundly paradoxical.* I've already mentioned in passing the paradox that on the surface of life we live in a world of separate things, but at the depths all is one. At first such spiritual paradoxes can sound like mystical mumbo jumbo. So I want to ground our discussion of paradox in the empirical discoveries of hardnosed science, before using paralogical thinking to cast new light on the insights of spirituality.

The Wave-Particle Paradox

I want to focus on one particular paradox that scientists have found informs reality on a very deep level. When physicists studied the nature of light they discovered something extraordinary. If an experiment is set up one way, light seems to be comprised of elementary particles. But if the experiment is set up in another way, light appears to behave as a wave.

So is light a wave or particles? According to quantum physics it's both at once. Light can be seen as *both* a wave *and* particles, depending on how you look at it. Physicists call this paradox the 'wave-particle duality'.

This is all very hard to understand, so don't be surprised if you feel bamboozled. You should be feeling bamboozled, because it is genuinely bamboozling. The Danish scientist Niels Bohr, who was one of the founding fathers of quantum physics, famously remarked:

If you think you can talk about quantum theory without feeling dizzy, you haven't understood the first thing about it.

THE GLORIOUS BOTH/AND

The quantum physicists found that, on a deep level, reality has to be understood as inherently paradoxical. This has huge implications. It means we can't think about the deep mysteries of life using normal logic, because normal logic treats paradox as... well... illogical. We need a way of thinking that can embrace paradox. We need to think *paralogically*.

The great psychologist Carl Jung contrasted what he called the niggardly either/or with the glorious both/and. This is a simple way of differentiating logical and paralogical thinking.

Logical thinking is either/or thinking.

Paralogical thinking is both/and thinking.

Logical thinking says that light is *either* a wave *or* particles. It can't be both. Paralogical thinking says that light can be *both* a wave *and* particles, because life is inherently paradoxical. Niels Bohr explains:

> There are trivial truths and there are great truths. The opposite of a trivial truth is plainly false. The opposite of a great truth is also true.

This is a wonderful statement of the difference between logical thinking and paralogical thinking. Niels Bohr says that we need to think in different ways, depending on whether we are looking for 'trivial truths' or 'great truths'. If we want to understand the surface of life, logical thinking works perfectly. But to understand the depths of things we need to think paralogically.

Logical thinking is based on the principle that something is *either* true *or* it isn't true, so the opposite of a logical truth is plainly false.

Paralogical thinking is based on the realization that on a deep level life is paradoxical, so the opposite of a paralogical truth is also true.

Paradoxity

Now I need to add one more new idea to our conceptual repertoire, which can help us more easily discuss things paralogically, and that's the idea of 'paradoxity'. When we think paralogically we eventually arrive at a paradoxity. We see the paradoxity of something when we understand it from two opposite perspectives at once. For example, the paradoxity of light is that it appears as a wave and as particles, depending on how you set up the experiment.

> We reach the conclusion of our logical deliberations when we decide that *either* this *or* that is true.

> We reach the conclusion of our paralogical deliberations when we grasp the 'paradoxity' of the situation, by seeing that opposite perspectives are *both* true.

I have coined the word 'paradoxity' because I want to avoid the confusion caused by different ways of understanding the more familiar word 'paradox'. From a logical perspective, paradoxes are problems to be solved. But from a paralogical perspective a 'paradoxity' is the resolution of a problem.

Paralogical thinking allows us to embrace paradox. Indeed, rather than try and avoid paradoxes, we seek to understand the paradoxity of whatever we are thinking about. Niels Bohr once said:

> How wonderful that we have met with a paradox. Now we have some hope of making progress.

Paralogical Vision

I want to suggest a simple analogy to help you understand the value of paralogical thinking. It's an interesting fact that we look at the world with two eyes, rather than one big eye in the middle of the forehead like a cyclops. The reason for this is that if we had only one eye we'd perceive a flat world. Looking at things with two eyes is what gives us depth perception.

> Logical either/or thinking is like looking out of one eye or the other.

> Paralogical both/and thinking is like looking out of both eyes.

> When we think paralogically we see things from two complementary perspectives at once and this gives depth to our understanding of life.

When we look at the world, what each eye sees is different, but they combine to create a single vision of reality that has depth. In the same way, when we think paralogically we see things in different ways that complement each other to create a single vision of reality that has depth.

When I discuss philosophy with people who adopt an either/or approach to understanding the depths of life, I often find myself in the paradoxical position of agreeing with what they're saying, but also feeling they're missing half the truth. So I sometimes quote the cheeky words of the great Niels Bohr who once remarked:

> No, no, you're not thinking; you're just being logical.

THE PRIMAL PARADOX

Niels Bohr was a very interesting man. He was one of the most influential scientists of all time and winner of a Nobel Prize for physics. Yet when he designed his own coat of arms he chose to put on it a spiritual symbol from ancient China. This symbol is commonly known as the yin/yang symbol, but it is properly called the '*taijitu*', which means 'diagram of the supreme ultimate'. Now there's a big claim to live up to!

The *taijitu* is a symbolic representation of the essential paradoxity of reality. It encodes the ancient Taoist understanding that reality is characterized by the primal polarity of yin and yang, represented by black and white tadpole shapes. Yin and yang are opposites which paradoxically coexist and complement each other. This is why there's a dot of white in the black tadpole and vice versa.

Niels Bohr clearly felt the yin/yang symbol captured the paradoxical understanding of reality he had arrived at through his scientific discoveries. And he made this plain, by adding on his coat of arms the Latin motto:

> contraria sunt complementa
> opposites are complementary

This is an idea that has been important to many of the greatest philosophers, who often referred to it as the *coincidentia oppositorum* or 'union of opposites'. The essential idea is that existence is a primal oneness that is arising as complementary opposites. Werner Heisenberg, another of the founding fathers of quantum physicists, puts the primal paradox of existence like this:

> Unity and complementarity constitute reality.

Complementary Perspectives

'Hang on' I hear you saying warily. Or perhaps it's not you? Perhaps it's my imaginary philosophical sparring partner Rational Richard who wants to take issue with all of this. Clever Dick, as he's known to his friends, helps keep me on the intellectual straight and narrow by questioning my conceptual flights of fancy.

Tim: Nice to see you Dick… have you popped in for some philosophical chat?

Dick: Yes. What you've been saying is worrying me. If we believe contradictory things we'll end up in a right mess.

Tim: Paralogical thinking doesn't mean being contradictory. Quantum physics shows that to understand light we need to see it from two perspectives at once… as both a wave and particles. But it's important to understand that, although these two perspectives seem to be *contradictory*, they are actually *complementary*.

Dick: Why do you say that?

Tim: When we examine light in one way, it appears as particles. When we examine light in another way, it appears as a wave. This is a paradoxity but it's not a contradiction, because we are looking at light in two different ways, not the same way.

Dick: So if we said light is a wave and particles it would be a logical contradiction. But if we say light is a wave and particles depending on the way we look at it… then that's a paradoxity.

Tim: Exactly. Paralogical thinking means understanding reality from opposite points of view that complement each other.

Dick: Well I still think logical thinking is the best way to deal with life. It makes clear sense of things and we'd be lost without it. We need to be more logical, not less logical, in my opinion.

Tim: I agree. Logical thinking is very important. But life is paradoxical so we need two ways of thinking about it.

Dick: What can that possibly mean?!

Tim: You can get what I'm saying by looking at the two forms of physics that scientists use to understand reality. Scientists distinguish 'Newtonian physics' and 'quantum physics', because they are very different. When dealing with the everyday world, the logical laws of physics discovered by Newton work perfectly. But when we go deeper into the nature of things we need the paradoxical insights of quantum physics, which don't fit with Newton's laws at all.

Dick: That's a paradox I admit.

Tim: In the same way, logical either/or thinking is a very useful tool to help us negotiate the everyday world, but it won't do if we want to understand the depths of life. For this we need paralogical both/and thinking.

Dick: Well I kind of get it and I'm kind of confused... damn it... now you've got me talking in paradoxes!

Tim: Don't worry. Paralogical thinking will make more sense as we apply it throughout our journey in this book.

THE ESSENTIAL MESSAGE

Let me take you through the essential message of this chapter one more time, because it can be slippery to hold at first.

Reality is fundamentally paradoxical.

This means we can't understand the depths of existence with either/or logical thinking.

We need to use paralogical thinking, which says something can be *both* this *and* that, depending on how we look at it.

Paralogical thinking sees reality from two opposite yet complementary perspectives at once, and arrives at an understanding of the 'paradoxity' of whatever is being examined.

We don't have to choose between *either* logical thinking *or* paralogical thinking. They can both help us understand life.

We need to use logical thinking when we're dealing with surface things and paralogical thinking when we're dealing with the depths of life.

When we perceive reality with both eyes open we see reality in depth.

PART I

A JOURNEY INTO THE DEEP MYSTERY

CHAPTER 6

THINGS ARE NOT WHAT THEY SEEM

In this part of the book we're going to explore the deep mystery of existence, because it's when we become conscious of how mysterious life is, that the mystery experience arises. We're going to start by looking at some of the astonishing discoveries of science, which reveal how paradoxical and puzzling the universe really is.

For thousands of years the great spiritual explorers of life have made the audacious claim that things are not what they seem to be. There is a deeper level to reality that lies behind the superficial appearances. In recent centuries the great scientific explorers of life have shown that this is true. When we look below the surface of things we discover that reality is much more amazing than we normally realize. And it's characterized by paradoxity.

I want to examine the scientific view of the universe, because it compels us to question our common-sense assumptions about life. And we need to question our most basic assumptions if we want to dive into the mystery experience. We need to think in new ways if we want to experience life with greater depth.

I find that contemplating the insights of science wakes me up just as much as contemplating the insights of spirituality, because the world that science reveals is WOW! Let's begin our exploration of the fantastical nature of reality with a simple paradoxity we're all familiar with.

The Earth and the Sun

Throughout most of history human beings have assumed that the Earth is stationary and the Sun travels across the sky. That's how it appears to us, and for most purposes this way of thinking still works. We continue to talk about the Sun rising and setting to mark the beginning and end of the day.

Yet actually, of course, we've found that the Earth is a spinning sphere which orbits the Sun. This may seem obvious now, but when this was first discovered it was a mind-blowing sensation, because it flies in the face of common sense.

From an everyday perspective the Sun goes around the Earth. But from a scientific perspective the Earth goes around the Sun. This points to an important realization. For most purposes our common-sense picture of the world works well. But to penetrate the depths of life we need to be willing to see things in shocking new ways.

Am I Still Here?

I've been sitting here for the last hour preparing to write this chapter for you. Or have I? It feels as if I've been in the same place, because I've been sitting on the same chair in front of the same computer. But actually my chair is glued by gravity to a spinning ball that's hurtling around the Sun at a speed of 67,000 miles per hour. So I'm not in the same place at all. I'm 67,000 miles away from where I was sitting an hour ago! Or am I?

Our Sun is orbiting around the centre of the Milky Way galaxy and an orbit takes about 226,000,000 years to complete. So the last time there was a living creature where I am right now, it wasn't a human being sitting in front of a computer, it was a dinosaur plodding around a prehistoric jungle. From this perspective the idea that I've been 'here' for hours is ludicrous, because no one has ever been 'here' before.

If that isn't paradoxical enough for you… get this! There really is no 'here' at all. Einstein showed that space and time don't exist in the way we think they do. They exist together as two aspects of a primal paradoxity he called 'space-time'. This means I really can't talk about *where* I am without also talking about *when* I am and vice versa. And it's completely impossible to be in the same space-time twice. So in one way I'm still here… but actually I'm somewhere else… except really there is no 'here' or 'elsewhere'. What a buzz!

One and Many

According to current scientific theory, the universe popped into existence about 13 billion years ago when something came from nothing. This is the moment time started and space first appeared, because space-time came into existence. Scientists call this ultimate magic trick the 'big bang', which is a beautifully ironic name, because the big bang was infinitesimally small, and it made no sound as there was no one to hear it!

The big bang happened when the 'singularity' exploded and the universe came into existence. Like the firing of some cosmic starting-gun, this signalled the start of a process of evolution that has led to us being here to discuss the 'big bang'.

What is the singularity? We could say it's the primal oneness that has evolved into the multifarious variety of life. The fundamental simplicity which is the source of the astonishing complexity of the universe. The nothing which contained the potential for everything. It's extremely paradoxical, so it's hard to get your head around!

One thing that seems clear, however, is that if everything has come from the singularity, essentially everything *is* the singularity. On the surface we appear to be separate individuals in a world of separate things. But essentially the universe is the singularity evolving into complex forms. You and I are the singularity looking at itself... thinking about itself... confused about itself. Can you get that paradoxity?

Incomprehensibly Big and Incomprehensibly Small

We used to believe that the Earth was the centre of the universe, which was lit by the Sun during the day and a celestial canopy of stars at night. I'm sure the night sky seemed unbelievably big to our ancestors, but compared to our current understanding of things the universe they looked at was tiny.

Through our scientific studies we've come to the stunning realization that our mighty Sun is an insignificant star in a galaxy containing more than 100 billion stars! Can you feel how big an expansion of understanding that is? Then, only 100 years ago, we discovered that we'd still been thinking far too small, because the universe is much more than just our particular galaxy. The universe contains more than 100 billion galaxies!

Then we realized that the universe was expanding and came up with the theory of the big bang. Having understood the universe was incomprehensibly big, we realized it had once been incomprehensibly small. An infinitesimally small point had appeared in the middle of nothing, which had expanded to become 100 billion galaxies. Is that a WOW or what?!

Everywhere from Nowhere

Scientists often say that the universe was once the size of a pea. Of course it was originally much smaller than that, but I like the idea of the universe as a pea. It makes me feel like I could pop it in my mouth and swallow the whole thing... gulp!

Where did the universe come from? Well... nowhere. There was no space before the big bang. It was the moment that space-time came into existence. So how can we conceive of the universe as expanding, when there was no space for it to expand into? And how can we conceive of the universe beginning, when there was no time before the beginning? Ouch... my head is hurting... in an enjoyable sort of way!

And here's another thing. If space is expanding there must surely be a place somewhere in the universe where the big bang happened and everything is expanding from there? But it's not like that, because the big bang created space. Space is a pea that has grown into the universe. The centre of the universe from which it is expanding is not somewhere... it's everywhere. You are the centre of the universe and so am I.

Everything is Nothing

Here's another paradoxity that really rocks my boat. The physical world we live in isn't there. The solid objects we manipulate with our solid hands are mostly nothing. Seemingly concrete things are made up of infinitesimally small atoms swirling around in an immense void. And these atoms are made up of unimaginably small subatomic particles dancing in vast emptiness.

Our seemingly solid world is mostly 'ghostly empty space', as the great physicist Sir Arthur Eddington put it. The latest calculation is that 99.9999999999999 per cent of the world you're experiencing right now is actually emptiness. Physicists set out to understand what things are made of and found out they are made of nothing.

Nothing is appearing as everything right now. Can you get the paradoxity of that? I seem to be a solid body sitting here writing these words, but really I'm mostly emptiness. What an affront to common sense! If we could take away the empty space then all the subatomic particles in every one of the seven billion people on our planet would be about the size of a grain of rice. Can you feel that WOW?!

How Old Am I?

I think of myself as this body called 'Tim', which has been making its way through the world for the last 52 years. But science has shown that 98 per cent of the atoms in my body are replaced every year. Indeed, there isn't a single atom in my body today that was part of my body 10 years ago. My body isn't 52 years old, it's 10 years old at most! That really messes with my sense of identity. Clearly in one way I'm the same body, but physically I'm not the same body at all. How about that for a paradoxity?!

What We See and What We Don't

We think that we can see reality. It's this wonderful world in which we live. Right? But as scientists have studied the nature of things they've realized we aren't seeing much of reality at all. The visible spectrum, from violet to red, that we can see with our eyes is a small part of a much bigger electromagnetic spectrum that we don't perceive.

Imagine the visible spectrum as one octave on a piano keyboard that represents the whole electromagnetic spectrum. How big do you think the keyboard would be? Think big. Think very big, because the keyboard would be hundreds of thousands of miles long. And all we see would be just one octave on it!

We think we see reality, but actually we hardly notice it. Now we've reached the point where scientists have concluded that what we experience as matter is pretty insignificant compared to mysterious 'dark matter' and 'dark energy'. Less than 5 per cent of the universe is ordinary matter. The rest is… well we don't know what the rest is.

Abstract and Concrete

If that messes with your melon consider this. Physicists have found that the best way to comprehend the nature of the physical universe is to use mathematics. But numbers don't exist in the physical universe. You can't see or touch or hear a number. You can look at two apples, but you can't look at 'two'. Numbers are abstract ideas, not concrete things. Physics is the study of physical reality, but to understand physical reality it uses numbers that don't exist in physical reality!

The great insight at the heart of science is that nature obeys 'laws'. But the laws of nature don't exist in nature. They are abstract equations. For example Einstein's famous equation $E = MC^2$ explains the relationship between energy and mass. But the equation itself is made of neither energy nor mass. The laws of nature exist, but not in the same way that nature exists. We need to understand the universe paralogically as *both* an abstract and concrete reality.

The Observer and the Observed

And here's something even more astonishing. We think of reality as an objective world that obeys the laws of nature. This means we can predict how things will behave. If I drop my coffee cup it will fall down, not up. If I drop it again it will behave in the same way. Yet on a deeper level things aren't so predicable, because the idea of objective reality ceases to make sense.

According to the 'uncertainty principle' of quantum physics, on an elementary level the physical universe is a collection of possibilities. Scientists have discovered that there has to be a conscious observer to 'collapse' the quantum possibilities, which stops particles being in two places at once and creates a world we can examine and measure.

So on the surface, reality seems to be objective and we can predict the way things work. But at the depths is a realm of possibilities and what exists depends on the presence of a subjective observer. 'Curiouser and curiouser' as Alice said in Wonderland.

Subjective Thoughts and the Objective World

The scientific view of the universe is so far from common sense it seems bonkers, yet here we are doing our best to understand it. And we're able to think about such things because we have a lump of clever porridge in our heads, which inexplicably gives rise to intangible thoughts.

Our thoughts are very mysterious, because they don't exist in the objective world. They are subjective rather than objective realities. We think about the mysteries of the objective world with subjective ideas that have no existence in the objective world. There's an interesting thought… whatever a thought may be?!

The universe is unimaginably big, but our imagination is also unimaginably big. By counting the number of neural configurations possible in a human brain, scientists have estimated the number of possible thoughts a brain could have as 10 to the power of 70,000,000,000,000! That's an extremely big number when you realize that it's estimated that there are only 10 to the power of 80 atoms in the entire universe. No wonder when we allow ourselves to think in new ways a whole new reality opens up before us!

RELATIVE KNOWLEDGE AND ABSOLUTE MYSTERY

The history of scientific discovery has been a constant process of discovering that things are not the way we thought they were. Science has taught us, again and again, that what seems certain today will change tomorrow. The story that science tells about reality is continually evolving and this often means revolutionary changes in our understanding.

The more we've learned, the more we've come to appreciate the depths of the mystery of life. For previous generations the mystery was what lay beyond the woods, the seashore, the edge of the world. As our knowledge has increased we've solved those particular mysteries, yet found ourselves faced with much bigger ones.

Even if science could, one day, completely explain how our universe unfolded from the primal singularity, we'd still be left with the biggest mystery of all. What is a 'singularity' exactly?! And what business did it have creating a cosmos with you and I in it to wonder about these things?!

Our relative knowledge has increased but the deep mystery remains undiminished. To think we really *know* what is going on is utterly ludicrous. If we spent a lifetime of 80 years trying to puzzle it out, we'd have about 4,000 weeks to understand this incomprehensibly enormous, intricate, paradoxical universe. When I contemplate this it fills me with deep humility in the face of the grandeur of reality.

The universe that science has revealed is more mind-boggling in its bigness, smallness, and strangeness than our ancestors could have imagined. We are discovering more all the time at an ever-accelerating rate. Yet the big question remains. What is life? We just don't know!

GETTING THE SCIENTIFIC VISION

How does life look if we really take on board the paradoxical discoveries of modern science? Let's go through some of the fascinating both/and paradoxities we have been exploring again.

We can and can't be in the same place twice.

We are and we aren't separate individuals.

The centre of the universe is here and everywhere.

The world is and isn't made up of solid physical objects.

The body does and doesn't have a continuous identity.

We do and don't see the world around us.

Nature does and doesn't obey deterministic laws.

Reality does and doesn't exist objectively.

We do and don't know what life is.

For everyday purposes we need to believe that here is here, solid objects are solid objects, nature obeys deterministic laws, and reality is objective. If we didn't approach life in these common-sense ways we'd go mad... so be careful!

Yet if we look below the surface of things another dimension of reality is revealed. This is the great discovery of science. And it's paralogically complementary to the message of spirituality, which also teaches that if we look beyond the superficial appearances a deeper reality is revealed.

The great scientific explorers of life have discovered the hidden depths of reality by closely examining our shared objective experience of the world. The great spiritual explorers of life have discovered the hidden depths of reality by closely examining their individual subjective experience of living.

Science and spirituality seem to be very different approaches to life, but they lead to the same astonishing conclusion. Our common-sense understanding of things is inadequate, because life is much more than it seems to be.

CHAPTER 7

THE DEEP MYSTERY

In this chapter I want to focus on the profound realization that, when we look at the depths of things, we really don't know what life is. This is the doorway into the mystery experience.

I've spent my whole life wondering what life is. After five decades of passionate exploration, which has included some serious study and in-depth spiritual practice, an honest attempt at radical soul-searching and a monumental amount of philosophical chat, I've come to a fascinating conclusion. What is life? *I don't know.*

I'm a pretty smart guy. I can read philosophical books and discuss quantum physics. But it seems to me that all my clever opinions float like flotsam on a vast sea of uncertainty. The edifice of information I've erected totters on the foundation of the ultimate enigma of existence… *that anything exists at all.*

The mystery of life is so enormous it takes my breath away and leaves me speechless. It's not some riddle I will one day unravel, but real magic to be marvelled at. It's not a darkness my intellect can illuminate, but a dazzling radiance so splendid that my most brilliant ideas seem dull.

I may go about my daily life as if I know what's going on, but the truth is I really don't know what life is. Nobody does.

What! Nobody?

Nobody knows.

Not even the guys in white coats?

Nope.

What about the pope?

Are you kidding?

Or my enlightened guru?

You obviously haven't spent enough time with him.

Or some really smart philosopher like Socrates?

He was famous precisely for knowing he didn't know!

Well Jesus then?

He didn't really exist… haven't you read my bestseller about Christianity?!

There's got to be some special person somewhere who's got the whole thing sorted out?

Look. I'm not saying nobody knows just because I don't know and I can't imagine anyone smarter than Tim. I'm saying it because I've come to realize that it's impossible to know what life is.

What do you mean?

Could we ever really explain the mystery of life with words? Would it take a sentence? Or a paragraph? Or a book? Or a whole library of books? Could any amount of words explain away the mystery?

I guess not.

Human beings have created a mountain of words to explain the nature of reality, but under all the words the mystery of life remains as magnificent as ever.

So we can never say what life is with words.

Exactly. And that's why, as the great mythologist Joseph Campbell once said, 'The person who thinks he has found the ultimate truth is wrong.'

So it isn't just me. Nobody knows what's really going on.

In the ancient Hindu Rig Veda it says 'Who knows the truth? Only the God who sees in the highest heaven. He only knows. Or perhaps not even he knows?'

DEEP KNOWING

The paradoxity of our predicament is that we *both* know *and* don't know what life is. On the surface of life we have a working knowledge of things. Yet life remains a deep mystery. And when we become conscious of the deep mystery, the mystery experience spontaneously arises.

This is how it is for me. When I wonder about the depths of life I find myself becoming inarticulate. It's as if I'm trying to formulate a primal question that is so enormous it's impossible to express. A question which is deeper than thought... something felt... something of the heart.

I could try to say it like this... What's going on?... What is life?... What is this moment right now? Then I want to add... Who am I?... What is it to be alive?... And what should I do about it? Or perhaps I would be better to just stammer... what... how... why?!

Science offers many great insights into the nature of life that fascinate my mind, but it doesn't answer the inarticulate question of the heart. The books I read are full of valuable information, but words can't answer my wordless question. It seems to me that all my ideas about life form a net of concepts which I cast into the ocean of mystery to catch the water.

Yet as I wonder deeply about life, I find myself immersed in the deep mystery. Then something astonishing happens. The inarticulate question of the heart dissolves into the ocean of mystery. And I feel I've found the answer I'm looking for.

But this answer, like the question, is more of a feeling than a thought. I can't really express the inarticulate question, because it's too deep for words. I can't really express the inarticulate answer, because it's too deep for words.

It is one of the great paradoxities of life that not-knowing leads to the 'deep knowing' that the ancients called 'gnosis'. As the poet Robert Frost writes so beautifully:

> We dance around in a ring, and suppose,
> But the Secret sits in the middle and knows.

In my experience, when I know that I don't know, there's a wordless knowing of what-is before words. A silent knowing that arises in the mind as intuitive wisdom. A passionate knowing that arises in the heart as boundless love.

I started my spiritual journey because life was a mystery that I wanted to solve. But I've discovered that the question is the answer. *Life is a mystery*. That's what life *is*. And when I know the mystery, I know what life is, so intimately, that words are unnecessary.

THE MYSTERY AND THE STORY

Life is a mystery about which we tell stories. We all have a personal story about what life is, which we use to help us navigate our lives. A story that helps us understand what's going on… that gives us a sense of who we are… that gives life meaning. Our stories are wonderful. I love listening to people's stories. I'd love to hear your story.

We need a story to help us understand life, because if we didn't have a life-narrative we'd be lost. The problem is that we can easily mistake the story for reality. We can invest so heavily in our beliefs about life that we forget that we really don't know what life is. We can become so caught up in our opinions that we miss the breathtaking mystery. And when this happens, life becomes mundane and empty of wonder.

When I become embroiled with my story I find myself living in a sort of trance. I'm certain I know what's going on, even though I really don't. I exist in a state of numbness that I call 'normality' and I feel only half alive. But when I wake up I can see that my story is just a story. If I look deeper I discover that hidden behind my story is the pristine, virgin, untouchable mystery. And that's when the mystery experience spontaneously arises.

If you want to spiritually awaken to the WOW you need to see through your story to the deep mystery. But please don't misunderstand me. I'm not suggesting you abandon your story. Having a life-narrative is essential and the more coherent it is the better. Philosophy can be seen as the art of creating a better narrative to live by.

If we didn't have a story we'd be lost and confused, rather than awake to the wonder of life. But it's not an either/or choice. We can approach things paralogically and be conscious of *both* the story *and* the mystery. We can see that on the surface of life we need a narrative to help us understand our experience. But at the depths we don't know what life is.

It amuses me how I can bob along on the surface of life, thinking I know what's going on, then suddenly remember the deep mystery. And when this happens everything changes, because my state of consciousness is profoundly transformed. I become deep awake… super-conscious… really alive. When I know that I don't know… life becomes WOW.

Fearing the Mystery and Loving the Mystery

Yet sometimes the mystery seems terrifying. When I wake up alone at night the world can seem ominously strange. The realization that I don't know what's going on makes me panic. I don't want to dive into the mystery because it's so deep I'm frightened I'll drown. I want to push the mystery away and cling to the known for dear life. I want to close down, not open up.

When I feel terrified of the mystery of life I try to distract myself with superficialities. I numb myself with banality. I cosset myself with vapidity. This is a high price to pay because my life goes dead on me. The irony is I don't need to be frightened, because when I immerse myself in the mystery it's utterly safe… like coming home.

The mystery is only terrifying when I tell myself scary stories about the unknown. When I'm frightened of the mystery I'm not actually immersed in the mystery at all. Rather, I'm projecting imaginary monsters into the void. Then the unknown becomes a danger waiting to assail me in the shadows.

But actually the mystery isn't frightening. How could it be when I don't know what the mystery is? So when I stop clinging to my frightening story and truly immerse myself in not-knowing, there is no fear. Quite the opposite. There is relief and wonder. If I simply relax into the mystery I find myself free from the anxiety that can dominate me in my story. My story is still there, of course, because it must be. But it's transformed from a horror story into a mystery story.

When the Story Breaks Down

It's perfectly safe to step out of our story into the mystery. But if we start to feel we're losing touch with our story altogether, this can be awful. If the story that we use to negotiate life starts to disintegrate we feel totally disorientated and start to panic. This is what happens when we experience a mental breakdown. Our story breaks down and we feel that we're losing the plot.

I know many people for whom a breakdown has become a *breakthrough* to a deeper experience of living. But the distress we experience when we aren't anchored in the story is very disturbing. This is why I've been encouraging you to be conscious of *both* your story *and* the mystery.

Paradoxically, it's easier to relax into the mystery when we have a strong sense of our story. In my experience, when I am conscious that I *both* know *and* don't know what life is, I fall in love with the magnificent enigma of existence. I feel the mystery around me like a warm embrace and within me like a reassuring presence. I am far from terrified. I am wonderstruck.

THE TRUTH THAT WILL SET YOU FREE

So here's the paralogical message I want to share with you. At the heart of all we think we know is the deep mystery. And at the heart of the deep mystery lies a deep knowing that is so immediate it can't be mediated by words. A silent certainty that all is well. An unshakeable conviction that all that really matters is love.

This is the sublimely comical insight that has been passed down to us through countless generations of men and women who've dared to be spiritual explorers. The simple realization which seems like nothing but changes everything. The truth that will set you free.

Not-knowing is the doorway to all you can truly know and all you need to know.

Enter there.

Because that's where the party is.

CHAPTER 8

DEEP WONDERING
- WOW Experiment -

In this chapter I want to share with you a WOW experiment that takes wondering to a deeper level. If you take your time and really engage with the WOW experiments in this book, they will profoundly transform your state of consciousness. Don't worry if this doesn't happen straight away. Keep playing with these experiments and you may find yourself surprised. Often the mystery experience arises when we least expect it.

Spiritual awakening is as easy as not-knowing. In this chapter I want you to see the truth of this audacious statement for yourself. I want to invite you to wonder so deeply about life that you find yourself in a profound state of not-knowing... and to experience what happens to your state of consciousness.

Please don't misunderstand me. I'm not asking you to pretend you don't know anything, because that would be absurd. I'm not asking you to reject the wealth of human understanding, because that would lead to ignorance not wisdom. I want you to take a paralogical approach, which means recognizing that you *both* know *and* you don't know what life is.

The paradoxity of our predicament is that we need a story to make sense of life, but to experience the WOW we *also* need to know that we really don't know what's going on. The art of awakening is to be conscious of *both* the story *and* the mystery.

Most of us are so wrapped up in the story that we're unconscious of the deep mystery. So in this WOW experiment I want you to put your ideas to one side for a while and focus on not-knowing. I want you to step out of your story and dive into the deep mystery, because this is when the deep awake state naturally arises.

Socrates was honoured as the wisest man in the ancient world, because he knew he knew nothing. That's quite an achievement. Most of us suspect we don't really know what life is. But really *knowing* you don't know takes some work. It requires you to clearly see that your story is just a story; and to become conscious of the deep mystery at its foundation.

The Taoist sage Lao Tzu explained that 'in the pursuit of learning we come to know more and more'. But if we want to awaken we need to 'know less and less until things simply are as they are'. We need to let go of all our beliefs about life, which obscure the wordless reality of what-is.

In one of his poems Walt Whitman announces:

It is time to explain myself – let us stand up.
What is known I strip away,

> I launch all men and women forward with me into the
> Unknown.

Let's follow Uncle Walt into the deep mystery. Let's walk through the doorway of not-knowing to the WOW. Our ideas about life form a conceptual veil, which prevents us appreciating how exquisitely mysterious life really is. Let's see what happens if we part the veil and kiss the bride.

NOT-KNOWING

In our previous WOW experiment we wondered at the marvels of the world we live in. In this WOW experiment I want to explore deep wondering, so that we become immersed in the deep mystery. I wish I could be with you to personally guide you into the mystery. But that's not possible. So, instead, I'm going to share with you how it is for me when I enter a profound state of not-knowing. You can follow this process with me. Then you can try the experiment for yourself.

> I am sitting quietly and relaxing my body and mind.

> I am rousing myself from the numbness I call 'normal' by wondering at the amazing world I live in, which I so often take for granted.

> I am conscious of the story that I tell myself about who I am and what's going on.

> I am acknowledging how important my story is, but I'm clearly seeing that it's a story… a collection of concepts that I use to understand my life.

> I am conscious that I *both* know *and* don't know what life is.

> On the surface I have a working understanding of life… but I am reaching below the surface to the depths… and focusing on not-knowing.

> I am wondering deeply about what it is to be alive.

I am conscious of the inarticulate question of the heart that has no answer in words.

I am letting the inarticulate question lead me into the deep mystery of life.

I really don't know what this amazing experience of life actually is.

And as I realize this there is a wonderful sense of ecstatic liberation.

There is a lightness of being that feels like weightless dancing in endless space.

I am deep awake and intensely alive.

I am swimming in the numinous stillness of the deep mystery.

There is a deep knowing of the what-is before words.

There is a primal love of being.

I am dissolving into the mystery experience.

KNOWING THE MYSTERY

Now, you experiment with immersing yourself in the deep mystery. Take this experiment slowly and savour the experience. Be patient with yourself if your mind keeps bringing you back into your story. These WOW experiments can be difficult at first, but get much easier as you become familiar with a deeper way of experiencing life. Immersing yourself in the mystery is like free diving. The more you practise, the deeper you can go and the longer you can stay there.

Wondering

Be still and relax your body.

Bring your attention into the present moment and wonder at the world around you.

The Story

Be conscious of your story and acknowledge its importance. Yet also recognize that your story is only a story.

Be conscious that you *both* know *and* don't know what life is.

Not-Knowing

Now let go of the story and become intensely conscious of not-knowing.

Be conscious of the inarticulate question of the heart and let it lead you into the deep mystery of life.

Go below the surface of things and dive into the unfathomable depths.

Be conscious of the wordless mystery of what-is.

Feel the ecstatic wonder of not-knowing.

No ideas… just the WOW of being alive.

The Mystery

Dissolve into the deep mystery.

Be one with the deep mystery.

Be in love with the deep mystery.

CHAPTER 9

SCIENCE AND SPIRITUALITY

When we dive into the deep mystery we become deep awake. But this is impossible while we're certain we know what life is.

Many people today see spirituality as outmoded nonsense and reject the possibility of awakening, because they're convinced that science is on the verge of solving the mysteries of the universe. So in this chapter I want to critically examine this misunderstanding of science.

Science and spirituality are often seen in opposition to each other, which can make people feel they need to choose one or other perspective. I want to suggest that they are paralogically complementary ways of understanding life, so we can embrace both.

Tim: Hi Dick. Nice of you to pop into my imagination. Is there's something that's bugging you?

Dick: Yeah. I think any scientist would find your idea that no one really knows what's going on, completely laughable.

Tim: Actually, I think you'll find that the greatest scientists were profoundly conscious of the deep mystery.

Dick: Really? I think all this mystical stuff you're going on about is much too religious for any serious scientist. They're not going to abandon the awesome knowledge that science has given us to let go into 'not-knowing' and experience some nebulous WOW!

Tim: You don't have to abandon a scientific understanding of the world to awaken. You simply need to also recognize that underneath all we 'know' lies the pristine mystery of life.

Dick: You say that rationality is a good thing, so I don't understand why you're so enamoured with spirituality? Why not take a scientific approach to life? That's the real cutting edge of human culture.

Tim: I think science is amazing, but I don't think it can tell us everything about the human condition. Science and spirituality both reveal something important about life. I don't think it's an either/or choice. We can embrace both.

Dick: Rubbish. Science has been at war with religion for centuries. They're obviously not compatible.

Tim: Science certainly isn't compatible with superstitious, superficial types of spirituality. But deep spirituality doesn't contradict the findings of science.

Dick: So *you* say… but what do you know? Nothing by your own admission!

Tim: You're right. It would be better if you heard this from a well-respected scientist, rather than a quirky stand-up philosopher.

Dick: I don't think you'll find any serious scientist would go along with the ridiculous idea that hardnosed science is compatible with flaky spirituality.

Tim: Why don't we invite Albert Einstein to join our conversation, so you can ask him. No scientist is more widely respected than Einstein. He's a scientific superstar.

Dick: But he's dead.

Tim: Yes. So that means he'll only be able to say things he's already said before.

Dick: How do you mean?

Tim: I mean you'll be talking to a sequence of quotes.

Dick: But it really will be things the great man said... not you putting words into his mouth. Right?

Tim: I wouldn't dare.

Dick: In that case let's do it.

Tim: Great. I adore Uncle Albert, with his wild white hair and love of playing the violin. Let's welcome him in and see what he has to say about all of this.

A CONVERSATION WITH UNCLE ALBERT

Dick: So, Professor Einstein, will you kindly confirm for me that life is a mystery that we're well on our way to solving, thanks to the power of the scientific method.

Uncle Albert: 'The human mind is not capable of grasping the universe. We are like a little child entering a huge library. The walls are covered to the ceilings with books in many different tongues. The child knows that someone must have written these books. It does not know who or how. It does not understand the languages in which they are written. But the child notes a definite plan in the arrangement of the books – a mysterious order which it does not comprehend, but only dimly suspects.'

Dick: But we're understanding more and more all the time.

Uncle Albert: 'Measured objectively, what a man can wrest from Truth by passionate striving is utterly infinitesimal. But the striving frees us from the bonds of the self and makes us comrades of those who are the best and the greatest.'

Dick: Nevertheless, science gives us real knowledge about the truth of things.

Uncle Albert: 'Whoever undertakes to set himself up as a judge of Truth and Knowledge is shipwrecked by the laughter of the gods.'

Dick: But science has mapped reality with mathematical equations that help us manipulate reality. They really work because they're about the real world.

Uncle Albert: 'As far as the laws of mathematics refer to reality, they are not certain, as far as they are certain, they do not refer to reality.'

Dick: The fact remains that science is about the way it actually is… here and now in this concrete reality.

Uncle Albert: 'Time and space are modes by which we think and not conditions in which we live.'

Dick: What?!

Uncle Albert: 'Reality is merely an illusion, albeit a very persistent one.'

Dick: Look mate… I did science at school… everything can be reduced to physical matter. That's what really exists.

Uncle Albert: 'No, this trick won't work… How on earth are you ever going to explain in terms of chemistry and physics so important a biological phenomenon as first love?'

Dick: I thought scientists were materialists.

Uncle Albert: 'There is no place in this new kind of physics both for the field and the matter, for the field is the only reality. The field is the sole governing agency of the particle.'

Dick: Yeah… whatever… my point is that science is completely different to all that spiritual mumbo jumbo.

Uncle Albert: 'Let us not forget that human knowledge and skills alone cannot lead humanity to a happy and dignified life… What humanity owes to personalities like Buddha, Moses, and Jesus ranks for me higher than all the achievements of the enquiring and constructive mind. What these blessed men have given us we must guard and try to keep alive with all our strength if humanity is not to lose its dignity, the security of its existence, and its joy in living.'

Dick: Listen pal! Buddha didn't discover any of the laws of nature, he just got fat sitting around meditating all day. That doesn't lead to objective knowledge. All that spiritual stuff is subjective feelings and floaty intuitions.

Uncle Albert: 'The intuitive mind is a sacred gift and the rational mind is a faithful servant. We have created a society that honours the servant and has forgotten the gift.'

Dick: But what I'm trying to say is that science is about hard facts not just imagination.

Uncle Albert: 'Imagination is more important than knowledge. For knowledge is limited, whereas imagination embraces the entire world, stimulating progress, giving birth to evolution.'

Dick: I thought scientists were rationalists not intuitives.

Uncle Albert: 'The mind can proceed only so far upon what it knows and can prove. There comes a point where the mind takes a higher plane of knowledge, but can never prove how it got there. All great discoveries have involved such a leap.'

Dick: All right. But I can't accept this notion that we can intuitively 'deep-know' some gnosis that we can never say how we know. That's absurd.

Uncle Albert: 'If at first the idea is not absurd then there is no hope for it.'

Dick: But I want sensible answers. It's important to have something tangible to hang on to.

Uncle Albert: 'The important thing is not to stop questioning… One cannot help but be in awe when one contemplates the mysteries of eternity, of life, of the marvellous structure of reality.'

Dick: OK. But that doesn't mean you've got to become some sort of wonder-junkie and sit around wondering at how wonderful the wondrous universe is!

Uncle Albert: 'The most beautiful and deepest experience a man can have is the sense of the mysterious. It is the underlying principle of religion as well as all serious endeavour in art and science. He who can no longer pause to wonder and stand rapt in awe, is as good as dead; his eyes are closed.'

Dick: I don't mind a bit of wonder and awe every now and then. But I'm not going along with the silly idea that we need to become like little kids playing in the great sandpit of the cosmic mystery.

Uncle Albert: 'The pursuit of truth and beauty is a sphere of activity in which we are permitted to remain children all our lives.'

Dick: Very nice you sweet old codger. But let's say it like it is… This idea of the mystery experience… that's just spiritual twaddle.

Uncle Albert: 'To sense that behind anything that can be experienced there is something that our mind cannot grasp and whose beauty and sublimity reaches us only indirectly and as a feeble reflection – this knowledge, this feeling… that is the core of the true religious sentiment.'

Dick: What the hell has 'religious sentiment' got to do with science?

Uncle Albert: 'I maintain that cosmic religiousness is the strongest and most noble driving force of scientific research.'

Dick: But science is opposed to religion. They've been at each other's throats for centuries.

Uncle Albert: 'Well, I do not think that it is necessarily the case that science and religion are natural opposites. In fact, I think that there is a very close connection between the two. Further, I think that science without religion is lame and, conversely, that religion without science is blind. Both are important and should work hand-in-hand.'

Dick: Yeah… all very inclusive and open-minded… but the bottom line is that science is about solving the mysteries of life, while spirituality seems to be content with wallowing around in some sort of mystical not-knowing.

Uncle Albert: 'If you try and penetrate with your limited means the secrets of nature, you will find that, behind all the discernible concatenations, there remains something subtle, intangible and inexplicable. Veneration for this force beyond anything that we can comprehend is my religion. To that extent I am, in point of fact, religious.'

Dick: What? But you're meant to be a scientist!

Uncle Albert: 'Everyone who is seriously involved in the pursuit of science becomes convinced that a spirit is manifest in the laws of the universe – a spirit vastly superior to that of man.'

Dick: Science isn't about some vastly superior spirit for God's sake. It's about studying the physical world.

Uncle Albert: 'The divine reveals itself in the physical world.'

Dick: Man! You're sounding like a religious nutcase.

Uncle Albert: 'I am a deeply religious nonbeliever… This is a somewhat new kind of religion.'

Dick: No wonder you look like a mad professor… you really are a mad professor! You're the biggest name in science, but you're into some sort of cosmic religious feeling. I'm not sure what you really believe in.

Uncle Albert: 'I believe in mystery.'

REDUCTIONISM

When people view spirituality and science as in opposition to each other, it's usually because they don't really understand either spirituality or science. They see spirituality as superstitious nonsense and they confuse science with bland 'reductionism'. But reductionism isn't science. It's a flawed way of interpreting the findings of science.

Reductionist thinking is the opposite of paralogical thinking. Paralogical thinking says that to understand the fullness of reality we need to look at it in different ways. Reductionist thinking gives us an impoverished view of reality by insisting that we look at it in only one way. Here are some common reductionist ideas.

The universe is really *just* elementary particles.

Consciousness is really *just* the by-product of a piece of meat.

The feeling of love is really *just* chemicals in the body.

The birds may sing beautifully, but they're really *just* marking their territory.

When I hear someone use the word '*just*' in this way, they're usually being reductionist, because the universe is never *just* this or that... it is also so much more. So here are my responses to the reductionist claims above.

It's true that the universe is made up of elementary particles, but it can't be reduced to elementary particles. This misses the most amazing thing about the universe, which is that when parts combine to form a whole, the whole is greater than the parts.

Consciousness may correlate with the firing of neurons, but it can't be reduced to the activity of the brain. You're experiencing ideas right now, but if you could look inside your brain you wouldn't find a single idea. Ideas are non-physical things, which can't be reduced to physical things.

Emotional states may correlate with chemicals in the body, but being in love can't be reduced to chemicals. If you'd never felt love you wouldn't come to understand love simply by reading a paper on the chemistry involved. You'd need to *feel* love for yourself.

It's an interesting observation that birds sing to mark their territory, but this doesn't explain why birdsong sounds so beautiful. It doesn't account for the wonder of the dawn chorus. Birdsong may be functional, but it's also transcendental.

Reductionism kills wonder, because it reduces the universe to so much less than it is. Reductionism solves the mystery of life by pretending it isn't there. It's reductionists who've created the bleak picture of the universe as a meaningless accident. But this is not what science has revealed. It's a reductionist interpretation of what science has revealed.

A Theory of Everything

Reductionists are convinced that science is all we need to understand reality. Indeed, many believe that science is on the verge of a 'theory of everything', which will bind together the different strands of physics into a coherent whole. This would be exciting if it happens. Yet even if physicists did arrive at the longed-for 'theory of everything', the mystery of life would remain.

Professor Stephen Hawking explained in *A Brief History of Time* that a 'theory of everything' would necessarily be a set of equations and we would still be left with the great question:

> What is it that breathes fire into the equations and makes a universe for them to describe?

And, of course, a so-called 'theory of everything' wouldn't actually be a theory of *everything*. It would be a theory of how physics works. It wouldn't explain the beauty of music or the feeling of grief or the wonder of the WOW.

THE MEDIUM AND THE MESSAGE

Imagine that you've given a DVD of Frank Capra's classic movie *It's a Wonderful Life* to a friend. Later you ask 'What did you make of the movie?' and you're surprised to hear your friend reply:

> I've examined the DVD in great detail and found that it cleverly encodes digital information in such a way that it projects the illusion of colour and movement onto a screen.

All true and erudite, but surely missing the point! A movie may be digital information, but it's not *just* digital information. Above all it's a story. And the story is what we're really interested in. That's obvious isn't it?

In the same way, the universe may be made up of atoms bouncing around like billiard balls, or quantum particles coming in and out of existence, or superstrings weaving some vast web of appearances. But above all, surely, life is a story. The story of you. The story of me. The story of nature. The story of endlessly unfolding possibilities.

It seems to me that physics has done a marvellous job describing the physical universe, which is the medium through which the story of life is being told. But we're still left needing to understand the story.

A movie tells a story through the medium of digital information on a DVD. But if we want to understand the meaning of the story... feel its transforming power... be emotionally moved and intellectually challenged... it won't help to analyse the medium through which it's being told. We need to really get into the story.

It's similar with life. Science can tell us about the medium through which the story of life is being told, but it can't help us navigate the dramatic narrative of our individual lives. It can reduce life to mathematical equations, but it can't tell us how to live. It can inform us about how the universe works, but it can't reveal what life means. To find meaning in life we need to appreciate the story.

Subjective Meaning

If lots of your friends watched *It's a Wonderful Life* and you asked them what they made of the movie, you'd get different responses. Some would find it full of poignant optimism. Others would find it sentimental and ridiculous. Some would say it was OK. Others would say it was a masterpiece. Your friends could argue about who was right, giving reasons for their views. But no one would be right, because they're all subjective opinions.

It's similar with life. Science investigates how the universe works and offers us objective knowledge. But we all have our own subjective interpretations of the story of life. The deep spirituality we're exploring in this book offers an interpretation of the story of life that can lead us to a deep knowing of the depths of existence. But the gnosis can't be proven objectively like scientific theory. It's something we must know for ourselves.

COMPLEMENTARY STORIES

I've compared life to a story, but that's only a metaphor. Life isn't actually a story. Life is a mystery about which we tell stories. Science and spirituality offer us very different stories about life, but I want to suggest they are paralogically complementary, so we can embrace both.

Science helps us explore the objective mysteries of life. Spirituality helps us explore the subjective mysteries of life. Science is essentially a collective enterprise through which we come to understand how the universe works. Spirituality is essentially an individual enterprise though which we come to understand the meaning of life.

The scientific story on its own is not enough. It can't bring meaning to life, because meaning is subjective and science only deals with the objective world. But when we look with the two eyes of paralogical vision we can see that we live in both a mechanical reality and a meaningful reality. It's not either/or. It's both at once. That's the paradoxity of existence.

Most of us actually adopt a paralogical approach to our lives all the time. If we argued with a lover and they started throwing plates at us, we'd understand that the plates were smashing on the floor because of the laws of gravity. But we'd also attempt to understand the meaning of the event within the story of our lives, by asking who was at fault and what it told us about ourselves. We'd question how we'd got into such a situation and what it meant for the future.

Deep Science and Deep Spirituality

The great task of our age is to harmonize the subjective insights of spirituality and the objective insights of science. We need to embrace the paradoxity that there are objective and subjective ways of knowing. We can look outside ourselves for answers and we can look within ourselves for answers.

If we interpret science in a reductionist way and spirituality in a superstitious way, they're certainly not compatible. But deep science and deep spirituality are perfectly compatible. They're both rational, because they tell their particular stories about the mystery for good reasons, grounded in genuine experience. And they offer complementary perspectives on the paradoxity of life.

Of course many thinking people disagree with this approach. Indeed, militant rationalists have recently become extremely vocal in their opposition to spirituality. They see that huge numbers of people are still clinging to the sort of irrational religion that dominated our understanding of the world before the advent of science. They argue that people like me, who see spirituality and science as complementary, are trying to co-opt the authority of science to validate a primitive way of seeing the world.

This misses the important fact that people cling to out-dated religion because it gives them something that science can't. It addresses the great questions of our existence. It brings meaning to life. It offers an experience of the numinous. If we want to enable people to go beyond irrational religion, we need to offer more than rational science in exchange. We need to also offer a form of deep spirituality that brings to life the perennial wisdom at the heart of religion in a way that complements the wisdom of science.

DICK'S DOUBTS

Dick: Your intellectual gymnastics don't impress me I'm afraid. You say that science and spirituality are complementary stories about life. But that just isn't true. Science isn't a story. It tells the truth about the way things really are. Science isn't complementary to spirituality. It's the right way of seeing the world as opposed to the wrong way!

Tim: I had a feeling you might say that, so I've brought together three great quantum physicists for you to talk this through with.

Dick: Great. Albert had some very funny ideas. But then he's obviously an eccentric. I mean to say… he went to pick up his Nobel Prize without wearing socks. I could do with talking to some scientists who've got their heads screwed on.

Tim: These quantum guys are among the greatest scientific minds of all time. They've all won a Nobel Prize for physics. Let me introduce you to Werner Heisenberg, Wolfgang Pauli and, of course, Niels Bohr, whose ideas on paradox we discussed earlier.

Dick: Not the great Dane again! This suddenly doesn't sound so promising.

Tim: Of course they're all dead now, so they'll only be able to repeat things they've said before, as with our previous chat with Uncle Albert.

The Quantum Physicists

Dick: All right gentlemen… help me out here. I'm trying to convince Tim that science is much more than a story. It's concerned with the way things actually are. As physicists I'm sure you must agree with that. After all it's your job to work out how nature really is.

Niels Bohr: 'It is wrong to think that the task of physics is to find out how nature is. Physics concerns what we say about nature.'

Dick: But what science says about nature is hard fact. For example, reality is made up of atoms. That's not a story.

Niels Bohr: 'When it comes to atoms, language can only be used as in poetry.'

Dick: So how come physics enables us to build rockets and go to the Moon? You can't do that with poetry! Science helps us understand how things affect other things.

Werner Heisenberg: 'Quantum theory provides us with a striking illustration of the fact that we can fully understand a connection though we can only speak of it in images and parables.'

Dick: But surely physics doesn't deal in parables! The scientific method allows us to study nature in a neutral and unbiased fashion to arrive at a definitive picture of the universe.

Werner Heisenberg: 'What we observe is not nature itself, but nature exposed to our method of questioning.'

Dick: I don't think I can be making myself clear. What I'm saying is that we live in a real world and science explains how reality *really* is.

Wolfgang Pauli: 'The layman always means, when he says "reality", that he is speaking of something self-evidently known; whereas to me it seems the most important and exceedingly difficult task of our time is to work on the construction of a new idea of reality.'

Dick: Isn't that exactly what science has done?

Werner Heisenberg: 'The existing scientific concepts cover always only a very limited part of reality, and the other part that has not yet been understood is infinite.'

Dick: But we're progressively pushing back the frontiers of our ignorance. I mean… we've nearly understood the whole thing from the big bang onwards.

Werner Heisenberg: 'I for one no longer understand what we mean when we say we have understood nature.'

Dick: I realize that reality has turned out to be pretty strange, with all those quantum possibilities and whatnot. But the fact remains we're slowly coming to understand the universe.

Werner Heisenberg: 'Not only is the universe stranger than we think, it is stranger than we can think.'

Dick: But it says on the internet that more than 50 million scientific papers have been published. That must mean we've understood a whole load about reality.

Werner Heisenberg: 'The reality we can put into words is never reality itself.'

Dick: Don't give me that philosophical twaddle. The fact is that since we've freed ourselves from primitive superstitions and started thinking rationally, we've been getting to the truth of things.

Werner Heisenberg: 'It will never be possible by pure reason to arrive at some absolute truth.'

Dick: That's as may be. But everyone knows that rational science has had to fight against irrational religion for centuries. Now it's emerged triumphant we can reject spirituality as anachronistic nonsense. That's the main point I want to make.

Werner Heisenberg: 'In the history of science, ever since the famous trial of Galileo, it has repeatedly been claimed that scientific truth cannot be reconciled with the religious interpretation of the world. Although I am now convinced that scientific truth is unassailable in its own field, I have never found it possible to dismiss the content of religious thinking as simply part of an outmoded phase in the consciousness of mankind, a part we shall have to give up from now on. Thus in the course of my life I have repeatedly been compelled to ponder on the relationship of these two regions of thought, for I have never been able to doubt the reality of that to which they point.'

Dick: Well I'm shocked. Surely you don't go along with that Professor Pauli?

Wolfgang Pauli: 'I consider the ambition of overcoming opposites, including also a synthesis embracing both rational understanding and the mystical experience of unity, to be the mythos spoken or unspoken of our present day and age.'

Dick: But the mystical experience of unity isn't going to help us take forward scientific knowledge for heaven's sake!

Wolfgang Pauli: 'I confess, that very different from you, I do find sometimes scientific inspiration in mysticism... but this is counterbalanced by an immediate sense for mathematics.'

Dick: All very paralogical I'm sure! I suppose you think reality is a paradoxity or whatever.

Wolfgang Pauli: 'It seems significant that according to quantum physics the indestructibility of energy on one hand – which expresses its timeless existence – and the appearance of energy in space and time on the other hand correspond to two complementary aspects of reality.'

Dick: Man! You guys have been lost in your equations for so long you're no longer living in the real world.

Niels Bohr: 'Everything we call real is made of things that cannot be regarded as real.'

Dick: Yeah?! Well real things seem pretty real to me! I don't think you know what you're talking about!

Niels Bohr: 'Every sentence I utter must be understood not as an affirmation, but as a question.'

Dick: Look amigo… I've had it with all the paradoxes! You physicists have got the most crackpot ideas I've ever heard. In my opinion the universe is a physical reality that exists for no reason, in which human beings have evolved by chance.

Niels Bohr: 'Your theory is crazy, but it's not crazy enough to be true.'

Dick: Most amusing I'm sure. But I'm trying to discuss the nature of reality here.

Niels Bohr: 'There are some things so serious you have to laugh at them.'

Dick: Laugh all you like, but the truth is this: The more people have come to understand science, the more people have realized we don't need all that religious baloney about God and the mystery.

Werner Heisenberg: 'The first gulp from the glass of natural sciences will turn you into an atheist, but at the bottom of the glass God is waiting for you.'

A THINKING PERSON'S GUIDE TO NOT THINKING

We've critically examined a superficial understanding of science, which overestimates the power of the rational mind. Now I want to critically examine a superficial understanding of spirituality, which makes the opposite error, by rejecting the rational mind. I want to make it clear that awakening to the mystery doesn't require us to stop thinking clearly about things.

In this chapter I'd like do some thinking about thinking. For some spiritual traditions the thinking mind is a problem because it prevents us from awakening. In my experience this can be true. My mind creates the story that helps me navigate my life. But if I get caught up in the story I become convinced I know what's going on. Then I don't notice the deep mystery of life. And this means I stay only superficially awake, rather than becoming deep awake.

The mind spins a web of words, which we become caught up in and can't escape. This is why thinking has come to have a bad name in spiritual circles. But it seems to me that this is a one-sided view of the mind. Thinking has a good side and a bad side… as everything does.

On my spiritual journey I've been told many times that the mind is a problem I need to overcome. I need to stop thinking if I want to awaken. The mind is the villain that distracts me when I'm meditating. Thinking keeps me embroiled with my opinions, which prevents a deeper form of knowing. And if I dare to doubt the dubious nature of my thoughts, well that's just my nasty mind trying to stop me waking up. The message is clear… the thinking mind… boo… hiss… bad guy!

It seems to me that this demonizing of the mind is a profound mistake. It's absolutely true, of course, that when we get lost in our habitual thoughts it makes it harder to awaken. This is a valuable insight, but it's only half the story. I take a paralogical approach. To me the mind is a wonderful tool with which to create and criticize my story of life. But I don't want to be *only* conscious of the mind and the story it weaves for me. To become deep awake I *also* need to be conscious of the deep mystery.

Many spiritual traditions treat the mind as the enemy. But it seems to me that this is a crazy idea, which people take seriously precisely because they're not thinking about things enough! As we've matured from children into adults we've worked hard to develop the ability to think, and here's some spiritual teacher telling us it's all been a big mistake. Surely that can't be right?!

There's a little game I play when I want to check out if a

spiritual teaching makes sense. I ask myself if I would share the idea with my children. If the answer is 'no' then I usually find there's something missing from the teaching. This is a technique I'll return to many times in this book and I want to use it now by asking this: Would I tell my kids that the mind is a problem and that they should do their best to stop thinking?

The answer is obvious... definitely not! I encourage my kids to think more, not less. I want them to learn how to think clearly and imaginatively. I want them to develop a coherent story about life. But I also want them to grasp the paradoxity of the mind. So I would explain to them that the mind is a great gift, but that it can also cause all sorts of problems if we get carried away by the wrong thoughts. That's a both/and approach that works for me.

Struggling with the Mind

The demonizing of the mind makes it harder to awaken. If we believe that to awaken we must try to stop thinking, we become forever engrossed with battling the mind. And this prevents us seeing how easy it is to wake up, by simply becoming conscious of the deep mystery *as well as* the story.

When we're told that we must silence the mind, yet it stubbornly continues to perform its thinking function, we blame ourselves for our failure. Or, more accurately, the mind starts to berate itself for its failure to stop being the mind! But the mind can't stop thinking any more than the heart can stop beating. That's what it does. And thank goodness for that. If we stopped thinking we wouldn't be enlightened... we'd be stupid!

The mind can seem like a spiritual adversary because when we're lost in the mind it's hard to spiritually awaken. But the mind isn't really the bogeyman it's portrayed to be. When I examine the experience of thinking I find it's similar to talking. Thinking is simply talking to myself within the privacy of my own psyche.

Just as it drives me mad when I'm with someone who won't stop talking, it also drives me mad when I won't stop talking to myself. I need to be quiet as well as talk. I need to be with the silence as well as the ideas that arise within it. Then I can be conscious of the mystery as well as the story.

In my experience, when I'm troubled by constant, anxious inner chatter, I simply need to find something more interesting to focus on. Such as how wonderful it feels to let go into the mystery! When I do this I start to wake up and my worries dissolve. But if I attempt to get rid of the anxious chatter by stopping the thoughts, it doesn't work, because my worries just keep returning. Acknowledging the paradoxity of the mind works much better.

When I take this approach I first acknowledge that my mind is trying to do a necessary job for me, even when it seems out of control. The mind is thinking about my story so I can have a better time of things. It's imagining the future to help me avoid unpleasant experiences. It's analysing the past to help me learn from past mistakes. I need it to continue to do that. So before I dive into the deep mystery I'm clear with myself that I'll return to fully engage with the thinking process.

Then I'm free to take some time off from thinking to refresh myself in the mystery. And when I come back to my story and engage with the mind again I see the dilemmas of my story in a whole new light. My thoughts become less anxious and more considered. And when my mind is calm my attention can dance between my story and the deep mystery, because I am conscious of both.

CHILDISH SPIRITUALITY

Believing that the thinking mind is a hindrance on the journey of awakening leads to a regressive form of childish spirituality. Most of us are so embroiled with the grown-up world that we long for the joyous simplicity of childhood, so this approach to spirituality can be very appealing. But it seems to me to be disastrous.

In my experience when I'm deep awake I feel like a little child playing in the mystery. But I'm not *just* childlike. Being deep awake is not regressing to an earlier stage of my journey through life. It's progressing to a place where I can be *both* a thoughtful adult dealing with the challenges of life *and* like a child playing in the mystery.

Being an adult without also being a child means we miss out on the joy of life. Being a child without also being an adult means we can't handle the practicalities of life. But we don't have to choose one or the other. We can be both at once. We can mature out of childhood into adulthood, yet remain conscious of our innocent heart that was there right from the start.

Unfortunately many spiritual seekers become confused about this. The American philosopher Ken Wilber writes about what he calls the 'pre/trans fallacy', an understanding of which he regards as essential if we want to awaken. He explains:

> The essence of the pre/trans fallacy is itself fairly simple: since both prerational states and transrational states are, in their own ways, nonrational, they appear similar or even identical to the untutored eye.

The deep awake state is 'transrational'. It *transcends* and *includes* the rational state. It's a more expansive state of consciousness in which we can be rational, but we're also conscious of the deep mystery. This is completely different to the prerational state, in which we have yet to become really rational.

Understanding that the awakened state is transrational rather than irrational is essential if we want to spiritually evolve rather than regress to a childlike state that we mistake for wisdom. The problem is that much of modern spirituality is decidedly pre-rational. Let's look at some of the consequences of adopting this immature approach to awakening.

Irrational Optimism

I meet many spiritual people who've adopted a childlike optimism that life will simply look after them, just as a parent tends to a child. Having faith in life is wonderful, but this naïve positivity misses the obvious fact that life takes care of us through our own thoughts and actions. We're involved in the process and we need to take responsibility for that. We need to *both* have faith *and* think about what we're doing. As the Sufis advise… 'trust in Allah but tether your camel'.

Numerous people have approached me with wildly optimistic plans to arrange some huge event that will change the world, which they want me to become involved with. Their enthusiasm is very inspiring. They have a vision that they're willing to follow wherever it leads, which I admire immensely. They have unshakable faith in the goodness of life, which is extremely contagious. Yet something is wrong.

What's wrong is that they're missing a necessary paralogical perspective on life. They have regressed into the state we inhabited as children in which we expect Father Christmas to magically bring us what we want. They believe that if they intend hard enough… believe in the vision without allowing in doubts… don't think about things and just let them happen… then life will simply shower blessings upon them.

This may work for a while, but it ends in failure and disappointment, which leads to feeling disenchanted with life. This is why I suggest taking a paralogical approach, by *both* following our intuitive visions *and* engaging the rational mind to make them happen.

Please don't misunderstand me. Confidence in the benevolence of life is a great thing. When we face difficult challenges the thinking mind is not enough to get us through. We need faith in the fundamental goodness of existence, which spontaneously arises in the deep awake state.

While I've been writing this book, for example, my little girl was hospitalized with severe appendicitis. Thinking couldn't relieve my intense concern for her wellbeing. Rather, I needed to let go into the mystery and fill her with confidence that everything would be OK.

I entered a state of not-knowing in which I was present and loving. But I was extremely grateful that the surgeon who was operating on her knew exactly what he was doing. I was counting on the fact that he was going to think carefully about things and not simply have faith that it would all turn out for the best.

Miracles

We become spiritually childish because we feel starved of miracles. The adult world has exiled wonder, so we long for the aliveness of childhood when life was magical. But this means that when we come across strange tales of supernatural happenings we swallow them whole without chewing. We don't stop to cautiously consider if we're being sold a lot of baloney. We want to believe, because it makes us feel good.

Please don't get me wrong. I'm not saying that life isn't magical, because it most certainly is. Strange miracles do happen. I've witnessed more than I can remember. I love seeing the inexplicable wonder of life.

At one of my mystery experience retreats, for example, I took everyone outside on New Year's Eve, so we could release sky candles into the crisp night sky. It was a 'blue moon' that night and perfectly still. Everyone was brimming with love and we felt like little children. Then we noticed that an exquisite rainbow corona was circling the moon above us.

As we watched in breathless astonishment the shape of the corona changed to form an eye in the sky with the moon as its pupil. It was utterly magical. If so many of us hadn't witnessed it all together I think we may have doubted it happened. Yet it surely did.

Once in a blue moon miracles happen. I don't know how this eye in the sky occurred, but I suspect there's a rational explanation. Yet, that it happened when it did, made it *also* miraculous.

I value the rational mind but that doesn't mean I want to cut myself off from the miraculous nature of life. I don't want to dismiss the amazing synchronicities of life, which suggest a hidden pattern and meaning to events. It's rather that I've come to see everything as miraculous. Indeed, it seems to me, the fact that I can attempt to understand life rationally is truly miraculous.

Albert Einstein once said:

> There are two ways to live your life. One is as though
> nothing is a miracle. The other is as though everything is
> a miracle.

Very paralogical Albert… I agree with both perspectives.

Gullibility

When we reject the rational mind we don't become wise, we
become gullible. So it's no surprise that childish spirituality leads
to people believing all sorts of silly nonsense. If you don't think
too hard about it, you can buy into any story you like the sound of.
Being open to new possibilities is wonderful. But when you throw
away your 'bullshit detector' you become open to any old mumbo
jumbo.

I met a lovely man recently who told me he'd just come across
a new guru in town. He'd been very impressed when this Indian
teacher had confided that the time was coming when he would
manifest in three places at once in front of millions of his followers.
The man wondered what I made of this amazing prediction. I told
him my bullshit detector was 'bleeping' so loudly it was giving me
a headache. I'm open to anything, but I'd have to see some pretty
convincing evidence before I just took that on trust.

Without a bullshit detector we're truly lost. We can end up following channelled wisdom on how to live from disembodied spirits
and aliens from the Pleiades. I don't say this to denigrate channelling. I investigated this phenomenon in some depth when I was
younger and I found myself listening to people channelling some
deep and inspiring stuff. But largely it was rubbish.

Yet other people seemed inordinately impressed. I soon realized this was because they wanted to believe and were dismissing
their rational doubts as negativity. This is why people rarely choose
to ask the difficult questions that can puncture the illusion. No one
is saying:

OK. So you're an alien entity who comes from an advanced civilization and you want to help us evolve out of our primitive human state. That's great. Thanks for that. But can I just check you out to make sure you're for real. Can you give me some new scientific equation that we haven't arrived at yet? That should be easy for you in such an advanced stage of development. And then I can take the equation along to Professor Hawking at Oxford and blow him away, which will mean everyone will start listening to the urgent wisdom you are desperately trying to transmit to us... through your chosen channel... Petuli Lightworker.

Alas, this doesn't happen much because, as every child knows, it's more fun to just believe.

Spiritual Glamour

When we're spiritually childish we become easily enamoured with spiritual glamour. We like our teachers to have exotic names and wear exotic clothes. We want our masters to be 'fully enlightened', although we don't stop to ask ourselves what this could possibly mean. Even better, we want a guru who's an incarnation of God, come to rescue us if we trust in his grace. We're looking for daddy to take care of us. I know... I've been there!

These days, however, I feel very different. Now I'm attracted to teachers who know they are also students... who don't pretend to be perfect... who feel safe enough to show their human vulnerability. Indeed, it seems obvious to me that if I want to judge a teacher I need to examine their students. How many have they taught so well that the students no longer need the teacher? Surely that's a teacher's job?

The danger of being spiritually childish is that we end up in a cult around a paternal figure who actually has no interest in us ever growing up. When we follow a teacher who claims to be an ultimate authority, this undermines our ability to become our own authority, which is what needs to happen if we are to awaken.

When we become spiritual children we become stuck at an infantile level of development. We don't come to individualize as a person with a unique perspective. We start to talk in the same way as the teacher and dress like all the other disciples. We lose our precious individuality in a group trance that we mistake for awakening.

If we're spiritually childish it's easy to believe any appealing fantasy that serves us, and resent the rational mind that seeks to disillusion us. I've met many people who're convinced the spiritual group they belong to has been chosen to save the world. They believe that they're following the special master and that makes them feel special. And they need to feel special just as children need to feel special. The irony, of course, is that we're all special already, because each one of us is a unique thing in the world. And the more we individuate by thinking for ourselves, the more special we become.

The Latest Fad

When we're spirituality childish we easily buy into the latest spiritual fad. Last week it was 'The Age of Aquarius is coming'. This week it's 'the world is going to end in 2012'. You may well be reading this after 2012, in which case I'm confident there will be another day approaching soon that will herald the apocalypse or a wonderful collective awakening.

Over the decades of exploring spirituality I've seen an endless succession of spiritual fads come and go. At one time 'Immortalism' was in vogue. Now it's the 'Law of Attraction'. And it's not that I'm saying we shouldn't investigate these ideas. On the contrary, it seems to me we should fully examine such amazing possibilities, because they may have something to them. But we should do so using *both* the intuitive heart *and* the rational mind.

Recently there has been a spiritual health fad for fasting and detoxing. My wife Debbie has been detoxing and was told it's bad to drink coffee, but it's a good idea to have a coffee enema. Having done the fast and the coffee enema she says it's been great for her, so these things can really work. But when you're told to stop putting coffee in your mouth and put it up your bum instead, you at least need to stop and think about it first. Or the next thing you know they'll be offering enemas in Starbucks!

THE PARALOGICAL ALTERNATIVE

If we want to spiritually awaken we need to remember our child-like essence that wonders at the world. But it's important that we take a paralogical approach, so we're conscious of ourselves as a child as well as an adult... not instead. Then we can enjoy the magic of life and function in the practical world.

It's the ability to think which characterizes the adult mind. When we stop thinking carefully about things we regress to a pre-rational childish state. When we become deep awake, however, we transcend and include the rational mind within a more expansive state of consciousness. We're conscious of ourselves as a playful child and a thinking adult.

The deep awake state doesn't negate the mind. In my experience it allows me to think more deeply about things. It sets my mind free so that it functions with intuitive ease. Waking up to the WOW doesn't make my brain turn to jelly, so I spout sweet nonsense wearing a silly smile... although I should confess that I can be pretty fluffy sometimes, because when I'm really immersed in the mystery experience, the deep love is all that really matters! ;-)

CHAPTER 11

ENTERING
- WOW Experiment -

We've seen that we need a story to help us negotiate our lives. We've come to the conclusion that awakening doesn't require us to become irrational or unscientific. We've explored what a blessing it is that we can think about things.

Having acknowledged the importance of the mind, we're now ready to transcend the mind, and dive deeper into the mystery experience.

In this chapter I'm going to invite you to experiment with focusing on your sensual experience in the present moment. This will still your mind and help you step out of your story, so that you can immerse yourself in the wonder of the WOW.

When we're conscious of the deep mystery we become deep awake. But it can be difficult to stay conscious of the mystery if the mind keeps pulling us back to the story. So in this WOW experiment I want to share with you a simple of way of 'entering' deeply into the mystery of the moment, so that the mind relaxes and becomes quiet. But first I want to tell you an old Zen story.

> A Zen master was walking with one of his students who asked him: 'How can I awaken?'
>
> The master was quiet for a moment and then he replied: 'Can you hear that babbling brook?... Enter there.'

I love this story because in my imagination the student is looking for a clever spiritual teaching, but the master suggests that he can awaken by simply focusing his attention on the sound of the brook which has been babbling away in the background during their conversation. The master is telling him to become profoundly conscious of what he's already experiencing, by 'entering' into his sensual experience in the present moment.

I've found 'entering' my sensual experience to be a powerful way of awakening. When I enter into the immediacy of my sensual experience it becomes a doorway to the deep awake state. Suddenly my everyday world, which may previously have seemed banal, is transformed into something mysterious and exquisite. My senses come alive, my body becomes deeply relaxed and I feel intensely present.

Professor Semir Zeki, a neurobiologist at University College London, has recently discovered that when we look at beauty the same areas of the brain are activated as when we fall in love. This doesn't surprise me, because I've found that when I enter my immediate sensual experience, all that I'm sensing becomes utterly wondrous, and I fall in love with the moment.

The Practice of Entering
The practice of 'entering' builds on our previous WOW

experiments to make deep wondering easier and more effective. It involves *really* listening, looking and feeling, so that we profoundly appreciate how wonderful our sensations are. In my experience, when I enter the sensuality of the moment it's intensely pleasurable, so it's easy to let go of my story and dive into the mystery. My mind begins to become quiet and the mystery experience spontaneously arises.

'Entering' is a practice you can use at any time to dive into the mystery, because it simply requires you to become profoundly conscious of what you are experiencing in the here and now. You can enter the enjoyment of tasting. You can enter the magic of music. You can enter the delight of touching another human being. You can enter your present experience of looking at this page.

Sensual Breathing

I find entering the sensuality of breathing is particularly powerful. I regularly practise 'sensual breathing', so I've developed the ability to enter deeply into my breath. And this brings me back to life when I've forgotten how much I love being.

Many spiritual traditions teach the practice of meditating on the breath. But to call it a 'practice' can make it sound like an arduous thing to do. Actually 'practising' sensual breathing is wonderful. In my 20s I spent a year meditating most of the time. What I discovered was that sinking into my breath feels really good.

The sensual delight of breathing is something that meditation teachers often seem to overlook. Focusing on the breath can then seem like a demanding challenge, rather than a pleasure to savour. But in my experience it can be utterly beautiful to bathe in the bliss of simply breathing.

SENSUAL ALIVENESS

The practice of 'entering' is simple and it works. As with our previous WOW experiment, I'm going to share with you how it is for me when I enter the sensual moment. You can go through the practice with me and then you can try it out for yourself.

Wondering

I am sitting quietly and relaxing.

I am waking myself up by wondering.

I am marvelling at the splendour and beauty of the world around me.

I am wondering so deeply that I am entering a state of profound not-knowing.

I am stepping out of my story and into the mystery of the moment.

Now I am focusing my attention on my immediate sensual experience.

Sensual Listening

I can hear a bird singing in the garden and I'm entering the sound.

I am *really* listening.

I am noticing the textures and cadences of the singing.

And as I listen deeply my state of consciousness is changing.

It feels exquisite to listen… as if I am listening for the first time.

My immediate experience seems utterly mysterious and full of wonder.

My attention is focused yet soft… as if I am caressing the sound.

The edges between the various sounds I can hear are melting away and there is one beautiful flow of sound arising within awareness.

It feels as if I am becoming one with the river of sound.

The whole world is ringing with vibrating sound... and I am the sound.

Sensual Looking

As I look out the window I can see the bright-pink blossom on the tree in my garden.

It reminds me of Dennis Potter before he died, looking at the blossom in his garden and seeing it as if for the first time.

I am entering the pink blossom.

I am really looking.

I am becoming very still and intensely present.

I am entering into the delicate textures of the flowers.

I am entering into the vibrant pinkness of the petals.

I feel as if I have never seen anything so pink before.

I feel as if I may never see anything so beautiful again.

I feel as if I am seeing things as they really are... magical... miraculous... mysterious.

I am so close and intimate with the colour of the blossom that I feel one with the blossom.

I am in love with the blossom.

Sensual Breathing

Now I am noticing the feeling of my body sitting here on this chair. I am conscious of the air on my skin.

I am conscious of my breath as it rises and falls.

I am entering my breath.

I am conscious of the sensual flow of air in and out of my body.

I am sinking into my breath and it's becoming intensely pleasurable to simply breathe.

The air feels thick and my body is vibrating with energy.

To simply be here breathing is the most fulfilling experience I could possibly imagine.

I am dissolving into breathing.

I feel as if the universe is breathing me.

I am one with the sensation of breathing which is arising within awareness.

My body is softening and it feels good to simply be.

I feel immersed in mystery.

I am in love with this moment just as it is.

I am in love with being.

I've stopped the practice now, but the feeling of profound connectedness and delicious sensuality is still overwhelming. I'm not wearing any shoes and I can feel my feet gently stroking the carpet and it feels wonderful. I'm sipping a coffee and the taste is electric. It feels great to be alive.

THE SENSUALITY OF THE MOMENT

Now I want to invite you to enter your sensual experience. When I lead this exercise at my mystery experience retreats I always put on some beautiful music, because music is magic. Nothing transforms consciousness so quickly. And, although I'm a musician myself, I really have no idea how it does that. Music is very mysterious.

For this exercise I usually play something gentle, ambient and deep, such as *Für Alina* by the minimalist composer Arvo Pärt. I don't want the music to become overwhelming, just to seduce people out of the numbness of normality into a state of sensual aliveness. When you do this experiment you don't need to use music, but it's something you may want to play with.

I urge you to keep experimenting with this practice, because the more often you 'enter' the sensual moment, the deeper you'll go into the mystery. If you become troubled by distracting thoughts, simply focus on how pleasurable it is to pay attention to your sensual experience, and the mind will gradually become still.

Wondering

Become quiet and comfortable… relaxed and alert.

Wonder at the world around you and enter a state of profound not-knowing.

Step out of your story into the mystery of the moment.

Then focus your attention on your sensual experience in the here and now.

Sensual Listening

Be conscious of listening and *enter there*.

Listen intently to the flow of sound… the loud sounds… the subtle sounds.

Be conscious of the timbres of the different sounds.

What is it to hear something?

Appreciate how exquisite it is to listen.

Listen as if you had been deaf all your life and are listening for the first time.

Listen as if you are hearing for the last time.

Listen so intimately that you feel one with the sound arising within awareness.

Be in love with listening.

Sensual Looking

Be conscious of looking and *enter there*.

Really look at what is before you.

Be conscious of the shapes... the colours... the textures.

What is it to see something? How is looking different from listening?

Appreciate how amazing it is to look at something.

Look as if you had been blind all your life and are looking for the first time.

Look as if you are seeing for the last time.

Look so intimately that you feel one with the sensation of seeing.

Be in love with looking.

Sensual Breathing

Be conscious of feeling in the present moment and *enter there*.

Feel your body letting go and loosening up.

Feel the air on your skin.

What is it to feel something? What is it like to experience this particular quality of sensation?

Focus on your breath coming into and out of your body.

Dissolve into your breath and become conscious of how utterly delicious it feels to breathe.

Feel your breath so intimately that you are one with the sensation of breathing arising within awareness.

Be in love with breathing.

Be in love with being.

THE MYSTERY OF THE MOMENT

In this chapter I'm going to explore how we can use the practice of 'entering' to awaken to the mystery of the moment in our everyday lives. I'm also going to continue my critique of superficial spiritual ideas, which can make it much harder to awaken.

I exist right now and my story tells me what's going on. In my case what's going on is that I'm writing this book for you. I've just made breakfast and got my kids off to school. Before me lies a day of coaxing words into a comprehensible order, so that I can help you dive deeper into the mystery experience.

I love my story but today it's making me feel uncomfortable. I'm concerned about the fact that I'm behind schedule writing this book. I'm aware of the problems that could arise if I don't deliver this manuscript to deadline. Yet I really want to make this book as good as possible and that takes time.

I've allowed myself to become consumed by this story, so I've been getting anxious about the future. Then I've been regretting things that have happened in the past, which have left me in this predicament. And my anxiety and regret are ruining my experience of the present moment.

I'm not enjoying feeling like this, so I'm going to change my perspective on the moment. I'm putting my story on one side and placing my attention on the delicious sensuality of my breath flowing into and out of my body. My mind is quieting and I'm seeing through the anxiety of my story. Who knows what is really going on? My life has rarely worked out as I planned. It's no good fighting the way things are. Much better to be at peace with what-is.

Now I'm sinking below my surface agitation into the deep mystery. I'm conscious of a vast stillness... a primal peace... a reassuring sense that all is well. I feel intensely present. My body is relaxing and I'm feeling easy. I'm conscious of the miracle that I exist right now and how good it feels to simply be. I'm appreciative of the everyday wonders that surround me. The weariness caused by my worries is passing and I feel refreshed.

Yet there's something stopping me just staying here in the mystery of the moment. Thoughts are reminding me that time is passing and I have so much to do today. But I don't feel resentful for the disturbance, because I'm grateful for the reminder. I could say to myself 'Well it's better for me when I hang out in the mystery, so who cares about stupid deadlines'... but that doesn't feel right. I want to be a responsible person who meets his commitments to others, because being responsible is being loving.

So now I'm bringing my attention back to the challenges in my story. They haven't changed, but my state of consciousness has. I feel alive and present, not overwhelmed by the burdens of practical life. The adventure of Tim has led me to this moment. This is the way it is. Life is an unspeakable miracle... and in the story of my life I'm facing these challenges. OK... bring 'em on. I'm ready to play!

HOW LONG IS NOW?

I've found that an extremely simple and effective way to transform my state of consciousness is to use the practice of 'entering'. This brings my attention to the immediacy of my sensual experience, so that I become intensely conscious of the here and now. Then I can step out of my story in time and into the mystery of the moment. And when I become immersed in the mystery, this changes how I see my story.

To understand why this practice works so well we need to examine the paradoxity of the 'now'. I've done this before in my book *How Long Is Now?* and I want to return to some of these ideas again, because they can help us both wake up to the WOW and deal with the dilemmas of everyday life.

I love the question 'how long is now?', because it elicits two opposite responses. On the one hand the 'now' seems infinitely brief. I can never catch the moment, because as soon as I've thought about it, the moment has moved on. On the other hand, it's always now. The past and future exist as memory and possibility. The perpetual now is what *is*.

So is the moment too brief to catch or so long it's always now? Examine your experience right now and I think you will find that it's both. Time is an ever-changing flow of experience that's arising in the perpetual now. The moment exists in time, but it also has a timeless quality.

As with all paradoxities we need to be conscious of both of

these perspectives, not just one or the other. The problem is that most of us see the moment from only one perspective. We're conscious of the moment in time, because we're interested in where we've come from and where we're going. We aren't conscious of the timeless moment, because we haven't got time for that!

If we do pay attention to the timeless moment, however, our state of consciousness changes because we come out of the story into the mystery. This is because the story exists in time. The story is how we understand life with thoughts. And thoughts are a sequence of words in time. You can easily see this... if... you... read... this... sentence... slowly... because... you... don't... know... what... I... am... going... to... say... until... the... sentence... ends. And that takes time.

When we bring our attention into the timeless now, we don't understand life with words. We experience the glorious immediacy of being alive in the present moment. We are no longer dominated by concerns about the past and future... and this can be a great relief.

The story is a narrative that allows us to understand the present in the context of where we've come from and where we're going. We need this perspective to negotiate the ever-changing flow of events. But to become deep awake we *also* need to profoundly appreciate the here and now.

When we're caught up in the story of time we experience regret about the past and anxiety about the future. We become harried by worried thoughts and permanently stressed. But when we come into the timeless now there is no story. In the mystery of the moment we find a deep peace that lies below the surface agitation. We allow life to simply be as it is.

In my experience, when I enter the present moment I find myself in a relaxed state of childlike wonder... spacious openness... naked presence... profound not-knowing. The Zen master Shunryu Suzuki calls this 'beginners mind'.

In the state of beginners mind I see what-is with fresh eyes, uncontaminated by my previous experience. I'm not just an

informed adult who's on a journey through time. I'm also an innocent child playing in the perpetual now, not expecting thngs to
make sense by conforming to the patterns of the past.

PASSION AND PEACE

I remember discovering the power of being conscious of the
mystery of the moment in my early 20s. I'd spent many months in
meditative retreat, which was wonderful, but my peace had been
shattered by a big argument with the girl I was in love with. It
looked as if our relationship was over and I was in extreme emotional turmoil. I found myself sitting by the open window of the
little cottage I was living in, listening to the babbling brook outside,
full of regret and anxiety.

Then I remembered the Zen story I shared with you earlier, so
I entered the sound of the brook. I let go into the melodies of the
water dancing over the rocks. And as I became intensely conscious
of the present moment I found my state of consciousness started
to change. In the moment there was no story… no regret… no
anxiety… no suffering. And I found myself immersed in a deep
and poignant stillness.

When thoughts about my heartbreak arose, I found myself
back in the story of my lamentable past and frightening future. But
as soon as I let go into the timeless *now*… there was the deep peace
again. Then back to the story… and there was the suffering. Then
back to allowing things to simply be… and there was deep peace.

The more this kept happening, the more I hated my story
and longed to be liberated into the mystery of the moment. But
somehow I couldn't manage to push my story away. It kept coming
back and bringing the emotional pain with it.

Actually it's more accurate to say that some part of me wanted
to keep returning to the story, because it felt inauthentic to simply
ignore how I was feeling. When I pushed away my story, I was
pushing away the reality of my love for the girl who was leaving
me. And I wasn't prepared to do that. Not even to avoid suffering.

As long as I was caught up in an either/or way of looking at the moment, I found myself constantly vacillating between being consumed with agitation and surprised by deep peace. Then I saw another possibility.

I took some time to fully acknowledge how I felt about what was happening in the story of Tim. I honoured my heartbreak. I acknowledged my regret and fear. Then I chose to put my story aside for a while. I consciously decided to take a break from time and refresh myself in the timeless peace of the present.

I let go into the mystery of the moment so deeply, there was only the music of the babbling brook, caressing away my cares. My heart opened and I felt a profound love of being. I felt the deep knowing that all is well, despite appearances. I stayed with the timeless moment until my state of consciousness had been transformed. And then, when it felt intuitively right to do so, I brought my attention back to the story. But now I saw my predicament with new eyes and knew how to make things right.

IN AND OUT OF TIME

The point I want to make here is paralogical. On the one hand, the simple way to wake up from the story is to become conscious of the mystery of the moment. But it's important not to take an either/or approach, because we also need to be conscious of the story in time as well.

There is a current fad in spirituality for 'being in the now' *instead* of thinking about time. I meet a lot of people whose mantra has become '*just* be in the present moment'. But we can't *just* be in the present moment. If we actually stopped thinking about time we wouldn't know who we are and what happened yesterday. We'd become amnesiac. And that's not a sign of spiritual awakening. It's a challenging medical condition we'd all like to avoid.

When we try to push away one pole of a paradoxity it doesn't make it easier to become conscious of the other pole. It makes it more difficult. If we try to become conscious of the timeless moment by exiling our concerns with time, we set ourselves an impossible task.

The simple solution, which makes awakening much easier, is to take a both/and approach. We need to acknowledge that being conscious of time is not a curse, it's a great blessing. And we *also* need to be conscious of the wonder of the present moment. Then we can move our attention freely between time and the now, dealing with the unfolding challenges of our lives whilst also appreciating the mystery of the moment.

Child and Adult

Previously I mentioned that I test out spiritual teachings by asking myself if I would share them with my children. So let me now ask: Would I tell my kids that they should stop thinking about time and just live in the moment? The answer is clear. No I certainly would not!

As a parent I encourage my kids to become *more* conscious of time. I want them to think about school the next day, even when they're enjoying staying up late. I want them to do their homework, so they have an education to help them in the future. I want them to clean their teeth, so they remain healthy when they're older.

I want my kids to take responsibility for what they've done in the past and think about what lies before them in the future. Does this mean I'm hampering their spiritual awakening? Should I really be letting them just exist in the moment? Surely not?!

Children naturally exist in the present moment, which is both good and bad. On the good side they can easily enjoy the play of simply being here and now. But they can't cope with the practical demands of living in time. That's why they need adults to look after them.

Growing up is a journey into time. You and I have made that journey. And now we're finally *in* the story of time it seems perverse to say we should stop being concerned with the past and the future. That doesn't make any sense. Was the whole process of growing up a regrettable error?

The process of life necessitates that we grow up out of the present moment into the story of time. Yet we pay a price for coming into time, because we lose the primal sense of being in the moment that we experienced as a child. And this makes our grown-up world a very serious, anxiety-ridden place to live in. Yet the childlike joy of being present is still there if we look below the surface, waiting for us to remember.

Spiritual awakening is reconnecting with our childlike essence. But this doesn't mean *just* becoming like a child again. I expect, like me, you've met people who have chosen to take this path and… let's be honest… they can be a right royal pain in the butt. Adults who behave just like children aren't deep awake. They're immature, selfish, ineffective and unreliable. Just like kids! But what is endearing in children is far from endearing in adults, because we expect more. We expect self-reliance and responsibility to others. And rightly so.

Conversely, however, if we meet adults who've smothered their childlike essence with layer after layer of grown-up worries, they are uptight, fretful people who seem to have forgotten that the joy of life lies in simply appreciating the present moment.

Taking a paralogical approach to this dilemma allows us to be *both* a responsible grown-up in time *and* a little child playing in the perpetual present. We don't have to choose between the two. We can be conscious of *both* the flow of time *and* the timeless now. And when we do, life becomes WOW.

CHAPTER 13

THE ADVENTURE OF AWAKENING
- WOW Experiment -

In this chapter I'm going to encourage you to experiment with awakening to the mystery of the moment during your everyday life.

To end this part of our journey into the mystery experience I'd like to invite you to accept a life-changing challenge. While you're reading this book, pay attention to your state of consciousness, and regularly choose to step out of your story into the deep mystery. If you live your life in time *also* conscious of the perpetual now, you'll find that it transforms your experience of living into an adventure of awakening. Give it a go and see for yourself.

The Paradoxity of Attention

It may sound difficult to be conscious of *both* the story in time *and* the mystery of the moment, but it becomes much easier if you understand the paralogical nature of your attention. To help you understand this I'd like you to first examine the paralogical nature of your eyesight, which is similar and easier to recognize.

Examine your vision and you'll see that it focuses on a point around which you experience unfocused, peripheral vision.

Right now my vision is focused on the computer screen before me, but in my peripheral vision I can see the garden through the window, yet it's indistinct and out of focus. I am presuming you're experiencing something similar. Yes?

Now examine your attention and you'll find that it also has a point of focus and a more diffuse, peripheral quality.

Right now my attention is focused on the words I'm writing, but in my peripheral attention I'm aware that it's getting late and I'll need to stop soon. I'm presuming that your attention is focused on reading this book. But in your peripheral attention you are conscious of whatever else is going on in your life right now.

For me the art of awakening is to move the focus of my attention between the mystery and the story, whilst retaining the other pole in my peripheral attention. This means that when I focus on the mystery, my story is in my peripheral attention. And when I focus on my story, the mystery is in my peripheral attention.

At first it can be hard to do this. On my spiritual journey I initially found that when I focused on the story I forgot all about the mystery. But now I'm familiar with the mystery experience, it's easier to keep the mystery in my peripheral attention when I focus on the story, so I can return my focus to the mystery when I choose to. This means I can allow the focus of my attention to flow between the story and the mystery.

Fluid not Fixed

During a mystery experience retreat over New Year we held a party to celebrate a new beginning. My little girl came along and immediately picked up on the deep love we were feeling. When I came to tuck her into bed that night she told me 'Daddy I'm drunk on love'. That's how it feels to be immersed in the deep mystery. It's my favourite feeling. But feeling intoxicated isn't always appropriate.

If I want to meet with my accountant, the focus of my attention needs to be in the practical world. When I'm swimming in deep love the whole idea of 'money' seems utterly absurd. I'm playing in the moment, enjoying time off from time. This is a welcome holiday from the practical challenges of life. But sooner or later I must focus my attention on my everyday world to continue the human journey.

When I'm deep awake, my attention is fluid, not fixed, so I can respond to the changing demands of life. Sometimes I find myself diving into the WOW. Sometimes I focus on my story, and the mystery is present in the background. The focus of my attention flows between the paralogical poles.

WHAT STATE AM I IN?

Awakening is easy because it simply requires us to become conscious of the mystery of the moment. The tricky thing is noticing when we're only superficially awake, so that we can choose to become deep awake. When we're living in the semi-conscious state we call 'normal' it's hard to recognize how unconscious we are.

And that's because we're largely unconscious! It's a paralogical Catch 22!

The secret is to develop the habit of noticing how awake you are. Instead of just paying attention to what's happening in your life story and responding habitually to the unfolding narrative, you need to stop and ask yourself 'What state of consciousness am I in?'

What you think and do is important, but your thoughts and actions arise from your state of consciousness, so this is *extremely* important and paying it attention will profoundly transform your life for the better.

As you cultivate the habit of paying attention to your state of consciousness you'll find yourself noticing when you're only superficially awake. Then if you want to become deep awake you can. Here are some signs to look out for, that mean you're only superficially awake.

If you're certain you know what's going on... you're superficially awake.

If life seems banal and lacking in magic... you're superficially awake.

If you're so caught up in trying to get somewhere that you're ignoring the mystery of the moment... you're superficially awake.

If you've become so serious that you can't laugh about life... you're superficially awake.

If you're missing the fact that your life is an astonishing adventure... you're superficially awake.

Paying attention to your state of consciousness is like pinching yourself in a dream so that you wake up. It disrupts the unconscious flow of life to allow a conscious change of perspective.

A WOW Word

The trick to awakening in everyday life is to notice when you're only semi-conscious and respond immediately, because it's very easy to fall asleep again before you've even attempted to become deep awake. Something that can help with this is to have a WOW word. This is a word or phrase that you say to yourself as soon as you notice you're asleep in the story, so that you can trigger a change in your state of consciousness.

For example, sometimes I use the WOW word 'breathe'. When I notice I'm only superficially awake I repeat this word to bring my attention to my breath and trigger the process of becoming deep awake. Other words and phrases I use to initiate an awakening are… wake up… don't know… be present… love… be real… sink into the mystery.

I suggest you find a WOW word that appeals to you and try it out. You can write your WOW word on post-it notes and leave messages for yourself around your home or place of work. People will think you're weird… but what the hell! I did this for years and it works well as a reminder. But you'll need to keep changing the notes, otherwise you'll find yourself looking at them without seeing them. We quickly habituate to things.

I suggest you constantly experiment with ways to remind yourself that it's possible to awaken. In my 20s I went as far as creating messages for my unconscious self. I took an endless tape and a pillow speaker designed for teaching people foreign languages in their sleep. I replaced the French verbs with messages reminding myself to be conscious of my breath. Then I slept with the tape playing all night. I'm not suggesting you do this, because it didn't really help. But it was worth a try! It's always worth experimenting with ways to awaken.

REMEMBERING TO WONDER

So here's what I'm encouraging you to do.

> Throughout your day, pay attention to your state of consciousness as much as you can.

When you discover you're only superficially awake, seize the moment to become deep awake.

Wondering

Focus you attention on the wonder of life.

Be conscious that you really don't know what's going on.

Focus your attention on not-knowing.

Entering

Enter the immediacy of your sensual experience in the here and now.

Become conscious of the delicious feeling of your breath coming into and leaving your body.

Focus your attention on the mystery of the moment.

Living in the Mystery

Then, when it feels intuitively right, return the focus of your attention to the practical world in time, but keep the mystery of the moment in your peripheral attention.

See your story with new eyes and engage creatively with your life.

Get on with your routine activities, but at the back of your mind remember what a miracle life is, so your everyday life becomes suffused with wonder.

Part II

A JOURNEY INTO THE DEEP SELF

CHAPTER 14

THE DEEP SELF

We're on a journey into the WOW of awakening that leads to the bliss of deep love. But to get to the depths of this wonderful feeling we need to understand life in a deeper way. This means that, in the next part of this book, we'll be traversing some challenging philosophical terrain.

The ideas we're going to explore are so far from common sense they can seem hard to grasp. Yet actually they simply describe the reality of the present moment. So you can check out the ideas by simply paying close attention to what you're experiencing as you read this book.

Our journey of awakening has led us below the surface of life to become conscious of the deep mystery. We've been focusing on the question 'what is life?'. Our next step on the journey is to make a paralogical switch of perspective and to focus on the question 'who am I?'. This is a profound question that can lead us deeper into the mystery experience.

When I ask myself the question 'who am I?' the obvious response is 'I am Tim'. Yet I'm not sure what that means. There are so many Tims. There's the Tim who is a philosopher writing this book. But he's quite different to the Tim who snuggles up in bed with his wife at the end of the day. Or the Tim who plays computer games with his children. Or the private Tim who no one else sees but Tim himself.

It amuses me that I even dress up in different clothes to clearly differentiate the different Tims. Shorts and a T-shirt for hanging out in the garden with the kids. A sharp suit for public presentations. Jeans and a jacket for going to the school for parents evening. Something more flamboyant for socializing with friends. The relief of no clothes at all for going to bed.

I have many different personas. The word '*persona*' means 'mask'. I wear many different masks. But who is underneath the mask? What happens if I perform a philosophical striptease and peel away all these passing identities? Who am I then? What is my naked self?

WHO AM I?

As I have studied my own nature over the years, I've discovered there are two paralogically opposite ways of seeing who I am. I can look at myself *objectively* and *subjectively*. How I answer the question 'who am I?' depends on which perspective I adopt. Let me take you through it.

The Objective Perspective
First I'm going to examine my objective identity.

Objectively I am a person in the world, who puts on different personas to meet different situations.

In my imagination I am peeling off all my personas to reveal my fundamental nature.

Underneath all the roles I play and the clothes I wear I'm a naked body.

Objectively I am an *object* in the world.

The Subjective Perspective

Now I'm going to examine my subjective identity. Objectively what I am is easy to see, but subjectively what I am is a lot less tangible.

Subjectively I am the experiencer of this moment.

I am the mysterious presence I call 'I'.

I'm conscious of being the 'I' experiencing a stream of experiences right now.

But what is the 'I'?

The 'I' is aware of this moment, so I could describe the 'I' as 'awareness'.

I am awareness witnessing an ever-changing flow of experiences that I call 'life'.

Subjectively I'm a *subject* who is witnessing the world.

The Paradoxity of Identity

I have found that there are two paralogical poles to my identity.

My objective identity is a body in the world.

My subjective identity is the 'I' that is aware of my body in the world.

So which am I? A subject or an object? When I examine the reality of the moment, I see that I am clearly both. Most of us think of ourselves as just a body in the world. We're conscious of the objective perspective. Spirituality encourages us to pay attention to the elusive subjective perspective. It urges us to 'look within', because then we become conscious of the deep self.

AN EXISTENTIAL RIDDLE

I want to share with you two of my favourite quotes which point to the deep self. The first comes from the Gnostic 'Gospel of Thomas' and the second from the Hindu 'Chandogya Upanishad'. I like putting these quotes together because, although they come from very different cultures, they're both saying exactly the same thing, which I find fascinating.

In the first Jesus announces:

> I will reveal to you
> what can't be seen,
> what can't be heard,
> what can't be touched,
> what can't be thought.

What is he on about? Is he being deliberately abstruse? The second quote makes things a bit clearer. It's in the form of a riddle. See if you can find the answer.

> What is it that can't be seen,
> but which makes seeing possible?
> What is it that can't be heard,
> but which makes hearing possible?
> What is it that can't be known,
> but which makes knowledge possible?
> What is it that can't be thought,
> but which makes thinking possible?

So what is the answer to this existential riddle? I suggest the answer is obvious. What is it that can't be seen or heard or touched or thought? It is the mysterious 'I' that is seeing and hearing and touching and thinking. It is 'awareness' that is conscious of all that we experience.

So here's my response to the riddle.

Awareness experiences seeing,
but has no colour or shape.
Awareness experiences hearing,
but makes no sound.
Awareness experiences touching,
but has no tangible form.
Awareness experiences thinking,
but isn't a thought.

The great secret found at the heart of all the great spiritual traditions of the world is this. If you pay close attention to your identity, you will discover your subjective nature as the mysterious 'I' of awareness. This is your deep self. It is what the Hindu philosophers call the 'atman', the Buddhist masters call your 'buddha-nature', and the Christian mystics call your 'spirit'. The word 'spirit' means essence. The word 'essence' comes from the Latin '*esse*' meaning 'to be'. Your deep self is your *being*. It is what you *are*.

DEEP-KNOWING THE DEEP SELF

We spiritually awaken by becoming conscious of our spiritual nature. We become deep awake by deep-knowing the deep self. This can seem a tricky thing to do, so I'm going to describe how it is for me when I pay attention to the ineffable 'I' of awareness.

I can't see or hear or touch awareness, so it's extremely mysterious.

I'm familiar with being conscious of what I'm experiencing,

but my deep self is not something I'm experiencing. It's the experiencer of all I'm experiencing.

I'm familiar with paying attention to my unfolding story, but my deep self isn't part of my story. It's the presence of awareness witnessing the story.

I can't know the deep self as an object in my experience, because the deep self is the subject. I can only *deep-know* the deep self by recognizing my essential subjectivity.

I deep-know the deep self by knowing the knower.

A Blind Feeling of Being

A mystical Christian text called 'The Cloud of Unknowing' teaches that to awaken to our spiritual nature we need to become conscious of 'a naked conception and a blind feeling of being'. I find this very helpful. Let me take you through it.

Deep-knowing the deep self can seem difficult, but actually it simply requires me to pay attention to something utterly obvious. *I know I exist.*

To become conscious of the deep self I need to let go of my ideas about myself and focus on a 'naked conception' of who I am.

I need to be conscious of a 'blind feeling of being'.

I need to sink my attention into the deep knowing *that I am.*

Being Conscious of Being Conscious

The deep self is ineffable, because it isn't something we can see or hear or touch. Yet it is also obvious, because it is our essential *being*. To help you explore your deeper nature, I'm going to describe how it feels when I deep-know the deep self.

I am conscious of a flow of sensations and thoughts right now.

Normally I pay attention to what I am experiencing, but I'm choosing to be intensely conscious of my subjective nature as the *experiencer*.

I am conscious that I am conscious.

I am conscious of *being*.

How does this feel?

It feels as if I am a mysterious presence which is always present.

I am an unchanging stillness witnessing an ever-changing flow of experiences.

In the flow of experiences I appear to be a person called 'Tim'.

But essentially I am awareness witnessing the unfolding adventures of Tim.

This is my deep self.

NAKED BODY AND NAKED BEING

My identity seems to be a complex of different personas that I adopt to play different roles in my life. But when I pay close attention I can see there is a simple paradoxity to my naked identity.

Objectively, underneath all the clothes I wear to define my different personas, I am a naked body.

Subjectively, I am the presence of awareness, which is the constant background to all my experiences. This is my naked *being*.

As with all paradoxities these two opposite perspectives appear to be contradictory but are actually complementary.

The body is what I *appear* to be.

Awareness is what I *am*.

The Surface Self and the Deep Self

I'm going to describe the paradoxity of my identity one more time
and I invite you to check if it's also like this for you.

On the surface of my identity I appear to be a body called
'Tim'.

At the depths of my identity I am awareness witnessing Tim's
adventures.

On the surface my body exists in the world of the senses.

At the depths I am awareness which can't been seen or heard
or touched.

On the surface I appear to be a physical object.

At the depths I am essentially a spiritual subject.

CHAPTER 15

WHERE IS AWARENESS?

We've become conscious of the deep self as the presence of awareness. In this chapter I want to explore the mysterious nature of awareness to show you something truly amazing.

Objectively I'm a physical body. Subjectively I'm the presence of awareness. My body is sitting here in front of this computer. But where is awareness? If you looked into my eyes you'd connect with the presence of awareness, which would seem to be inside my head. But is that really true?

In my imagination I'm bending down in front of you so you can take a look. There's a big zip in my head, which I'm opening up to invite you to reach in and find awareness. You are searching with your hand amongst all the gooey porridge inside my head. And then you find it and pull it out to show the world... Tim's awareness... not as big as you might have expected!

It would be fun for that to happen. But it isn't going to, because awareness isn't inside my head. You can search about in my brain with a microscope, but you'll never find awareness. This is because awareness is not a thing in the world. It's not something we can see or hear or touch.

So where is awareness? Here's an interesting paralogical possibility to consider. Awareness can't be found within the world because it's the other way around. The world exists within awareness. Awareness isn't within my experience. My experience is arising within awareness. Let me take you through it.

Right now I am awareness experiencing a flow of thoughts and sensations.

It's easy to understand that thoughts are arising within awareness, but it's equally true that sensations are arising within awareness as well.

Everything I see, hear, and touch is a sensation arising within awareness.

I am listening to the sound of the wind blowing in the garden. This sound is arising within awareness. If it wasn't I wouldn't be conscious of it.

I am looking at a big pink poster of the artists Gilbert and

George on my office wall. The colour is arising within awareness. If it wasn't I wouldn't be conscious of it.

I am enjoying the mellow flavour of the coffee I am drinking. The taste is arising within awareness. If it wasn't I wouldn't be conscious of it.

Everything I am experiencing is arising within awareness.

As a body I appear to exist within the world, but essentially I am awareness and the world exists within me.

The Spacious Presence of Awareness

The deep teaching of spirituality is that essentially you don't exist in the world at all. Your essential nature is the presence of awareness within which everything is arising. It can seem a strange idea at first, but I invite you to try it out and see what happens.

Stop imagining that you are just the physical body you appear to be.

Instead, imagine yourself to be a spacious presence within which your experience is arising.

When I first became open to this possibility, I found it too subtle to hold on to for long, but as I have experimented with it I have found that it has profoundly transformed my experience of life. Now, when I examine the present moment I can immediately see that both these paralogical statements are true:

There is an objective reality to my sense of being a physical body.

There is a subjective reality to my sense of being the spacious presence of awareness.

THE LIFE-DREAM

Many spiritual traditions compare life to a dream. At first this can seem an outrageous idea, but it suggests an interesting answer to the question 'where is awareness?'

The Dreaming State

Let's first consider the answer we would give to this question from the perspective of the dreaming state.

> In the dreaming state, awareness isn't inside the head of the dream-character I appear to be in the dream.

> The dreamer isn't in the dream. The dream is arising within awareness.

> Awareness is a spacious presence that is nowhere in the dream and everywhere in the dream.

The Waking State

It seems to me that things are similar in the waking state.

> In the waking state, awareness isn't inside the head of the person I appear to be in the life story.

> Awareness isn't in the life story at all, because all that I'm experiencing is arising within awareness.

> Awareness is a spacious presence that is nowhere and everywhere.

> Ah… so that's where it is!

Dreaming and Waking

Could life really be like a dream? Based on personal observations and the discoveries of science, I've come to see that the dreaming and waking state are more akin to each other than we normally acknowledge. Here are some statements I've found to be true of both states.

In the dreaming state and the waking state I think I know what's going on, but really I don't.

In the dreaming state and the waking state I appear to experience a world of solid things, but they aren't really there… as science has shown.

In the dreaming state and the waking state the world I inhabit seems to have real existence in space and time, but actually this is an illusion.

In the dreaming state and the waking state I appear to be a character in a story, but my deeper identity is awareness witnessing the story.

In the dreaming state and the waking state I appear to be a physical body, but essentially I am intangible awareness.

In the dreaming state and the waking state I experience seeing, hearing and touching, but I can't see or hear or touch my deeper identity as awareness.

In the dreaming state and the waking state I am the spacious presence of awareness, within which all of my experiences are arising.

Lucid Dreaming

Comparing the waking state to the dreaming state helps me understand the deep awake state, because it seems to me that it's similar to the state of lucid dreaming. Let me explain.

Often when I dream at night I'm unconsciously engrossed in the dream.

But if I become more conscious I sometimes realize that I'm dreaming.

This is called 'lucid dreaming'.

When I dream lucidly I can clearly see the paradoxity of my identity.

From one perspective I appear to be a character in my dream story.

From another perspective I am the awareness within which the dream is arising.

When I dream lucidly the dream continues as before, but my experience of dreaming is transformed, because I see that I am *both* in the dream *and* not in the dream.

Lucid Living

Something similar to lucid dreaming happens while I'm awake.

Often I'm unconsciously engrossed with my life story.

But if I become more conscious I realize that life is like a dream.

I call this an experience of 'lucid living', because it's comparable to lucid dreaming.

When I live lucidly I see the paradoxity of my identity.

From one perspective I appear to be a person within my life story.

From another perspective I am spacious awareness within which my experience of life is arising.

When I live lucidly my life story continues as before, but my experience of living is transformed, because I see that I am *both* in the world *and* not in the world.

THE PARALOGICAL EXPERIENCE OF LUCIDITY

When I live lucidly I see the paradoxity of my identity. I see that I am *both* separate *and* not-separate from life. I experience the adventures of Tim, who is a separate individual in the world. But

I deep-know myself to be the spacious presence of awareness, within which the world is arising. I see that my essential nature as awareness is one with life, just like a dreamer is one with a dream. And when I deep-know that I am one with life, I experience an intimate connectedness with everything and everyone. I feel an all-embracing love for life.

Safe Vulnerability

When I live lucidly I feel that I am *both* vulnerable *and* safe. My human self is delicate and easily damaged. But the deep self can't be harmed, because it doesn't exist in the world. Understanding this gives rise to a reassuring sense that all is well.

I feel that what happens in my life really matters and really doesn't matter. From the perspective of the life-dream, how things unfold is of great consequence to Tim and I really want to honour this. But from a deeper perspective I see that there's nothing to worry about. The world is a passing show. All the challenges of my life are like dramas in a story.

When I see that I'm essentially safe, I'm no longer a hostage to fear. I can appreciate the story of Tim, with all its ups and downs, surprises and disappointments, beginnings and endings. When I know that fundamentally all is well, I feel courageous enough to really live my life.

Meaningless and Meaningful

When I live lucidly, the story of my life seems *both* meaningless *and* meaningful like a dream. On the surface, things may seem random and without consequence. But I sense a hidden meaning, which expresses itself symbolically in the flow of events. Strange synchro-nicities punctuate my adventures. Patterns emerge suggestive of a secret significance.

The more awake I am, the more dreamlike life becomes. The more I'm conscious that Tim is a character in the life-dream, the more magical his story is. Then the idea that life is simply the unfolding of chance events seems patently absurd. I may not be able to divine the meaning of events, but that something momentous is happening… of that I'm quietly confident.

Temporal and Eternal

When I live lucidly it becomes obvious that I *both* do *and* don't exist in time. Time is the flow of ever-changing forms which awareness is witnessing. As a person I am a form in the flow of time. But the deep self is outside time. It is timeless *being*.

I remember years ago at one of my seminars a lady in her 80s remarking: 'Tim. What you are saying gets easier to understand the older you get.' I said: 'That's interesting, why's that?' She said: 'Well I'm old now and my body has really changed, but I still feel that I'm essentially the same as when I was 18.'

I think most of us have this sense that our deep self is the same now as when we were much younger. I know I do. As I've grown from a child into middle age, my body and personality have changed considerably. But what I am hasn't changed. What I am is always fresh in the moment, untouched by the ravages of time. What I am is timeless awareness witnessing Tim's journey through time.

Mortal and Immortal

When I live lucidly I see that I am *both* mortal *and* immortal. The person I appear to be in time had a beginning and will come to an end. But the deep self isn't in time, just like a dreamer isn't in a dream. As a person I'm a body that is born to die. But the deep self can't die because it was never born. My essential *being* is immortal, because *being* by it's very nature must always *be*. And when I get that… it's a pretty huge WOW.

This intuition of immortality raises many profound philosophical questions, which I'm not going to address here. I certainly don't believe that becoming conscious of the timeless presence of *being* proves that we survive death as a conscious individual. However, understanding that essentially we don't exist in time makes this possibility credible.

My work as a counsellor with the terminally ill, and my experiences of being with loved ones who are dying, have confirmed for me the intuition of immortality that arises in the deep awake state. I suggest you become conscious of the deep self and examine your own intuitions.

The Sufi poet Rumi beautiful conveys how I've come to see death when he writes:

> The world is a passing dream,
> Which the sleeper is convinced is real,
> Until unexpectedly the dawn of death,
> Frees him from this fantasy.

CHAPTER 16

PRESENCING
- WOW Experiment -

In this chapter I want to invite you to experiment with a powerful practice I call 'presencing'. This will help you become conscious of yourself as the spacious presence of awareness within which the dream of life is arising right now.

Our next WOW experiment can help you deep-know the deep self. In the Gnostic 'Gospel of Thomas' Jesus teaches that to spiritually awaken you need to strip off all your clothes and stand on them naked like a little child. So if you'd like to get up and loosen your belt…

Only kidding. You don't have to do it literally. But it's a great metaphor, because to become conscious of your naked essence you need to peel away all your superficial identities to reveal the deep self. This is your innocent essential nature. It is what you have always been and always will be.

In this WOW experiment I want to invite you to become conscious of the deep self, which is the spacious presence of awareness within which all your experiences are arising like a dream. I call this 'presencing'.

I prefer the term 'presencing' to the term 'witnessing', which is often used to describe similar practices. This is because 'witnessing' can convey the idea that you need to imagine yourself as a little man inside your head, who's passively looking at your passing experience. Whereas what I am talking about is seeing that your essential nature doesn't exist inside your head at all!

Similar practices to 'presencing' are important in many spiritual traditions. Zen master Yuansou says:

> All the various teachings and practices of Zen are only
> to encourage you to individually look back into yourself
> and discover your original mind, so that you may know
> your essential nature and rest in a state of great peace and
> happiness.

Sound good? Let's do it. And it's not as difficult as you might think. Becoming conscious of the deep self simply requires you to pay attention to your sense of *being*, which is actually obvious. As Tibetan master Padma Sambhava explains so eloquently:

> It is your own awareness right now.

It is simple, natural, and clear.

Why say 'I don't understand what awareness is'?
There is nothing to think about, just permanent awareness.

Why say 'I don't see the reality of awareness'?
Awareness is the thinker of these thoughts.

Why say 'When I look I can't find it'?
No looking is necessary.

Why say 'Whatever I try doesn't work'?
It is enough to remain simple.

Why say 'I can't achieve this'?
The void of pure awareness is naturally present.

SPACIOUS AWARENESS

This WOW experiment builds on the practices that we previously explored to take us deeper into the mystery experience. When we practise 'presencing' we first enter our sensual experience. And then, as the Upanishads say so poetically, we become conscious of 'the self who is the enjoyer of the honey from the flowers of the senses'.

I'm going to take you through this practice in simple steps, so you can really get how it works. As you become familiar with awakening you'll find that these experiments come together to form one movement in consciousness. But to begin with it is worth going through the process step by step.

I'm going to describe how I experience 'presencing', so that you can explore the practice with me. Then you can experiment with it yourself. We've already looked closely at 'wondering' and 'entering', so I'll briefly describe these steps. However, I suggest you take a few moments now to use these practices to wake yourself up. Then you'll be more likely to experience 'presencing' for yourself while you read my description of what happens for me.

Wondering

I have recognized that I am only superficially awake, so I am waking myself up by experiencing a moment of wonder.

I am conscious that I really don't know what life is.

I am stepping out of my story into the mystery of the moment.

Entering

I am entering into my immediate sensual experience.

I am really looking and listening and feeling.

I am sensually alive to the pleasure of breathing.

Presencing

I am conscious of an ever-changing flow of experiences.

I am conscious of being conscious.

I am awareness witnessing this moment.

I am awareness that is looking, but can't be seen.

I am awareness that is listening, but can't be heard.

I am conscious of 'a naked conception and a blind feeling of *being*'.

It feels as if I'm sinking backwards and dissolving into vast emptiness.

I am conscious of being the spacious presence of awareness within which my experience is arising.

My sense of self is expanding until it has no edges.

Everything I am experiencing is arising within the spacious presence of awareness… just like a dream.

And then spontaneously everything becomes one.

I am one with the experiences that are arising within awareness… just as a dreamer is one with a dream… just as space is one with all it contains.

I am not separate from life… I am one with life.

I feel a wonderful sense of communion with everything and everyone.

I am deep-knowing my deep self and it feels good.

THE PRACTICE OF PRESENCING

Now you try this practice and see what happens. Take it slowly and savour the experience. These are the basic steps again. Read them through. Then put the book down and begin to experiment with presencing.

Wondering

Step out of your story and into the wonder of life.

Enter a state of profound not-knowing and immerse yourself in the mystery of the moment.

Entering

Enter the immediacy of your present sensations and become sensually alive.

Savour the delicious feeling of your breath entering and leaving your body.

Presencing

Be conscious of being conscious.

Be the presence of spacious awareness within which your experience is arising.

Presence the present moment.

At the end of Part I of this book I suggested you practise 'entering' the moment during your everyday life. Now I encourage you to deepen this daily practice by 'entering and presencing' the flow of your experience. Enter the moment so that you can become conscious of yourself as the spacious presence of awareness within which the moment is arising. Enter the deep mystery to know the deep self.

CHAPTER 17

WHO'S DREAMING THE LIFE-DREAM?

We've seen that life is like a dream, but who is the dreamer? In this chapter I'm going to explore the perennial spiritual teaching that life is the dream of God and suggest a new way of understanding this ancient idea.

The Hindu philosophers teach that life is the dream of Brahman. 'Brahman' is a name for God, so they're claiming that life is God's dream. In many mystical traditions we find the same idea. There is a primordial being, which is called 'Brahman' or 'God' or a host of other names. This supreme being is the primal awareness within which the dream of life is arising. Everything is a thought within one 'big mind' as the Zen masters say.

You and I are experiencing the life-dream right now. But this isn't my dream or your dream, because we are characters in the dream. The life-dream is God's dream. The primal awareness is dreaming itself to be you and me, and experiencing the dream through us. This is why we are both experiencing different perspectives on the same life-dream.

There is one awareness imagining itself to be everything and everyone, and meeting itself in all its many different disguises. In the words of Joseph Campbell, life is 'one great dream of a single dreamer in which all the dream characters dream too'. What an amazing vision!

The Neo-Platonic philosophers describe God as the 'mystery of being', which is in the process of 'becoming' all that is. The mystery of being is arising as all individual beings. This profound idea brings us to the greatest teaching found at the heart of the spiritual traditions of the world:

Atman is Brahman.

The soul is God.

The individual 'I' is one with the mystery of being.

In my experience this amazing teaching is true. If I look out at the dream of life I appear to be an individual 'I'. But if I bring my attention back onto itself, I deep-know the deep self as the primal awareness within which everything is arising. On the surface of life I appear to be Tim, but at the depths I am God.

I am often asked if I believe in God and I reply 'I don't believe in anything but God'. It's all God. We are all God. There is only God. God is not some distant figure somewhere in the sky. God is my own deepest nature and yours too. We are God playing a game of hide and seek. Pretending to be separate individuals and then awakening to our deeper nature, so that we realize something extraordinary. Essentially there is one of us. How exquisite!

THE FIELD OF BEING

Many people have problems with the word 'God', so I'd like to develop the ideas we've been exploring, using the concept of a 'field', which is central to physics. Scientists talk about fields such as the 'gravitational field' and the 'electromagnetic field', which reach throughout the whole of space. I want to use this concept for spiritual rather than scientific purposes to describe the mystery of being as an omnipresent 'field', because this can help us understand life in a whole new light.

> I want to suggest that the mystery of being is a field of unconscious awareness within which life is arising like a dream.

> The unconscious field of awareness becomes conscious through the particular forms it 'dreams' itself to be.

> The body is the means by which a centre of consciousness arises in the field of unconscious awareness.

> Consciousness isn't 'inside' the brain. Rather the brain allows the primal field of awareness to become conscious.

> Imagine the brain like a radio receiver. The music that a radio plays isn't in the radio. The radio tunes into an electromagnetic field of radio waves. And then we get to hear the music.

> In the same way the brain can be seen as 'tuning in' to the unconscious field of awareness. And that's when consciousness arises.

When a radio tunes into radio waves it creates a pocket of sound in a particular place within the silent electromagnetic field.

In the same way the brain creates a centre of consciousness that illuminates a 'bubble' of *conscious being* within the field of *unconscious being*.

A LOVE STORY

The fundamental motif at the heart of many ancient myths is that the primal oneness of being is manifesting as the multiplicity of life, so that it can come to know itself. As the Gnostic sage Simon Magus says in 'The Great Announcement':

> There is one power... begetting itself, increasing itself, seeking itself, finding itself... One root of the All.

In my imagination we're sitting together around a fire underneath a starry night sky, so that I can share with you my version of this myth. It's just a story but it resonates inside me like an ancient memory. It gives the human adventure the grandeur it deserves. And it helps me appreciate life in a deeper way. So come up close and I'll tell you an astonishing tale.

> In the beginning was the wordless.

> There was no one to think and nothing to think about.

> The primal field of awareness was unconscious, because there were no experiences to be conscious of.

> The field of awareness was like the presence of light without anything to illuminate, so paradoxically the light was dark.

> It is the nature of awareness to be aware, however, so the primal awareness imagined the dream of life.

The timeless possibility for everything imagined the flow of time through which everything came into being.

The mystery of *being* manifested its paralogical potentiality and the primal oneness appeared as the multiplicity of life.

The mystery of *being* manifested as the evolutionary process of *becoming*.

The field of unconscious awareness dreamt the story of life and progressively became more conscious through the evolving forms it imagined itself to be.

And so it came to be that the primal field of unconscious being arose as many centres of conscious being.

The Twist in the Tale

So far, so good. But this bring us to the twist that adds drama to our tale...

The problem arose that the primal awareness identified with each of the separate forms it appeared to be and didn't recognize its deeper identity as the oneness of being.

And here we are... that's you and me. Each one of us is the field of awareness believing itself to be just a separate individual.

This is not a satisfactory state of affairs, because when we're lost in separateness it's lonely and frightening.

We feel we're constantly missing something. And that's because we are.

Yet this underlying discontent pushes us to explore the depths of life.

We feel there must be more to life, so we start to wonder.

The Journey of Awakening

This begins our journey of spiritual awakening.

At some point on this journey we become conscious of the deep self and we recognize that our deepest *being* is the primal mystery of being.

You and I are centres of consciousness arising within the field of awareness, and when we realize this the primal oneness comes to know itself through us.

The unconscious field of awareness is coming to self-knowledge, by dreaming itself to be you and me on a journey of awakening.

Unconscious Oneness to Conscious Oneness

So the message of this fantastical story is this.

The primal oneness of unconscious awareness is arising as separate centres of consciousness, because through these centres of consciousness it can come to know that all is one.

Life is on a journey from *unconscious oneness* through *conscious separateness* to *conscious oneness*.

The Happy Ending

This brings us to the happy ending.

When we know that we are one with everything and everyone, we find ourselves in love with everything and everyone, because love is how oneness *feels*.

When we're conscious of the oneness of being, we fall in love with all beings.

We simply love *being*.

So our epic fable turns out to be a love story. And that's what makes it worth telling.

CHAPTER 18

DEEP PRESENCING
- WOW Experiment -

You and I are centres of consciousness arising within the unconscious field of awareness. In this chapter I want to return to the practice of presencing with this deeper understanding.

In our next WOW experiment I want to invite you to recognize your essential nature as the primal field of awareness, which is the source of everything, and presence the present moment from this deep perspective. Lao Tzu describes this practice beautifully when he teaches:

> Be the emptiness.
> Be the stillness.
> Watch everything come and go.
> Emerging from the source – returning to the source.
> This is the way of nature.
>
> Be the great peace.
> Be conscious of the source.
> This is the fulfilment of your destiny.
> Know that which never changes.
> This is awakening.

Consciously Separate and Unconsciously One

Before we dive into this practice I want to clarify something that can cause great confusion. I want to say this slowly because you'll find awakening to oneness becomes much easier if you get this.

When I'm deep awake I deep-know I am the primal field of awareness 'dreaming' itself to be all beings.

But this doesn't mean that I'm conscious of everything that's being experienced by all beings.

I am the unconscious field arising as an individual centre of consciousness, which is illuminating a particular 'bubble' of experiences.

I'm not conscious of the experiences being illuminated by other centres of consciousness.

Rather, I deep-know the paradoxity of my being. I am *consciously separate* and *unconsciously one* with all.

When I'm deep awake I am *conscious* of being the field of *unconscious* awareness.

CONSCIOUS OF BEING THE UNCONSCIOUS FIELD

As before, I'll describe what happens for me when I practise 'deep presencing'. Go through this process with me and then try it out on your own. Then make this a deeper level of your everyday practice of awakening

I will only briefly describe the stages of this process we've already examined in detail, but I encourage you to take a few moments to practise 'wondering and entering' before reading on. Then you'll be ready to experience 'deep presencing' for yourself, while I share my experience of this practice with you.

Wondering

I am wondering at the splendour of the universe.

I am conscious that I really don't know what life is.

Entering

I am entering my sensual experience in the present moment.

I am sinking into the delicious feeling of breathing.

Presencing

I'm focusing my attention on my sense of *being*.

I'm conscious of myself as the experiencer of all that I'm experiencing.

I am awareness presencing colours… sounds… feelings… thoughts.

I am conscious of being the mysterious deep self that can't be seen or heard or touched.

I am a spacious emptiness within which all of my experiences are arising like a dream.

Deep Presencing

As I become conscious of the deep self I feel a deep peace.

As I plumb the depths of my being, there is an oceanic feeling of oneness.

I can see that my essential *being* doesn't exist in time and space.

I am the primal field of awareness that is everywhere and nowhere.

I am conscious of the here and now, but I deep-know that my deepest being is the oneness of being.

I am unconscious awareness arising as a centre of consciousness, which is illuminating a 'bubble' of experiences within the unconscious field.

I am the field of awareness presencing a particular flow of experience that is arising right now.

I am the oneness of awareness 'dreaming' itself to be a particular individual.

My individual sense of being is one with the primal ground of being.

I am the oneness of being arising as all beings.

I am consciously individual *and* unconsciously one with all that is.

I am separate and not-separate from everything and everyone.

And this is an exquisite experience of all-embracing love.

MAD SCIENTISTS
DO MYSTICISM

Previously I suggested that a deep understanding of spirituality and a deep understanding of science are paralogically complementary perspectives on life.

We've been exploring the realization that life is like a dream arising within the primal field of awareness. This spiritual understanding of life seems a long way from a scientific understanding of life.

But in this chapter I want to show that many of the most respected scientists have seen the discoveries of science as endorsing the idea that the universe is like a thought arising in one great mind.

Tim: Hi Dick. I had a feeling you might pop in about now.

Dick: Yeah… it's all getting very mystical and that bothers me.

Tim: I know what you mean. But the words are just pointers to the mystery experience. The important thing is to actually experience the WOW of awakening for yourself.

Dick: I mean… this notion that life is a dream… it's just silly.

Tim: It's an analogy. We need analogies to understand life. But we need to be careful with them because they're only analogies.

Dick: Rational science doesn't need analogies. It tells it like it is.

Tim: But that's simply not true. After the momentous discoveries of Newton, for example, scientists thought of the universe as a great machine, with all the cogs deterministically turning away. But the universe isn't actually a machine. It was simply that human beings had become very good at building machines, so that was the natural analogy to draw on to explain things.

Dick: Well that's a good analogy.

Tim: But a rather soulless one don't you think? Anyway it's been discredited since we've moved beyond Newton to quantum physics.

Dick: So what analogies are scientists using these days?

Tim: All sorts. I've heard scientists compare the universe to a computer program or a hologram. Human beings always draw on their latest creations to give them some handle on the mysterious nature of life. We approach the unknown by analogy to the known.

Dick: But scientists understand life through mathematical formulas.

Tim: True… but that's also a type of analogy between the way the universe is and the way that numbers work.

Dick: But maths is sensible. Your dream analogy is ridiculous.

Tim: Really? I find the dream analogy very powerful, because it's an experiential analogy. I know what it's like to dream, so I can look at this moment and actually experience its dreamlike nature. I can see that I'm a character in the dream and also essentially the dreaming awareness.

Dick: I prefer to take a common-sense approach. Reality is reality. *This is it.*

Tim: I agree entirely Dick. But the big question is what exactly is 'this'?

Dick: Well it certainly isn't a dream… not according to science.

Tim: Actually many great physicists have explored the idea that the universe is arising like a thought within a primal mind.

Dick: I find that very unlikely.

Tim: Well why not talk to them yourself? Let's invite in the quantum physicists Max Planck and Erwin Schröedinger, both of whom won a Nobel Prize. And let's also have James Jeans and Arthur Eddington, both of whom were honoured with knighthoods for their contributions to physics.

Dick: Look… we've done this already with those other physicists and I didn't understand a word they said.

Tim: I know what you mean. I don't really understand what these guys are saying half the time. Their ideas don't fit with common sense, just like the ideas of the mystics don't fit with common sense. But I find that gives me an interesting new perspective on things. That's why I like hanging out with mystics and physicists.

Dick: I'm really not sure…

Tim: Give it a go… it'll blow your mind! Of course these guys are all dead, so as before you'll be speaking to a collection of quotes.

A Great Thought

Dick: OK. Respected professors… will you please confirm for me that reality is not like a dream in some universal mind. It's much more like a great machine.

Sir James Jeans: 'The stream of human knowledge is impartially heading towards a non-mechanical reality. The universe begins to look more like a great thought than like a great machine. Mind no longer appears as an accidental intruder into the realm of matter; we are beginning to suspect that we ought rather to hail it as the creator and governor of the realm of matter – not, of course, our individual minds, but the mind in which the atoms out of which our individual minds have grown exist as thoughts.'

Dick: But the universe is made of matter.

Max Planck: 'As a man who has devoted his whole life to the most clearheaded science, to the study of matter, I can tell you as a result of my research into atoms this much. There is no matter as such. All matter originates and exists only by virtue of a force which brings the particles of the atom to vibration. I must assume behind this force the existence of a conscious and intelligent mind. This mind is the matrix of all matter.'

Dick: That can't be right. The mind is something that arises from the brain. And the brain is a lump of matter. Matter is what really exists.

Max Planck: 'I regard consciousness as fundamental. I regard matter as derivative from consciousness. We cannot get behind consciousness. Everything that we talk about, everything that we regard as existing, postulates consciousness.'

Dick: How can you call yourself a physicist and believe that consciousness is fundamental? Physics by definition is about the physical world.

Sir Arthur Eddington: 'Physics is the study of the structure of consciousness. The "stuff" of the world is mindstuff.'

One Mind

Dick: You've been very quiet Professor Schröedinger. Do you agree with this crazy idea that life is like a dream, and we essentially exist outside of the physical world as the dreamer? That's just spiritual balderdash right?

Erwin Schröedinger: 'We do not belong to this material world that science constructs for us. We are not in it; we are outside. We are only spectators. The reason why we believe that we are in it, that we belong to the picture, is that our bodies are in the picture.'

Dick: But there isn't really one primal big mind. Surely you don't go along with that?

Erwin Schröedinger: 'The over-all number of minds is just one. I venture to call it indestructible since it has a peculiar timetable, namely mind is always now. There is really no before and after for mind. There is only a now that includes memories and expectations. But I grant that our language is not adequate to express this, and I also grant, should anyone wish to state it, that I am now talking religion, not science – a religion, however, not opposed to science, but supported by what disinterested scientific research has brought to the fore.'

Dick: 'Well all this just goes to prove that even great scientists are prone to flights of fantasy. There's obviously more than one mind. I'm a separate individual.

Erwin Schröedinger: 'The individual "I" is but an aspect of the whole which is identical to the universal "I" of which the world is also a projected aspect.'

Dick: Well Professor you're clearly out of your mind… so I'm very glad we have *different* minds!

Erwin Schröedinger: 'The multiplicity is only apparent, in truth there is only one mind.'

Dick: 'But the universe isn't some big oneness. It's made up of lots of very little particles.

Erwin Schröedinger: 'Particles are but wave-crests, a sort of froth on the deep ocean of the universe.'

Dick: Come down to Earth for a moment. You'll find the world clearly isn't all one, because it's full of variety.

Erwin Schröedinger: 'What seems to be a plurality is merely a series of aspects of one thing.'

Dick: Science will never solve the mystery of life with these mystical ideas of oneness.

Max Planck: 'Science cannot solve the ultimate mystery of nature.'

Dick: As far as I'm concerned that's exactly what it's done. Science has shown that I'm a physical body in a physical universe. And when I die that's it. No spiritual wish-fulfilling fantasies. Just the hard facts.

Erwin Schröedinger: 'If you have to face the body of a deceased friend whom you sorely miss, is it not soothing to realize that this body was never really the seat of his personality, but only symbolically, "for practical reference"?'

The Last Word

Dick: I've had enough. This guy Schröedinger is a weirdo! Didn't he get into trouble for keeping a cat in a box and not caring whether it was alive or dead?

Tim: It's a thought experiment that I don't think you've quite understood.

Dick: This whole conversation is freaking me out. Life isn't a dream. I'm a real body having a real conversation in a real world.

Tim: Actually Dick… I'm not sure how to tell you this… but you're my imaginary friend.

Dick: Ahhh! Will someone please tell me what's really going on?!

Tim: Sir Arthur would you like to have the last word? After decades of scientific study, what understanding have you arrived at? In your opinion what's really going on?

Sir Arthur Eddington: 'Something unknown is doing we don't know what.'

THE MYSTERY OF BEING

In Part I of this book we explored the deep mystery of life. In Part II we've been exploring the deep self within. In this chapter I want to suggest that the deep mystery and the deep self are different ways of seeing the primal mystery of being.

I want to use this insight to heal the schism between spirituality and science, because it seems to me that they are paralogically complementary perspectives on the mystery of being.

This will take us to the philosophical depths of the new way of awakening I've been articulating. What I'm saying may seem abstruse at first, but when you get the vision I think you'll find it's quite a WOW!

On our journey into the mystery experience we've explored the big questions 'what is life?' and 'who am I?' When we looked below the surface appearances of the universe we discovered the deep mystery. When we looked deeply within we discovered the deep self. Now I want to explore the idea that the deep mystery and the deep self are complementary ways of seeing the primal mystery of being. Let me take you through it.

The Objective Universe

Scientific exploration of the objective world has led to the realization that things are not what they seem to be.

On the surface of things we seem to live in a concrete world of solid things. But when science looks deeper the world of solid objects disappears.

Below the surface there is a fluid world of quantum possibilities.

And beyond that is the unknowable ultimate reality…
the deep mystery.

The deep mystery of what-is cannot be described…
we can only say that it exists.

The deep mystery is the mystery of *being*.

The Subjective Self

My spiritual explorations of the subjective self have led to the realization that I am not what I seem to be.

On the surface of things I seem to be a physical body. But if I look deeper into the nature of my identity I see that essentially I don't exist in the material world.

Below the surface of the self lies the fluid world of the psyche, full of intangible thoughts and imagined possibilities.

And beyond that is my essential being… the deep self.

The deep self cannot be described, because it can't be seen or heard or touched or imagined… I can only say that it exists.

The deep self is the mystery of *being*.

Whether I'm investigating the objective world or the subjective self, if I reach into the depths I discover the mystery of being. This is the primal ground of existence.

THE SPIRITUAL AND SCIENTIFIC PERSPECTIVES

The mystery of being is the primal ground from which everything is arising. We've been imagining the primal ground as unconscious awareness, within which life is arising like a dream. In philosophy this view of things has many names. For my purposes I'm going to call it simply the 'spiritual' perspective.

We've seen that some of the greatest scientists have agreed with the 'spiritual' view, but many other scientists take the opposite perspective. They see the primal ground of reality as made up of matter, albeit in a very abstract form. As this is the common understanding of science in our culture right now I'm going to call this view the 'scientific' perspective.

Before the development of modern physics, the scientific perspective took the form of crude 'materialism', which saw reality as made up of matter. Since the discovery that matter isn't really there, this has developed into a more subtle understanding of the ground of reality as 'energy', which is arising as physical matter.

The spiritual and scientific perspectives appear to contradict each other. But it seems to me that they're paralogically complementary views of the mystery of being. Let me explore this with you using the field analogy we've previously found helpful.

The Primal Field

From the spiritual perspective I see this.

The primal field of being is unconscious awareness, which has become conscious through the forms it 'dreams' itself to be.

From the scientific perspective I see this.

The primal field of being is the energetic substance of the universe, which has become conscious through evolving into complex physical forms.

So here's what we can say from both the spiritual and scientific perspectives.

The unconscious field of being becomes conscious through the individual forms that arise within it.

The body allows a centre of consciousness to emerge in the unconscious field, through which the field of being becomes conscious of being.

The oneness of being becomes conscious through the manyness of *beings*.

Separate and Not-Separate

From the spiritual perspective I see this.

I am the supreme being, conscious through 'Tim'.

I am the unconscious field of awareness individualized as a particular 'I'.

It seems as if my being is separate from the being of others, but actually my 'I' is intrinsically one with the being of all.

From the scientific perspective I see this.

I am the unconscious universe that has individualized into this particular conscious body.

I am the universe looking at itself.

The body seems separate from the universe, but it is actually intrinsically one with the universe and could have no independent existence.

So here's what I see from both the spiritual and scientific perspectives.

I am the unconscious oneness arising as a conscious individual.

I am the universal field of being, individualized as a particular being.

It seems as if my being is separate from the being of others, but actually every individual being is intrinsically one with the being of all.

I am separate and not-separate from all that is.

Space and Time

From the spiritual perspective I see this.

The primal awareness is an eternal presence that doesn't exist within space and time.

Space and time characterize the dream of separateness that is arising within awareness.

From the scientific perspective I see this.

Einstein has shown that the fundamental reality doesn't exist in space and time.

Yet we experience ourselves as existing in space and time.

So here's what I see from both the spiritual and scientific perspectives.

The primal field of unconscious being is everywhere and always.

The forms arising in space and time allow the unconscious field of being to become conscious, so consciousness is limited by space and time.

One and Many

Spiritual myths explore the idea that the primal oneness is becoming conscious of itself through appearing to be many separate individuals. ·

The scientific story of the evolving cosmos is a new version of this ancient myth. It relates how the oneness of unconscious nature has become conscious of itself through evolving into ever more complex forms, until it reaches the human form in which it is conscious of being conscious.

CONSCIOUSNESS AND THE BRAIN

Throughout the history of philosophy a great debate has raged between the 'spiritual' and 'scientific' perspectives on life. Over the centuries these perspectives have been understood in increasingly subtle ways and been given different names. But the fundamental debate has continued, because it's about the nature of the primal ground of reality.

In this section I'm going to discuss these two perspectives in their crude forms, which I will call 'materialism' and 'mentalism'. I want to do this because many people who are exploring spirituality struggle with trying to reconcile or choose between these perspectives.

This debate matters because it has huge implications for how we see the relationship between consciousness and the brain. Materialists see the brain as giving rise to consciousness, which seems to contradict the spiritual claim that essentially we're not the body. Here's the way the argument between materialism and mentalism often plays itself out.

Materialism

Materialists believe that matter is the ground of reality.

Materialists point to the fact that consciousness is clearly linked to the brain and argue that consciousness is a by-product of the physical body.

Materialists claim that subjective being arises from objective being. 'I' arises from 'it'.

Mentalism

Mentalists believe that consciousness is the ground of reality.

Mentalists point to the fact that consciousness is the prerequisite for all experience and argue that the physical world is like a great dream arising within consciousness.

Mentalists claim that objective being arises from subjective being. 'It' arises from 'I'.

It seems to me that both these perspectives are saying something important, yet they both seem problematic and out-dated. Let's start by looking at what's wrong with mentalism, because that's easy to see.

What's Wrong With Mentalism?

Mentalists see consciousness as the ground of reality. Yet the evidence is overwhelming that consciousness is linked to the brain. If I take a sleeping tablet right now I will alter the chemistry of my brain and very quickly consciousness will disappear. So how can consciousness be the ground of reality, when changing the chemistry of the brain can make consciousness disappear? That doesn't make sense.

Awareness and Consciousness

You may be surprised that I'm criticizing mentalism, because it sounds much like the philosophy I've been articulating in this book.

But there's a crucial difference. So before going any further I want to clarify this difference for you.

I distinguish the terms 'awareness' and 'consciousness', so that they refer to linked but distinct concepts. There's no standard way of using these terms, so people use them in different ways. Indeed, in previous books I've used them in different ways myself. This can cause all sorts of confusion if you're trying to compare what I'm saying here with what you've come across elsewhere. So let me take this opportunity to clearly state how I'm using these terms.

I use the term 'awareness' to describe the primal ground from which everything is arising like a dream. I use the term 'consciousness' to describe awareness when it is conscious of experience. The paradoxity of awareness is that it can be *both* conscious *and* unconscious. The unconscious field of awareness arises as centres of conscious awareness.

From a spiritual perspective I've been claiming that our experience arises within 'conscious awareness' like a dream. But I'm not saying that consciousness is the ground of reality. I'm saying that centres of consciousness arise within the field of unconscious awareness because of the physical body.

The primal ground is unconscious awareness that becomes conscious through the forms it 'dreams' itself to be. Give the body a sleeping tablet and awareness will cease to be conscious through the form. Indeed simply go to sleep and awareness will cease to be conscious through the form. The primal ground is not conscious awareness, which is what we experience ourselves to be in the waking state; but rather, unconscious awareness into which we dissolve in the deep sleep state.

What's Wrong with Materialism?

We've seen what's wrong with mentalism and clarified how it's different to the philosophy I'm articulating. Now let's look at what's wrong with the materialist perspective. Materialists claim that consciousness is a by-product of the brain, because matter is the ground of reality.

This is an attractive idea because it fits with common sense. But it's hard to take seriously since science has discovered that on a deep level 'matter' doesn't exist, which is why so many of the great physicists have rejected materialism completely. However, a more subtle form of materialism that sees matter arising from some sort of energetic field is still popular. But there are still many problems with this perspective. I'm going to focus on just one of them, because I enjoy this example.

When the quantum physicists looked deeply into the nature of matter, they discovered something astonishing. The quantum possibilities only come into a definite form when observed by consciousness. They concluded that consciousness 'collapses' the quantum possibilities into a seemingly solid universe. So, without the conscious observer the world as we know it doesn't exist.

This leaves us in a paralogical hall of mirrors. Let me take you through it.

Science has shown that consciousness is linked to the brain.

But science has also shown that the field of quantum possibilities only comes into a definite form when observed by consciousness.

So… hang on… that means unless consciousness collapses the quantum possibilities into a physical form there is no brain.

But if there is no brain there's no consciousness to collapse the quantum possibilities.

Holy moley… I'm getting dizzy!

Looked at one way, the brain creates consciousness. Looked at another way, consciousness creates the brain. How can we resolve this dilemma? By looking at things paralogically of course.

A PARALOGICAL ALTERNATIVE

I want to articulate a paralogical approach to the ground of reality.

I agree with the brilliant physicist David Bohm who writes:

> I would suggest that there is some ground, deeper and
> more subtle than are either mind or matter, and that they
> both enfold from this ground, which is the beginning and
> ending of everything.

This has been the underlying philosophy in this book, which I'm
clarifying in this chapter. I am suggesting that the ground of reality
is the mystery of being, which is actually a term for something so
mysterious we can't say what it is… only *that it is.*

Here's the way it looks to me.

> The mystery of being is the ground of reality.

> The mystery of being is a primal field of potentiality that is
> arising as everything.

> The paradoxity of being is that it manifests as subjective being
> and objective being… consciousness and matter… 'I' and 'it'.

'I' and 'It'

How can this help us understand the relationship between consciousness and the brain? I suggest they are the same thing seen
from different complementary paralogical perspectives.

> I is it and it is I.

> As life has evolved into more complex forms, greater con-
> sciousness has emerged at the same time, because conscious-
> ness and matter are the subjective and objective expressions
> of the paradoxity of being.

Two Perspectives on the Mystery of Being

In this book I've primarily been looking at the mystery of being
from a 'spiritual' perspective. So I've been imagining it as a field
of unconscious awareness, within which you and I are centres of

consciousness. In this chapter I've suggested that the mystery of being can equally be imagined as the primal 'energy' field that science speculates about.

Here's the way it looks to me.

The paradoxity of being is that it manifests as subjective being and objective being.

This means we can explore the mystery of being subjectively and objectively.

Spirituality examines things subjectively, so it sees the primal ground of reality as unconscious 'awareness' that arises as 'consciousness'.

Science examines things objectively, so it sees the ground of reality as 'energy' that arises as 'matter'.

So which is true? Both and neither.

The spiritual and scientific perspectives are paralogically complementary ways of thinking about the mystery of being.

Life is a paradoxical mystery that it can be helpful to see from both perspectives, but neither offer us the definitive truth… that's impossible!

Conscious Being and Unconscious Being

Don't be surprised if the ideas we've been exploring have made your head spin. I want to slightly rework Niels Bohr's famous remark about quantum physics and say:

If you think you can talk about the paradoxity of being without feeling dizzy, you haven't understood the first thing about it.

The depths of life are very difficult to understand with words. Yet the essential message that is important for our journey of awakening is simple. And it can be understood simultaneously from *both* spiritual *and* scientific perspectives.

> The mystery of being is a primal oneness that is arising as everything.

> You appear to be a separate individual, but essentially your being is one with the great mystery of being, which is manifesting as all beings.

> You are a centre of *conscious being* arising within the field of *unconscious being*.

THE *TAIJITU*

The ancient Taoist sages thought of the field of being as the mysterious 'Tao'. They taught that the primal oneness is fundamentally characterized by yin and yang, which symbolize the paradoxity of life. In our exploration of the primal field of being, we've found that it arises subjectively as consciousness and objectively as matter. Consciousness and matter are the yin and yang of the Tao of *being*.

Previously we discussed the amazing *taijitu* symbol, which shows that yin exists within yang, and vice versa. And this is exactly what we've discovered on our journey.

> Consciousness is hidden within matter.

> Matter is arising within consciousness.

> The objective world and the subjective self co-exist and create each other.

> Both are expressions of the primal field of being…
> the mysterious Tao.

The Next Big Paradigm Shift

It seems to me that the next big paradigm shift in the story we tell about life will be based on an understanding of the paradoxical nature of reality. This understanding of life becomes possible through paralogical thinking. And there is no better symbolic representation of paralogical thinking than the *taijitu*... 'the diagram of the supreme ultimate'.

We started our journey into paralogical thinking by discussing the wave-particle duality discovered by the quantum physicists. We explored Niels Bohr's ideas about paradox, which led him to choose the *taijitu* for his coat of arms. Contemplating this symbol again, now I can see why he was so attracted to it.

It's astonishing how the *taijitu* diagram anticipates the discovery of the wave-particle duality. If you place the symbol on its side, it creates the image of a wave flanked by two particles, one of which is white and the other black. This is quite extraordinary because physics has now found that all elementary particles come into existence with a complementary anti-particle of opposite charge, forming negative and positive pairs.

I've fallen in love with the depths of the symbol. It captures the essence of paralogical thinking. So I'm going to turn it on its side, to create the image of a wave, and claim it as a symbol for paralogical philosophy. Get the meaning of this symbol and you'll get the whole vision.

THE ANCIENT PRESENCE

Let's end this chapter with a wonderful description of the mystery of being by Lao Tzu, which echoes the passages from the 'Gospel of Thomas' and the 'Upanishads' that we looked at earlier.

> You can't see it, because it has no form.
> You can't hear it, because it makes no noise.
> You can't touch it, because it has no substance.
>
> It cannot be known in these ways,
> because it is the all-embracing oneness.

It is not high and light,
or low and dark.

Indefinable yet continually present.
It is nothing at all.
It is the formless form.
It is the imageless image.

It can't be grasped by the imagination.
It has no beginning and no end.

This is the essence of Tao.

Stay in harmony with this ancient presence,
And you will know the fullness of each present moment.

CHAPTER 21

DEEP AWAKE MEDITATION
- WOW Experiment -

In this chapter I want to invite you to immerse yourself in the mystery of being, by experimenting with deep awake meditation. This will take you to the depths of the mystery experience.

I'm also going to explore the paralogical relationship between the deep awake state and the deep sleep state, because it will help you understand what happens in meditation.

In our previous WOW experiment we explored deep presencing, which helped us become conscious of our shared essential nature as the field of being. This leads to the experience of lucid living, in which we see that life is like a dream arising within one primal awareness. In our next WOW experiment I want to invite you to dissolve your attention into the mystery of being, through the practice of deep awake meditation.

There are many methods of meditation and I've explored quite a few of them. The deep awake meditation I want to share with you is extremely simple. You need to find the right time to experiment with this practice, when you won't be disturbed and can let go into the mystery.

I've been encouraging you to engage with the process of awakening by experimenting with 'wondering, entering and presencing' while you're reading this book. Now I'd like to suggest you start regularly meditating, which will take your practice of 'presencing' to a deeper level.

Deep awake meditation involves 'dissolving' into the mystery of being. It's not usually appropriate to practise 'dissolving' while you're going about your daily business, because you need to keep returning the focus of your attention to the practical world. However, if you make the time to meditate and reach deep within, it becomes much easier to presence the moment during everyday life.

Here are the basic steps to follow to practise deep awake meditation:

Wondering

Wonder at the world and become conscious of the deep mystery.

Close your eyes. Be relaxed and alert.

Entering

Come out of your story in time, and enter your sensations in the present moment.

Focus your attention on how wonderful it feels to breathe.

Presencing

Become conscious of yourself as the spacious presence of awareness, within which the sensation of breathing is arising.

Become conscious of yourself as a conscious centre within the unconscious field of being.

Dissolving

Turn your attention deeply within and focus on the deep self.

Dissolve your attention into the primal ground of being.

DEEP SLEEP AND DEEP AWAKE

To help you understand what happens in meditation I want to explore the paralogical relationship between the deep awake state and the deep sleep state. I'm going to begin by examining what happens when we fall deep asleep.

The field of being can be seen as formless unconscious awareness, which becomes conscious through the forms it 'dreams' itself to be.

I am the primal oneness of awareness, conscious through Tim.

When I fall deep asleep each night, the conscious 'I' dissolves back into the primal unconscious awareness.

When I enter the deep sleep state I have no objective or subjective identity. There's no self... no other... no time. I exist but I'm not conscious that I exist.

I am compelled to dissolve my individual identity back into the unconscious oneness every night.

I arise the next day reinvigorated and refreshed from my time in the timeless nothingness.

As I wake up I occasionally experience a blissful afterglow of the deep sleep state. I feel as if I'm glimpsing how good it feels to be immersed in the deep oneness of being.

What Happens In Meditation

At the end of the day we *unconsciously* dissolve into the primal oneness by falling deep asleep.

Meditation allows us to *consciously* dissolve in the deep sleep state and become deep awake.

When we meditate we allow ourselves to *consciously* bathe in the blissful oneness of awareness.

In one of his poems the ecstatic Sufi Rumi explains:

> Every night you release the spirit
> from its body-prison
> and erase the mind of memory.
>
> Each night the bird is uncaged
> and the waking narrative pauses.
>
> Prisoners aren't in prison.
> Governors are powerless.
>
> No pain or aching.
> No worries about getting or losing.
> No fantasies about this or that person.
>
> The sage is in this state when awake.

SPIRITUAL SUSTENANCE

Becoming deep awake is consciously entering the deep sleep state, so I approach meditation in much the same way that I approach falling asleep. I can't make myself enter the deep sleep state and I can't make myself enter the deep awake state; but I can prepare the conditions which allow my state of consciousness to naturally change.

When I want to enter the deep sleep state I go through the familiar ritual of taking off all my clothes, turning off the lights, relaxing in a comfortable bed, closing my eyes and waiting to go unconscious. If I think about sleeping it just makes it harder. I simply need to relax and let things be.

When I practise deep awake meditation it's similar. I need to take off all my roles and personas and become conscious of the naked presence of my essential nature. I need to sit myself somewhere comfortable, relax my body and close my eyes, then allow the deep awake state to arise.

I can practise deep awake meditation anywhere. But it helps if I have a special meditation spot that I've come to associate with being deep awake, just as it's easier to sleep in a familiar bed. Joseph Campbell explains:

> Your sacred space is where you can find yourself again and again.

Regular Practice

It's possible to practise deep awake meditation for a few minutes, just as we sometimes briefly visit the deep sleep state by having a nap. But in the same way that it's essential we regularly have a good night's sleep, we also need to regularly dive into the deep awake state for a longer period. As the philosopher Alan Watts puts it:

> To go out of your mind at least once a day is tremendously important, because by going out of your mind you will come to your senses.

We need to regularly withdraw from life and sink into the field of being, from which we return refreshed and more conscious. This is a way of refuelling for the journey. We need to refuel physically by eating regularly. We need to refuel spiritually by meditating regularly.

When we've eaten well one day, we still become hungry the next. If we go too long without eating, our hunger will really start to hurt, as an urgent reminder that we need physical sustenance. It is the same with awakening. We inevitably start to become spiritually hungry unless we regularly feed the soul. And we can do this by practising deep awake meditation.

Practising for the Love of It

I call this practice 'meditation' because it's performed by closing your eyes, sitting quietly and going deep within. However, the word 'meditation' comes with a certain amount of baggage. It can sound like a serious spiritual endeavour, in which we earnestly try to become more awake. But I don't approach deep awake meditation in this way. I meditate because it is a wonderful thing to do. Alan Watts explains:

> We could say that meditation doesn't have a reason or doesn't have a purpose. In this respect it's unlike almost all other things we do except perhaps making music and dancing. When we make music we don't do it in order to reach a certain point, such as the end of the composition. If that were the purpose of music then obviously the fastest players would be the best. Also, when we are dancing we are not aiming to arrive at a particular place on the floor as in a journey. When we dance, the journey itself is the point, as when we play music the playing itself is the point. And exactly the same thing is true in meditation. Meditation is the discovery that the point of life is always arrived at in the immediate moment.

Many spiritual traditions encourage us to perform daily meditation to nurture our awakening. But, if you're like me, viewing regular practice as a spiritual 'discipline' can make the process of awakening sound like being back at school. A 'discipline' feels like something I'm confined by, when it's actually something that can set me free. I want to urge you to practise for the pleasure of it. Don't make meditation a spiritual chore!

MEDITATION AND THE MIND

When I practise meditation I need a simple focus for my attention to keep me conscious, otherwise I'll drift off into deep sleep instead of becoming deep awake. I find the breath is perfect for this. Sensual breathing is very pleasurable and I enjoy returning my attention to my breath if it starts to wander.

Inevitably my thoughts come and go. But I don't try to stop thinking. That's impossible. If my thoughts are agitated I simply become conscious that I'm listening to myself talking to myself. I pay attention to the silent presence which is listening. I become conscious of being spacious awareness within which the thoughts are arising.

In the same way that a puddle of water becomes transparent if you stop splashing in it and let the mud settle, so my thoughts becomes less agitated when I stop focusing my attention on them. Then my mind naturally becomes calm, which means I can easily sink into the mystery experience.

There was a time when I had a macho approach to meditation. I saw myself as a spiritual warrior fighting an internal battle to silence my thoughts. I viewed the thinking mind as an 'enemy' that I needed to subdue. But I don't approach meditation like that these days. Now I'm much kinder to myself. I simply allow things to be as they are. If my mind is agitated, I let it rage until it's spent. When my mind becomes still, I treasure the calm.

Sometimes when I enter the deep awake state, the mind becomes very clear and profound insights arise. When I was a macho meditator I saw this as my cunning mind offering me enticing ideas to distract me from my deeper purpose. Many spiritual traditions teach that the mind is so devious it will even use wisdom to keep you from awakening. These days this feels like nonsense to me. So when I become still and the mind becomes insightful I'm grateful for it. If an insight arises I may stop meditating and write the idea down, so that I can return to it later. Then I dive back into the formless presence.

I've spent long periods of my life exploring meditation so I'm often able to dive straight into the deep awake state. But this isn't always the case. If I pay too much attention to my thoughts, I find myself floating off into a dream. When I was a macho meditator I used to regard a dreamy meditation as a 'bad' meditation. These days I simply focus on what a dreamy meditation can teach me.

As I dream off, I examine how it feels to be sucked into a semi-conscious state. Sometimes it can be an effort to resist the inertia of falling asleep. It feels as if I have to extricate myself from a viscous stickiness and pull myself back to a more conscious state.

What fascinates me about this experience is that something similar happens all the time in my everyday life. I often get sucked into my story when I'm awake. And it feels as if my story is sticky, so it's hard to extricate myself. There is the dead weight of inertia pulling me into unconsciousness, which it takes an effort of will to resist.

This means that when I start to dream off in meditation, I no longer see it as some sort of spiritual failure. I see it as a wonderful opportunity to build the psychological 'muscles' which allow me to become more awake in my daily life.

Being deep awake is effortless, but waking up can take psychological effort. If you'd like to get a visceral understanding of this, simply lie down on the floor and then get up. Even if you are very fit you'll find you need to make some effort to get to your feet, but once you are up it's effortless. It's similar with spiritual awakening.

MY EXPERIENCE OF MEDITATION

For me, meditation is an opportunity to take time off from the pressures of living in time, and sink deeply into the mystery experience.

I can't force this, but I can be open to it. And when the mystery experience arises it feels like the most wonderful gift… undeserved and gratefully received.

I appreciate whatever I experience in meditation. Sometimes there's simply a sense of stillness and peace. Other times, meditation is so wonderful I find it very hard to put into words. I'm going to attempt to describe my experience of meditation, but I don't want to set up expectations for you. I simply want to share what happens for me… as one explorer of life to another.

When I practise meditation I dissolve into the deep mystery. Then I understand why the Gnostics call the mystery the 'fullness', because the emptiness is full of pulsating energy. The stillness is effervescent with vitality.

I understand why the Hindus talk about the primordial vibration of 'om', because I feel as if I'm merging with a low vibration that underlies all that is. I am consumed by ommmmmmm…

I understand why the Gnostics describe the mystery of being as a 'dazzling darkness', because the emptiness seems to be sparkling with 'dark light'.

I understand what people mean by the 'sound of the silence', because the silence has the sound of a million miniscule tinkling bells. And I feel submerged by waves of ringing, which are rising and falling in the void.

I understand what the devotional mystics mean by loving God as the divine 'Beloved', because I find myself falling in love with the vast unconscious field of being, which is the source of all.

When I reach within, it feels as if the deep self is reaching out to welcome me. It's as if we're lovers who've been longing to be together… to caress each other… to be one with each other.

I feel as if I am relaxing in the arms of the great Beloved. I feel one with the one I love... the oneness that I love... the one 'I' which *is* love.

DISSOLVING INTO THE MYSTERY OF BEING

I can't practise deep awake meditation right now and describe what happens, because it necessitates I withdraw my attention from the sensual world. So I'm going to remember my meditation yesterday as if it was happening now and share the experience with you. Then you can find the right time to experiment with deep awake meditation for yourself. I've gone through the steps involved earlier in this chapter.

I've retreated into the quiet of my bedroom where I won't be disturbed.

I am making my body comfortable.

I am becoming relaxed and alert.

I am conscious of the room around me and the sounds outside the window.

I am conscious of what a wonder life is and how mysterious it is to be alive.

I close my eyes and let go of my story.

I am intensely conscious of the present moment.

I enter the delicious sensation of breathing.

As I do this, my body begins to soften and my mind begins to calm.

I am entering the beautiful textures of my breath... the cool air coming into my body and the warm air leaving my body.

I am the spacious presence of awareness presencing breathing.

Now I am turning my attention deeply within.

I am conscious of 'a naked conception and a blind feeling of *being*'.

It feels to me as if I am sinking further and further back into the mystery of being.

I am dissolving my attention into the primal ground from which my conscious attention is arising.

I am immersed in the primordial vibration of the dazzling darkness.

The stillness is full of ommmmmmm…

The emptiness is alive with presence.

I am dancing in the vibrating stillness.

There's an oceanic feeling of oneness.

I feel as if I'm dissolving in an ocean of bliss.

I am enfolded within the safe arms of the Beloved.

All is one in boundless love.

CHAPTER 22

THE WONDERFUL SURPRISE

Awakening to the deep self is the most wonderful surprise, because it's an experience of exquisite aliveness and unconditional love.

Something has just happened that has interrupted my writing. I've been sitting here in front of my computer in floods of tears, unexpectedly overwhelmed by poignant love... like a gift of grace... and I want to share my surprise with you.

As I was writing the last chapter about how it feels to be immersed in the mystery, it made me remember a poem I'd written years ago in which I used similar images to express what I was experiencing in meditation. I was in my early 20s then and had retreated from the world for a year to explore the depths of my being. During this period the mystery experience really opened up for me. My life became a devotional love affair with the mystery.

I searched on my computer to see if I'd kept a copy of the poem, but it was written before there were personal computers, so of course it wasn't there. But I did stumble across a recording of the poem. At that time I wanted to be a musician and I'd set the poem to music. So I played the piece to hear the poem again. I wasn't prepared for what happened.

It wasn't that the music was anything special. It sounded like the dated work of an inexperienced composer. But as I listened to the words I began to sob uncontrollably as I realized how long I'd been attempting to convey my experience of the mystery.

In my imagination the young Tim was present beside me, so unformed and inexperienced, yet moved by the same strange impulse to write about the wonder of awakening. I felt his glorious passion, naïve sincerity, and determined commitment.

I felt my intimate connection to the 12-year-old boy who had glimpsed the mystery for the first time and set out on this adventure. I saw how he'd lost and found his way through the labyrinth of life... and brought me here to this moment... to this attempt to say the unsayable... to convey with clumsy words the inexpressible feeling of WOW.

When the track ended, another started playing. This was an old song I'd written called 'Life Itself'. Like so many of my songs it was an attempt to convey in music and words some fragment of my experience of all-embracing love. I wanted to take people to the mystery experience so we could be in love together.

The song sounded innocent and unpolished, but the genuineness of the young Tim reached through the decades. I think I'm going to transcribe the lyric for you.

> eyes cannot see it
> it cannot be heard
> hands cannot touch it
> it can't be put in words
>
> it's hidden by wanting
> it's hidden by fear
> its not in the future or in the past
> it's only now and here
>
> open your heart
> here it is… all you've ever wanted
> open your heart
> here and now… waiting… for you to open
>
> life itself
> open your heart to life itself

I'm starting to weep again as I type these words, because it's bringing back the feeling that made me write them when I was a young man. And it's the same feeling I am writing about in this book today, all these years later.

I'll be honest with you… writing this book hasn't always been an easy process. It's involved long hours sitting in front of a computer, missing my family and the simple joys of recreation. People often think a writer's life must be very romantic, but it's mainly spent patiently corralling uncooperative words into meaningful patterns. Yet as I sit here now, with my eyes wet and my heart wide open, I know why I'm choosing to put myself through this labour of love.

All my life I have been writing… singing… shouting about this awakening. I care about it so much. It has been my life and it is my life. All I've ever really wanted is to taste the sweetness of the mystery. This awakening is so beautiful… so precious… so natural. It unlocks the door of my heart and I feel such a love of life. I feel intensely grateful that I've had the good fortune to experience the WOW of life. And I know that all I can do to repay this great gift is to share it.

I don't want to sound gushy, but that's the way it is right now. I'm going to share with you the poem that initiated this experience. I'm no poet alas, but it's my inarticulate attempt as a young man to convey something of how it feels to become immersed in the mystery and dissolve into deep love. Thirty years later I am older, but the mystery experience feels the same… and forever new.

> my brimming heart held whole in full embrace
> flotsam upon the tides of breath
> washed in taste
> splashed with spume of light
> tossed by Tao's undulant pulse
> borne on swells of simple love
> falling into waiting arms
> surging up from depths of bliss
>
> eroded in the turmoil of your ocean presence
> waves of ringing break on rough rocks
> sucking back smooth pebbles
> grind grit to soft sand
> dissolving my grateful heart in your bounty

I LOVE EVERYBODY

When I dive deeply into the WOW of life it's an experience of deep love. This is why the mystery experience matters so much to me. This is why I'm writing this book for you. This is why I've made it my life's work to find new and effective ways to share the mystery experience with others. Love, by its very nature, wants to be shared. And when we share love… the love increases.

Waking up to oneness isn't a cold and colourless realization. It's an experience of profound communion with all that is, which transforms how it feels to appear as a person in the story of life. It's an experience of deep love that spontaneously arises when we *get* the great paradoxity that we're both separate and not-separate from one another. Love is the wonderful dance of being two *and* one.

I've had the great good fortune throughout my life to share the experience of deep love with a large number of people of different ages, temperaments and backgrounds. Some have been close friends and some strangers. Some have been long-time spiritual explorers and some have unexpectedly stumbled into the awakened state.

It makes no difference who we are, awakening is always the most wonderful surprise. The world becomes radiant with love. It is the same world but it's a new world. It's the familiar transformed by glory. Walt Whitman writes:

> I cannot be awake for nothing looks to me as it did before,
> Or else I am awake for the first time, and all before has
> been a mean sleep.

The dub punk musician Jah Wobble captures the magical rush of sudden awakening in a track called 'I Love Everybody', in which he rants about the transfiguration of the gritty London landscape into a transcendental vision:

> And now the buildings change.
> Now the people change.
> Everything changing.
> Spirit and matter most apparent.
> Realized there never was anything to worry about.
> To doubt was insane.
>
> The limited, callow, isolated individuals

living on housing estates in Chingford,
large detached houses in Kew,
tower blocks on the Tottenham marshes
… become my gods.

I see an accounts clerk from Tooting… *I see Zeus.*
A sanitary inspector from the London Borough of
    Haringey
… a Brahmin stands resplendent before me.

For five minutes *I LOVE EVERYBODY.*
There is only love. All action ceases.

The Mile End Road,
once a blood-stained battleground of Bacchanalian excess,
becomes the Garden of Gethsemane.
A bitter 72-year old ex-docker becomes the ever-
    compassionate Buddha.
A Cypriot minicab driver becomes St Francis of Assisi.
The 22-year-old Glaswegian checkout girl *is* the divine
    mother.

I love everybody. My spirit is free.

THE LUCENT SURPRISE

Recently I came across the work of the American poet James
Broughton for the first time. He describes the experience of awakening as the 'lucent surprise', which is a wonderfully evocative
phrase. He explains that 'we are all participants in the marvellous'.
I love that!

At a very young age 'Sunny Jim' experienced a life-transforming visit from his 'muse'. Describing this encounter years later,
Broughton wrote that his muse had told him…

> Despite what I might hear to the contrary the world was
> not a miserable prison, it was a playground for a nonstop
> tournament between stupidity and imagination. If I

followed the game sharply enough, I could be a useful spokesman for Big Joy.

This reminds me of my own experience as a boy, which has led me to aspire to be a spokesman for deep love. Here's one of Broughton's poems that captures beautifully the essence of the journey of awakening.

Not dawdling
not doubting
intrepid all the way
walk toward clarity
with sharp eye
With sharpened sword
clearcut the path
to the lucent surprise
of enlightenment
At every crossroad
be prepared to bump into wonder.

Part III

A JOURNEY INTO DEEP LOVE

THE HEART OF
THE MYSTERY

We began our journey by exploring the transformation of consciousness that occurs when we simply appreciate the wonder of the world around us. We followed the way of wonder into the deep mystery that lies at the foundation of all we think we know.

Then we turned inwards and discovered the same mystery at the heart of our own identity. And we explored the primal paradox that on the surface of life we appear to be separate individuals, while at the depths all is one.

Our pilgrimage has led us to deep love, which is the sacred ground towards which we have been heading all along. When we're conscious of ourselves as an individual expression of the primal oneness, it's an experience of all-encompassing love. This is the heart of the mystery experience.

We experience the mystery of being as a deep love that unites all things as one. The New Testament puts this beautifully in religious language when it declares:

> God is love
> and those that live in love
> live in God
> and God lives in them.

I remember coming to deep-know this was true during my awakening experience as a 12-year-old boy. Some weeks later, in a religious education lesson at school, the teacher invited in a priest to discuss Christianity. As part of our class discussion I suggested that all we really needed to understand was 'God is love'. The teacher and priest smiled condescendingly and one of them said: 'If only it were as simple as that.' But I was sure it truly was as simple as that. And I still am.

The presence of God is a reality in my life. But for me God isn't a great spirit that is separate from me. God is the primal oneness that is conscious through me. God is the mystery of being that is arising as all beings. And when I know God I experience a love that embraces all beings.

Religious traditions often portray God as a big person who decrees how we should live in holy books, which are the 'word of God'. But God doesn't speak to us. God is the primal silence that speaks *through* us. All words are human words and conditioned by the human experience of living in time. They are partial expressions of a truth that can never be articulated. There is no 'word of God', but if there were it would be only one word. And that word is 'love'.

Devotional Love
During the early years of my awakening I experienced an intense love affair with God, full of passionate longing when we felt apart, and deep communion when we found each other again. It is such

a precious feeling when, as the Christian mystic Hildegard von Bingen puts it, 'the mystery of God hugs you in its all-encompassing arms'.

Many spiritual traditions describe awakening as an experience of devotion to God. Other traditions maintain that having a devotional relationship with God characterizes a lesser awakening. It shows we're still enmeshed in the illusion of separateness, because in reality we are one with God.

In my experience, however, these two approaches are complementary not contradictory. Being one with God and being in love with God are paralogically different ways of experiencing the same awakened state. When I'm deep awake I see I am *both* separate *and* not-separate from all that is. I am one with the mystery of being *and* I'm this separate individual called 'Tim' who feels intense love for the mystery of being.

Loving Being

The great Christian mystic Meister Eckhart teaches that 'God is Being' and urges us to 'love God'. When I first read these lines I became full of insight. If God is *being*, then to love God is to love *being*. It is to love *being* here and now as Tim. It is to love the *being* of everything and everyone. It is to love all that is, simply because it is.

When I love *being*, it feels good to be. I know how much I want to exist. This love of *being* is something that permeates the whole of nature, which biologists call the 'survival instinct'. But it is much more than just the will to survive; it's an experience of the fundamental joy of living.

This love of *being* is always present, even when we're not conscious of it. And this is why to awaken to deep love we don't need to change ourselves or our lives. We simply need to become conscious of the ground of being that is perpetually present. And then there's the deep love waiting to welcome us with open arms.

A World of Wonders

When I'm deep awake I find myself in love with *both* the mystery of being *and* the exquisite world of appearances. I become awed by the beauty of the world. I become overcome with wonder at the multifarious richness of life. I see the numinous in nature.

The German scholar Rudolf Otto describes the feeling of communing with the natural world as:

> ... the sense of being immersed in the oneness of nature,
> so that man feels all the individuality, all the peculiarities
> of natural things in himself. He dances with the motes
> of dust and radiates with the sun; he rises with the dawn,
> surges with the wave, is fragrant with the rose, rapt with
> the nightingale: he knows and is all being, all strength, all
> joy, all desire, all pain in all things inseparably.

In mythological language when we fall in love with nature we're paying homage to the divine Goddess. She represents the mysterious appearances of life, just as God represents the mysterious essence of life. God is the life-dreamer. She is the life-dream. We are living in her sacred presence right now. She is everything we can see and hear and touch and taste. She is Mother Nature.

My deep love affair is with both God as the ground of being and Goddess as the appearances of being. The natural world is an objective expression of the unconscious oneness from which we have arisen. It is the unconscious foundation from which conscious bodies have evolved. When I see the numinous in nature, I see the mystery in the manifest.

Heaven on Earth

In the Gnostic 'Gospel of Thomas' Jesus proclaims:

> The Kingdom of Heaven is laid out upon the earth,
> but people do not see it.

Heaven and hell aren't afterlife rewards for good and bad behaviour, they are states of consciousness we inhabit here and now. In my experience, when I'm only superficially awake my life is at best banal and at worst full of suffering. But when I'm deep awake, life becomes magical. The everyday world becomes a lucent miracle shimmering with deep love. I see that heaven is truly here on Earth.

In the 'Gospel of Thomas' Jesus also teaches:

> The Kingdom is inside of you and it is outside of you.

If we reach deeply within or without, we discover the same mystery of being, which holds the world together in its loving embrace. Then we fall in love with being. And this transforms hell into heaven.

THE SPECTRUM OF LOVE

Deep love is not some ethereal experience, it's a tangible love I feel in my body. But deep love is much more than just a great feeling. It's a total relationship with reality. When I'm deep awake I feel deep love flowing out from the depths of my being into my heart to make me tender… into my mind to make me wise… into my body as sensual aliveness… and out into the world as compassionate action.

Deep love arises as a great spectrum of love that we can experience as affection for a friend… romantic love of a partner… the instinctual love of a child… the erotic love of sexual intimacy… the sensual love of pleasure… the engaged love of enjoying what we do.

Some spiritual traditions teach that these are lesser loves, which we must be willing to sacrifice if we want to experience the divine love of God. But it seems to me this is a terrible error born of either/or thinking.

The love I feel for my children is not a lesser form of love to my love of the mystery of being. It's a personal expression of the one love that contains all love within it. Deep love is a primal love that arises in my life as all my personal loves. Deep love embraces and completes all my personal loves.

From animal sex to transcendental devotion, love is the experience of the two becoming one while remaining two. When we love, we feel we are separate and not-separate from each other. And both are important because love is the relationship of unity, which can only arise because we are separate.

Alan Watts evocatively describes his experience of awakening to love:

> All at once it became obvious that the whole thing was love-play, where love means everything that the word can mean, a spectrum ranging from the red of erotic delight, through the green of human endearment, to the violet of divine charity, from Freud's libido to Dante's 'love that moves the sun and other stars'. All were so many colours issuing from a single white light.

THE HOLE IN THE SOUL

When I'm spiritually asleep there's always a feeling that something is missing. There's a hole in my soul that I don't know how to fill. I try to change my life so that things feel right, but nothing works. If I really pay attention, however, it becomes obvious that I'm longing for love. Without love my life is empty and meaningless.

The Buddha taught that the unawakened life is permeated by a type of suffering he called *dukkha*. *Dukkha* is an underlying unease and discontent. An existential SOS that arises from the knowledge of death. A fundamental sense of separateness from others. An alienation from the world.

The Gnostic Christians wrote about this debilitating alienation in texts such as 'Allogenes', which means 'The Stranger'. And this message resonates down the ages into the existentialist writer Camus' book *L'Étranger*. When we're lost in separateness we feel like a stranger in a strange land.

This perpetual sense of discomfort and alienation is hard to avoid because it arises from the fact that we are conscious individuals. To be conscious is to be separated off from the oneness of life as an observer of the world. We suffer from *dukkha* when we believe ourselves to be *only* a vulnerable human being, which is inevitably distressing.

We seek to alleviate this distress by making ourselves physically and financially secure. But we're never secure enough to withstand the storms of life. We seek to alleviate this distress by becoming important and respected. But we're never important enough to be overlooked by death. We seek to alleviate this distress by becoming successful and admired. But the emptiness within makes all our triumphs seem hollow. And then as the Indian poet Kabir says:

> Everything we do has some strange sense of failure in it.

Deep down, most of us know that only love can fill the hole in the soul. Only love can set us free from the debilitating *dukkha* that lurks in the shadows on even our sunniest days. Only love can truly mitigate all that is bad in life and allow us to truly celebrate all that is good.

We all crave love as if it's rare and hard to find, but there is no shortage of love if we look within to the source of love. The truth is, we live and breathe and have our being in an ocean of love. And when we understand this we can smile wryly at the irony of the human condition with wise Kabir who writes:

> I laugh when I hear that the fish in the water is thirsty.

Longing for Love

The hole in the soul is disturbing but it's also a blessing, because it demands that we fill it. And when our superficial attempts to fill the inner emptiness fail, we start to look deeper and become spiritual seekers. And when we spiritually awaken we find ourselves immersed in deep love. Then we know that this love is what we've been longing for all along.

When we know that really we're longing to feel deep love, we become filled with a deep desire to wake up to the deep self.

Longing for love is the fuel that can keep us going on the spiritual journey. Longing for love is missing the Beloved when we're apart and yearning to be reunited. Longing for love is aching to wake up.

When we know how much we want to wake up, we start to wake up. When we know how much we yearn for deep love, deep love reaches out to us. When we know that our deepest desire is to be immersed in the mystery, the mystery welcomes us in.

In one of his poems Kabir has God declare:

> When you *really* look for me,
> you will see me instantly.

On my mystery experience retreats I offer people the opportunity to dissolve into deep love, so when they return home they can remember how good this feels. This means that the next time they become troubled by the emptiness within, they can recall the deep awake state and become motivated to find it again, because they know they're really longing for love.

The deeper we go into the mystery experience, and the more frequently we return to it, the easier it becomes to remember how much we long to wake up when we've fallen asleep. When we recall times when we've been deep awake and in love with life, we naturally feel the desire to become more conscious again. And it's the authentic sincerity of this longing that gives us the energy and will to transform our state of consciousness.

Before the 'deep love initiation' that forms the heart of my mystery experience retreats, I ask people to make conscious their deep longing for love, because it is this longing which does all the work. On my own journey it has been this longing that has led me to continually experiment with ways to transform consciousness. It's this longing that motivated me to create the new way of awakening I'm sharing with you in this book.

Love is Worth Whatever it Takes
When we know how much we long for love, we'll do whatever

it takes to become deep awake. I'm very moved and inspired by the huge distances that people are willing to travel to attend my mystery experience retreats. I'm delighted to say that so far every person who's made such a remarkable effort has been very pleased they did. And that's because the mystery experience is worth the journey. It's what we've been looking for all our lives.

On my very first retreat a wonderful elderly gentleman and his lovely wife flew in to the UK from the USA. When we met on the first evening he announced:

> We've cancelled a cruise to come on this weekend, because I felt that at my time in life it was too important an opportunity to miss.

That was a little intimidating I must admit, especially on my first retreat! But he was so enthusiastic that I felt quietly confident that all I had to do was create the space for him to wake up and he surely would. At the end of our time together he told me it had been the best three days of his life, which touched me deeply. He returned with his wife a few years later and found this was an even richer experience. That's how it is with the WOW!

But you don't need to fly to the other side of the world to feel deep love. You don't need to attend a spiritual retreat. You simply need to be conscious of your longing for love… here and now… and dive into the mystery of being where the love is waiting. As Kabir says:

> Wherever you are is the entry point.

THE MAGIC THAT MAKES LIFE SWEET

When people come on my retreats it's my sincere aspiration that everyone experiences the natural wonder of deep love… and the majority of people do. As we fall in love together, we take each other deeper into the WOW, and there's no mistaking how this *feels*. The deep love vibrates in every cell of the body. When the time comes to leave we're immersed in deep love. The divisions dissolve and we relax into the naturalness of playing together in the blissful ocean of being.

I receive many inspiring emails from people telling me about their experiences and realizations. I want to share one that captures something of how it feels to taste the deep love. It's from an amazing man called Ian who runs a business out of Hong Kong and had flown in from his holiday home in France to attend one of my retreats in Glastonbury, England:

Dear Tim,

You, of all people, know why it is difficult to put into words any comment on an experience like this last weekend!! I am also sure that, notwithstanding, you are going to receive at least 46 other emails like this one!! I can only say that I now understand so many things I had read and never really understood before. How nothing changes and yet everything changes.

There is something very different seeing through these eyes now, and yet it is still me, but now it knows itself as that which it really is. Not something trapped or limited, but something totally free and unlimited. I had always been looking for it IN this 'dream' world and had therefore never been able to connect with it through the forms in the way you have shown. I now cannot even look in a mirror without seeing it instantly!!

Last night when we got back to France I was sitting in front of a roaring fire (in our freezing house!!) still glowing with the raw emotions of that parting session in Abbey House and I just had this overwhelming sense that Life was enjoying being me – watching the flames, feeling the warmth and the loving glow in my heart. There was both no-one here and of course someone here, both enjoying the fire!! WOW!!

I am also filled with stillness and find myself easily

slipping into the big space and the joy of just breathing that you highlighted for us. There is also the huge feeling of love and compassion for everyone else. Truly you must first love being and then be to love.

So, like many others, I feel that I came to Abbey House with a head full of ideas and wanting smart answers from you that would somehow cause some amazing change in me, and instead I was given such a deep experience of Love that makes all such ideas and questions somehow irrelevant or unnecessary. In the joy of that immersion in the ocean of Love, simply no words or understanding are necessary to feel it or be there. It was the last outcome of coming that I could have expected and yet it is everything I wanted from within the confused mist of my mental strivings.

If I was to try to sum it up, I would simply say that I came home and fell into Love. And I cannot thank you enough for opening the door to let me back into where I didn't even know I already was!!

While writing this book I received a wonderful email in which a lovely Irish woman called Therese shared how things had been for her after returning home after a mystery experience retreat:

> I am still basking in the afterglow. My yoga students are saying, 'Show us what you found in Glastonbury'. Others just take one look and smile, recognizing what they see. And being Irish, my family tease me. Tim – you are going to be a very rich man, if that is what you want, for you have found the magic that makes life sweet.

Unless I experience a big change of fortune I don't expect to become a rich man financially, but this is not important because I'm lucky enough to know that the greatest of riches is love.

From my first awakening to this present moment my ideas have changed and deepened, but the conviction that life is ultimately all about love has remained. I call myself a philosopher because I adore good ideas. But that's just a cover story to get people to take me seriously. Really I'm a love junkie.

I admitted this recently at the end of a mystery experience retreat and a wonderful woman called out 'You're not a love junkie… you're a dealer!' That's one of the nicest compliments I've ever had… and the funniest because it tells the truth. So here's what I'm really saying in this book:

Hey man! Are you looking for some deep love to fill the hole in your soul? I've got the real deal here and it's going for free. This is the magic that makes life sweet. This is the big WOW you've been waiting for. And when you taste it once you'll be hooked for life.

CONNECTING 'I TO I'
- WOW Experiment -

Spiritual awakening is an individual experience. But it's wonderful when we share the awakened state with others, because it amplifies the experience of deep love. The practices I want to explore in this chapter are very powerful ways of connecting 'deep self to deep self' with others, so that we find ourselves immersed in love.

In our previous WOW experiment I shared with you how to withdraw from the world into deep awake meditation. Now I want to share some practices that will bring your attention back into the world, so that you can connect with others in the deep awake state. These 'I to I' experiments are meditations that you practise with another person. But I'm also going to suggest ways you can experiment with these meditations on your own. And I'm going to end this chapter by exploring how you can use these practices in your everyday life.

'I to I' practices involve simply looking at each other… listening to each other… touching each other's fingertips. This is so simple it can sound like nothing special. Yet done with the right understanding these are incredibly transformative practices, because they allow us to connect as one *through* the separateness.

The first 'I to I' experiment is to come into the deep awake state with another person and look into their eyes. When I do this I am conscious of being the mysterious presence of awareness, which is looking but can't be seen. And I'm conscious that I'm connecting with the mysterious presence of awareness in the other person, which is looking but can't be seen.

If you've watched the movie *Avatar* you'll know the characters greet each other with the phrase 'I see you'. That's how it feels when I do this 'I to I' experiment. I really see the other person and they really see me. And at the depths of our being we know we are one.

In India, people use the greeting '*namaste*', which can be understood as meaning 'I acknowledge you from the place in me where you and I are one'. These 'I to I' practices enable us to acknowledge to each other that we are essentially one. And when this happens it's WOW.

In the Hindu tradition, meeting with a spiritual master is regarded as a great blessing, because we find ourselves becoming more awake. We resonate with the expanded state of consciousness inhabited by the great spiritual being we're with, which transforms our own state. This is known as *darshan*. In my experience, however, when we connect 'I to I' we can feel the joy of *darshan* with anyone, because actually we're all great spiritual beings. Walt Whitman describes how this feels when he writes:

> In the faces of men and women I see God, and in my own face in the glass.

Beautiful Otherness

When I use 'I to I' practices to connect deep self to deep self with another person, I find myself falling in love with their gorgeous individuality. I appreciate their unique humanity as a miraculous expression of the mystery of being. I see that what makes them so special is that they're different to me. I love the fact that we're separate as well as not-separate. Our separateness creates the colour that makes the world so beautiful. In the wonderful lyrics of the electronica band Bent:

> Beautiful otherness
> Love you because of this
> Lost in the loveliness
> Of your beautiful otherness.

SAFE INTIMACY

These 'I to I' practices are by far the most transformative practices I've ever used, which is why I've made them the heart of my mystery experience retreats. As I've developed and experimented with them, the results have astonished me. Nothing transforms consciousness so quickly and dramatically than simply communing deeply with another being.

When we awaken together, we find ourselves and find each other. We love others as they are, because we love ourselves as we are. Whether the other person is a friend or a stranger… a man or woman… young or old… we can't help but fall in love, because it feels totally natural to love and be loved.

Yet as I write this chapter I hesitate to share these practices with you, because the idea of such intimacy can seem intimidating. People often tell me that if they'd known about the 'I to I' practices, they'd have been too nervous to attend a retreat. Yet when they actually experience how safe and transformative they are, they're so pleased they did. A beautiful woman called Claire wrote:

> If I had known how it was going to happen I may not
> have come, but if I had known the outcome I would have
> taken baptism by fire for it.

This is so poetically put and captures the dilemma perfectly. We're normally so cut off from each other that the idea of connecting deeply with another person can seem scary. Yet actually when we connect as one it feels completely natural and utterly wonderful.

Deep Self to Deep Self

We habitually look from the perspective of the separate self, so when we gaze into each other's eyes it can seem intrusive. We may feel that someone is invading our private space, which makes us want to hide away rather than open up. And there can be an urge to giggle to cover the embarrassment of unfamiliar intimacy.

For 'I to I' practices to work, it's extremely important to create a safe environment in which we can relax and be ourselves. When we feel safe these practices become far from intimidating. Very quickly the experience becomes delightful… then completely intoxicating.

I always reassure people that 'I to I' practices are not invasive. When someone looks into your eyes they don't see into that secret place within, which is locked behind a door marked 'for my eyes only'. This is your private space and that's how it should be.

'I to I' practices are about seeing through the personal to the impersonal oneness and, from that expansive perspective, appreciating the uniqueness of our individuality. These practices don't help us get to know each other *personally*. To do that we need to hang out together… tell stories… laugh and cry… get drunk and become uninhibited… fall out and make up. All of which takes time.

'I to I' practices are about connecting in the timeless moment…
deep self to deep self. Getting to know each other in this way
doesn't take time. It happens the moment we look through the
separateness to the mystery of being.

'I TO I' PRACTICES

I prepare people for these practices by sharing many of the philosophical ideas and WOW experiments we've been exploring. So
I suggest you explore these practices with a spiritual friend who's
read this book.

In my imagination I'm going to recall the last time I experienced these practices and describe what happened. Then you can
try it for yourself when the time is right. I'm going to take you
through three 'I to I' practices, but I wouldn't normally use them
one after the other. Each practice is a powerful experience on its
own.

Preparation

Prepare for each of these 'I to I' practices by coming into the deep
awake state, using 'wondering, entering and presencing'.

> Sit comfortably with eyes closed and deeply relax.
>
> Wonder at the miracle of life and become conscious of the
> mystery of the moment.
>
> Enter the sensuality of breathing, so that the mind becomes
> still.
>
> Be the spacious presence of awareness, within which the
> experience of breathing is arising.
>
> Presence the flow of experience that is happening in the
> present moment.
>
> Become conscious of the mystery of being and deep-know the
> primal oneness.

'I to I' Looking

When I do this practice I often play music to help us let go into the safe intimacy of communion. My favourite piece for this exercise is 'Common Threads' by Bobby McFerrin, because it's so tender and inviting. I'm playing it now, which is vividly bringing back to me the experience of 'I to I' connection.

My partner and I are sitting opposite each other with our eyes closed.

I am entering and presencing the moment in the deep awake state.

Then I gently open my eyes and invite in the gaze of the person sitting before me.

First I'm conscious of what I can see… colours and shapes that make up the image of a beautiful face.

I focus on my partner's eyes and I know that I am connecting with another human being, full of hopes and fears… memories and dreams… just like me.

I am noticing that whilst the face is etched with their experiences of life, the eyes are strangely ageless.

It feels as if I am looking through the mature adult to see my partner as an innocent child.

I am looking through the separate self to the deep self.

I am conscious of being the presence of awareness connecting with the presence of awareness arising in another form.

I am awareness that cannot be seen… connecting through looking… with awareness that cannot be seen.

I am the mystery of being arising as Tim looking at the mystery of being arising as my partner.

My partner's face seems luminous and beautiful.

Sometimes it feels as if, when I look through one eye, I am connecting with the individual self and when I look thought the other eye I am connecting with universal being.

How delightful!

We are communing as one and two... separate and not-separate... the same and different.

We are dissolving into each other.

We are in love with each other.

'I to I' Listening

'I to I' listening can be wonderful in the silence, but I usually prefer to play a piece of moving music in the background. Two of my favourite pieces for this practice are 'Quanta Qualia' by Patrick Hawes and Hayley Westenra, and 'Full Moon Danse' by Andres Holte.

My partner and I are sitting close together with our eyes closed.

I am sinking into my breath and entering the deep awake state.

I am conscious of listening to the beautiful music, which feels like a river of sound flowing through time.

I am entering the music and savouring the sensuality of listening.

I am conscious of being the presence of awareness that is listening but can't be heard.

I am conscious of the deep self... the essential 'I' of being.

Now I am ready to express the deep knowing that I exist by softly saying the words '*I am*'.

There is a moment in which I hear the words arising from my lips and fading into the flow of sound.

Then my partner offers back to me the same words '*I am*'.

I hear the raw sound of a sweet human voice… different to mine… full of character and tempered by a life of experience.

Then I repeat '*I am*' and listen intensely as my partner echoes back '*I am*'.

I reach into the sound to grasp the meaning. I am listening to another person express the same deep knowing of *being* that I also feel within me.

We pass the words '*I am*' between us like a sacred mantra.

As I listen to my partner's '*I am*' I reach through the sound to the awareness from which the words are arising.

I am conscious of connecting with the mysterious presence of *being* in another form.

I am awareness that cannot be heard… connecting through sound… with awareness that cannot be heard.

The words '*I am*' flow between us and it feels as if we're performing a duet for one.

I'm no longer sure who is speaking and who's listening, because everything is happening of itself.

'*I am*' is rising and falling on one ocean of *being*.

I'm listening to oceanic *being* as it says '*I am*' through Tim.

I'm listening to oceanic *being* as it says '*I am*' through my partner.

I remember that '*I am*' is one of the great names of God in many spiritual traditions.

I am the oneness of God listening to itself… meeting itself…

recognizing itself… communing with itself… loving itself.

'I to I' Touching

'I to I' touching is an exquisite practice that allows us to explore being separate and not-separate, by dancing together in a simple and delicate way. For this practice the more relaxed you feel the better. I often suggest that people prepare by letting go of any tension in their muscles, so that they feel at ease in their bodies. This is an embodied experience. That's what's so great about it.

This practice definitely works best with music. A piece I often use is 'Benediction' from *The Prayer Cycle* by Jonathan Elias. It's full of moving intensity, which gives us permission to let our spirits soar.

My partner and I are standing in front of each other with our arms by our sides and our eyes closed, enjoying the stillness and the silence.

I am relaxing into my breath and letting go of the tension in my body, so that I feel open and at ease.

I am conscious of the feeling of my feet touching the carpet on which I'm standing.

I am connecting through touch with the whole Earth beneath me.

I am conscious of being the spacious presence of awareness within which my experience is arising.

Then I reach out my hands to lightly connect my fingertips with my partner's fingertips.

I feel the warm connection with another human body.

I am the presence of awareness that is conscious of touch… yet cannot be touched.

I am connecting with the presence of awareness that is conscious of touch… yet cannot be touched.

As the music starts to play it feels as if it's inviting us to move.

Without any conscious intention our hands are gently dancing together.

My hands are moving as one with my partner's hands.

The movement is happening of itself and I am following where it leads.

As the music moves us we naturally express its changing moods.

I can feel the pulse of life passing through the universe and animating our limbs.

There is a feeling of elation and liberation.

We are connecting as one and two in the great dance of life and that's WOW.

Our bodies feel open… our minds feel open… our hearts feel open.

We are swimming in an ocean of love.

The music builds in a crescendo and fades into stillness.

We put down our arms… yet remain strangely in motion.

It feels as if we're still dancing together even though we aren't touching.

We are always dancing together in the play of being two and one.

CONNECTING 'I TO I' WITH YOURSELF

If possible I encourage you to practise these 'I to I' experiments with a partner. However, you can adapt these practices, so that you can play with them on your own, which is also very powerful.

'I to I' Looking

Sit in front of a mirror.

Enter the deep awake state.

Be conscious of what you can see… the colours and shapes which form the image of your face in the glass.

Be conscious of yourself as the presence of awareness which is looking, but which cannot be seen.

Be conscious of yourself as the ineffable deep self looking at a reflection of your physical form.

Explore the paradoxity of being the looker and the looked-at.

Be conscious of yourself as the deep self and embrace the separate self with deep love.

'I to I' Listening

Sit alone in a place where you feel uninhibited.

Be conscious of listening to the sounds of life murmuring all around you in a million different voices.

Be conscious of the deep self that is listening but which can't be heard.

Gently start to hum or OM.

Let the sound arise from deep within you as a statement of the primal knowledge that you exist.

Be conscious that you are the person who is entoning and also the silent listener.

Reach through the sound to the deep self from which it is arising, as if you are circling back to meet yourself.

Dance in that circle of *being*… like a Sufi dervish ecstatic with love.

Recognize yourself as your own Beloved.

'I to I' Touching

Find somewhere that you feel uninhibited.

Play some expressive music which relaxes your body and opens your heart.

Stand quietly and enter the deep awake state.

Let go of the tension in your limbs and become sensually alive to the experience of touch.

Feel your feet rooting you to the Earth and the air caressing your skin.

Allow your body to be moved by the music.

Listen from the depths of your being and let the music's changing moods express themselves through you.

Be spacious awareness within which the dance is arising.

Feel the perpetual peace at the depths of your being and the joy of movement in the sensual world.

Be the movement and the stillness.

Be the never-changing delighting in changing.

Be timeless presence loving the flow of time.

CONNECTING 'I TO I' IN EVERYDAY LIFE

What's so wonderful about 'I to I' practices is that they simply involve looking, listening and touching, which is what we're already doing all the time. This means we can use these practices to transform our relationships with others in our everyday lives.

In my experience, when I'm superficially awake I connect with others superficially. But if I become conscious of the deep self within myself, I also become conscious of the deep self within others. Then I can connect 'I to I' with the people I meet in my everyday life.

It doesn't matter if the other person is only superficially awake. I can still see through the separateness to the deep self within them, and this changes how we interact. The other person feels they are being seen as they really are, and this can transform their state of consciousness.

States of consciousness are catching, because we resonate together. So when I connect deeply with someone, they often begin to wake up. And I like to think that they then go on to connect more deeply with other people that they meet, who may also be touched by the experience. And so a ripple of awakening spreads out into the world.

I'm going to describe ways that I connect 'I to I' with others in my everyday life, which I encourage you to experiment with as part of your exploration of awakening while you're reading this book. I'm not going to suggest you gaze into someone's eyes... or whisper to each other... or touch fingers and dance. In everyday life we can't formally practise 'I to I' connecting, because that would be pretty weird. But we can connect deep self to deep self nevertheless.

'I to I' Looking in Everyday Life

When I am with someone our eyes often meet. What I experience depends on my state of consciousness. If I am deep awake I see through the separateness to the mysterious presence of awareness that can't be seen. And there's a moment of deep connection. There's a moment of wonder.

'I to I' Listening in Everyday Life

When I am with someone we often talk to each other. What I experience depends on my state of consciousness. If I'm deep awake I can really listen. I can hear the timbre of their voice, which is telling me something. I can reach through the words to fully understand the meaning they carry. I can reach through the separateness to connect with the presence of awareness from which the words are arising.

'I to I' Touching in Everyday Life

In our culture we don't touch each other very much. Yet we long for the warmth of physical connection, which can so easily heal us of the suffering of separateness. And it takes only the gentlest of touches to connect. A squeeze of a hand. A passing pat on the shoulders. When I am deep awake I use these opportunities to reach through the tender sensation of touch and connect with the deep self in another human being.

Dancing With Life

When I practise the 'I to I' touching exercise with someone, we connect so deeply that we move as one to the music. I experience the dance of being separate and not-separate in a visceral way. Remembering how this feels changes how I approach my everyday life, because I can dance with my life in a similar fashion.

When I'm deep awake I feel that my life is flowing and I am flowing with it. I am responsive to the ever-changing moods of the music of life. The dance of being separate and not-separate unfolds spontaneously, so that I can't tell if I'm leading my life or life is leading me. I'm immersed in the timeless mystery and moving with the rhythm of time. I'm intensely present and in the groove.

THE EGO AS HERO

When we connect 'I to I' and share the deep love, we come to truly appreciate how beautiful we are. Yet many spiritual traditions teach that there is something within us that is inherently bad. We are afflicted with an ego that seeks to prevent us from awakening.

In this chapter I'm going to be critical of this ubiquitous idea. I'm going to suggest the ego is the hero, not the villain, of the story of life. And I'm going to examine our experience of inner conflict, which gives rise to the idea of an enemy within, so that we can love ourselves as we are.

Many spiritual traditions take an either/or approach to the paradoxity of identity. They teach that we need to reject our limited human self if we want to experience the expansive deep self. The separate self is seen as an obstacle to our awakening and is often referred to as the ego. This is such a popular idea that I'd like to take some time to explore why I think it's profoundly mistaken.

In my experience we don't need to eradicate the separate self to awaken to oneness. When I'm deep awake 'Tim' doesn't disappear in a puff of spiritual enlightenment. On the contrary, Tim comes to life. So in this chapter I want to suggest that the ego is actually necessary and desirable. This will be heresy for some spiritual folk. But for me, spiritual awakening is not about denying our humanity. I want to celebrate our individuality and appreciate the poignant beauty of the personal life.

The Individual 'I'

The idea of the ego as the villain of the spiritual journey is ubiquitous, but what is meant by the ego is understood in widely different ways. The Latin word *ego* simply means 'I'. From this perspective the ego is our sense of being an individual 'I'. For some spiritual traditions this is the ultimate illusion we need to see through if we are to discover the oneness of our deeper being.

On our journey in this book we've explored how the individual 'I' is arising from the oneness of being. But this doesn't mean that appearing to be an individual 'I' is an irrelevant illusion. There is a reality to the 'I' and the world of multiplicity it witnesses, just as much as there is a reality to the oneness of being in which there is no separateness. They are paralogically complementary perspectives on reality.

If the modern scientific story of evolution is to be believed then the universe has been steadily working towards manifesting the possibility of the individual 'I' for 13 billion years! Has that all been some enormous waste of time? Surely, far from being a pernicious illusion, the individual 'I' is the greatest achievement in the evolution of life?

In my experience, when I wake up to oneness the sense of being an individual 'I' doesn't vaporize away like a meaningless illusion. On the contrary, I see how important the 'I' truly is. The 'I' is arising within the primal field of unconscious being, as a separate centre of conscious being. If this were not the case I wouldn't be conscious at all… let alone spiritually awakened. So I certainly don't want to eradicate the 'I'. In fact I'd like to hang on to it for as long as possible. Because when there's no 'I' there's no consciousness.

Human Individuality

For some spiritual traditions the ego is not the 'I', but rather our human personality. When we identify with the person we appear to be we are unconscious of the deep self. The ego is our 'lower self', which connives to prevent us realizing that it isn't who we really are. When we act or think in ways we don't like… that's the ego playing up.

When I was younger I took this idea very seriously. But now it seems like the ultimate paranoid conspiracy theory. It doesn't awaken us, it merely encourages us to wage an internal civil war against ourselves. And that's disastrous.

We all have a sense of who we are as an individual person. We've spent our lives building up this personal self. Are we really now to conclude this was all a big mistake, because it turns out to be our greatest adversary on the journey of awakening? Surely not.

I check out spiritual teachings by asking myself if I'd share them with my children. So would I tell my little girl not to develop an ego? No I wouldn't. I want her to grow up with a clear sense of herself as a distinct individual. I want her to become a strong, independent woman, who knows who she is and can draw boundaries when necessary.

Of course if we are identified with *just* the separate self we can become 'egotistical', in the sense of the word 'ego' that implies we are selfish, self-obsessed and narcissistic. I'm not saying that's a good thing. I simply want to suggest that our individuality is something to celebrate not denigrate. And that as we awaken to deep love the separate self becomes a vehicle to express that love.

Indeed it seems to me that, far from being the problem, the personal self is our foundation in the world, from which we can spiritually awaken. It is a gloriously particular expression of the infinite potentiality of being, through which the primal oneness of awareness can experience life.

As we make our journey through life we all struggle to individualize ourselves as a particular person. We come into the world by picking up a picture of what reality is from those around us. We're conditioned by our family and culture. At this stage we exhibit the beginnings of individuality, but we're still largely unconscious. We really start to become individuals when we learn to question our conditioning.

When we doubt the received wisdom of our culture, we separate ourselves from the unconscious herd. This makes us different and can be isolating. But it's a necessary step on the path of awakening. If we are to experience life in a deeper way, we need to think for ourselves and see through the 'common nonsense' generally taken for granted.

So it seems to me that we become conscious by growing into *more* of an individual not *less* of an individual. Through this process we can become conscious enough to spiritually awaken. And this leads us to become conscious of the paradoxity of our identity. On the surface we appear to be a separate self, but at the depths all is one.

The Pathology of Depersonalization

We need a secure sense of our individuality if we are to awaken to the oneness of being. When this is not present the process of awakening becomes transformed into a pathology. For psychologists the condition of 'depersonalization' is a type of mental illness associated with extreme anxiety, not a higher state of consciousness.

People suffering from depersonalization feel that they have lost their sense of self. They describe living 'outside of the body' as 'an observer' who is 'detached from life'. They experience what psychologists call 'derealization', which is the experience that 'life is like a dream'. It sounds uncannily similar to the experience of awakening. But people suffering from this condition don't wake up to deep love. They find the experience of depersonalization extremely distressing.

There's a young man I know who's been suffering from depersonalization, which has made him very anxious. The irony for me is that while I've been writing this book about awakening, he's been reporting to me many similar experiences to those I've been describing. Except for him they are extremely negative.

Although he's not familiar with my philosophical ideas, he's been telling me that 'life seems like a dream'... 'I don't feel like I am a person'... 'I feel like a disembodied observer'... 'I can't stop paying attention to my breath'. And he's hated all of this. So I haven't been advising him to dive deeply into the experience and spiritually awaken. I've been doing the opposite. I've been trying to ground him in his separate self so the depersonalization passes, which is gradually happening.

First we need a robust sense of being a separate individual. When this is strong enough it can support a conscious awakening to our deeper being. When a strong separate self is absent, the natural process of awakening is transformed into the pathology of depersonalization. Many ancient spiritual traditions understood this, which is why they reserved the deep teachings of oneness for those who'd reached a mature age and created a strong sense of their individuality.

The Hero of the Story

Whether we see the ego as the individual 'I' or the personal self, it seems to me that the ego is not the enemy. Actually the ego is the hero of the life story. The ego is the separate self through which the universal self can experience the adventure of living. The ego is a character in the dream of life around which the life-dreamer weaves a cracking tale.

If I look at my own experience, Tim is clearly the hero of the story. He's the star of the show. Other people come and go, but Tim is in every scene. His wife Debbie plays romantic love interest. His best mate Pete plays comic sidekick. There's a whole load of extras who figure now and then. But Tim's the main man.

The paradoxity of life means that every one of us as an individual self is the hero of the story of life. Looked at from one perspective we appear to be irrelevant specks of dust in a vast universe, who are here for a moment and then gone. But from another perspective each one of us is the very centre of the universe. How wonderful!

When I understand that I am *both* an irrelevant speck *and* the star of the show, it makes me feel *both* humble *and* empowered. My desire in this book is to bring you to the same place, so that you can *both* become conscious of the oneness of being *and* feel empowered as a separate individual to be the hero of your life adventure.

INNER CONFLICT

If we want to waken we don't need to eradicate the ego. We simply need to be conscious of the deep self *as well.* But please don't misunderstand me. I'm not pretending that being a person isn't a mixed blessing. My own experience of being 'Tim' has been an amazing trip, but 'Tim' can also be a real pain in the butt.

It's because we experience the personal self as a source of continual problems that we are receptive to the idea that the ego is a bad thing. Who can't find parts of themselves they wish weren't there? It's like this for everyone I've ever met. So why is that and what can we do about it?

The problem we face is that the personal self is rarely individuated into one coherent persona, but is fragmented into a collection of different personas that don't always get on with each other. We have accumulated these disparate personas as we travel through life seeking ways to respond to our predicament. They can be seen as different bundles of responses to life that have taken on a sort of autonomous existence.

We often experience internal conflict between these personas, because they have different agendas, which can be extremely confusing. This gives credence to the idea of the evil ego. When our 'spiritual persona' gets pushed aside by another persona that is more interested in financial security or being important or hedonistic delights, then the spiritual persona feels it is engaged in a battle for supremacy with a traitor within.

We identify with whichever persona is dominant in consciousness and see the others as impostors. So if the spiritual persona is dominant, then the materialistic persona is the bad guy who is leading us away from the spiritual path. But if the materialistic persona is dominant, then the spiritual persona becomes just a silly distraction that stops us getting on with real life.

Actually, of course, we are not any *one* persona... we are *all* of them. When we realize this, the task becomes one of individuating the fragments into a coherent whole, which makes room for all the parts of who we are. This is impossible as long as we identify with any one persona. But it naturally starts to happen when we awaken to the deep self, because then we know our deepest identity isn't a person at all.

The Shadow

A particularly problematic source of internal strife is what is often referred to as the 'shadow'. The great psychologist Carl Jung, for whom this was an important concept, writes:

> The shadow personifies everything that the subject refuses to acknowledge about himself.

The shadow is the part of ourselves that we don't want to consciously acknowledge. The part we don't like. The part we'd prefer to repress than examine. For people who think of themselves as 'spiritual', the animal self with all its instinctual lusts can become the shadow. For people who think of themselves as 'selfless', selfish urges become the shadow. For people who think of themselves as 'calm', anger becomes the shadow. We all cast a shadow.

The shadow is a problem because what we repress comes back to bite us when we least expect it. This can happen at any time. One minute we're happily going about our business, then something happens to trigger the shadow. And we find ourselves behaving as if we're an entirely different person.

When I experience this it feels as if I've been hijacked by some unconscious part of myself. For example, I like to believe that I'm a tolerant and sensitive person. But a situation may suddenly arise when I find myself being annoyed and dismissive towards someone. Often someone I normally care about. It's as if I've become someone else. Someone I don't like.

When I'm overtaken by my shadow I find it hard to recognize this is happening, although it's perfectly obvious to everyone around me. I don't want to admit to myself I've been hijacked because I've become identified with the shadow. And the easiest way to avoid this awful fact is to project my shadow onto someone else. It is not me that's angry and insensitive… it's you!

The more I don't want to face the shadow the more unconscious I become, until I'm truly behaving in ways that at other times I would find appalling. Yet now my behaviour seems like a reasonable response to the unreasonable behaviour of those around me.

Being hijacked by the shadow is a disturbing experience I'd prefer to forget. So rather than face the way I've been, I prefer to repress any memory of how painful it felt. Once the storm has passed I go back to the idea of Tim as a reasonable sort of guy. Problem solved… until it happens again.

How can we prevent ourselves being hijacked by the shadow? The clue is in the name. We need to bring it into the light. We need to consciously acknowledge this part of ourselves. Only then will it stop unconsciously possessing us from time to time.

When we're conscious of the deep self and feel the deep love, it becomes much easier to acknowledge those parts of our personality that we would normally choose to ignore, because we're able to love ourselves as we are. And once we've consciously acknowledged the difficult parts of our personality, if they arise within us we can see them coming, so we're less likely to be overcome by them. We are conscious of what's happening, so we can choose a healthier option.

The Unloved Self

The experience of being overcome by some unconscious aspect of ourselves easily creates the idea of a devil within. The ancients saw this literally as demonic possession. Modern psychology has transformed this primitive conception into the idea of being possessed by the shadow.

This was a big step forward, but I also have reservations about calling the repressed part of ourselves the 'shadow'. It's an evocative term that captures the idea that the shadow is the darkness within us. But I also find it helpful to think of the shadow in a more approachable way as simply the 'unloved self'.

The shadow is that part of ourselves that we regard as unlovable, so we seek to repress it. And this unloved self is rooted in the unloved past. There are things we've experienced that were so painful that we don't want to remember them. There are ways that we've behaved that were so disturbing we push them to the back of our mind.

The unloved self is what we don't want to remember about our past. It is our hurt self that skulks in the shadows like a wounded animal. And mainly that's where it stays. Until a life situation reawakens the painful memory and we're involuntarily forced to play out the pain once again.

How can we prevent ourselves being overwhelmed by the unloved self? The clue is in the name. We need to love it. We need to care for our own wounded self as compassionately as we would care for someone else in great distress. We need to heal the pain of the past.

Many forms of modern psychology specialize in bringing the shadow into the light, so that we can love the unloved self. Their profound insights are beyond the scope of this book... but the simple secret that makes it possible to heal the wounded self is to become deep awake.

When we feel deep love we can embrace those parts of ourselves that normally seem unlovable. We can allow ourselves to remember the suffering we prefer to forget, which we've hidden away in a dark corner. We can accept what has happened to us. We can come to redeem the past by seeing it in a new way.

In redeeming the past we redeem the shadow, because we understand how the shadow has been cast. We empathize with the unloved self's point of view, so the shadow ceases to be an unconscious menace, and becomes an inner wound that we need to gently tend. When we become deep awake we can be kind to ourselves. And it is kindness which heals our hurt.

So the bad news is that there's a shadowy, unconscious, unloved part of ourselves that can cause us all sorts of grief. But the good news is that what we're unconscious of we can choose to make conscious. We can choose to bring the shadow into the light. This can be a painful process, but it leads us deeper into the mystery experience. Carl Jung explains:

> The shadow is a tight passage, a narrow door, whose painful constriction no one is spared who goes down to the deep well. But one must learn to know oneself in order to know who one is. For what comes after the door is, surprisingly enough, a boundless expanse full of unprecedented uncertainty, with apparently no inside and no outside, no above and no below, no here and no there, no mine and no thine, no good and no bad. It is the world of water, where all life floats in suspension; where the realm of the sympathetic system, the soul of everything living, begins; where I am indivisibly this and that; where I experience the other in myself and the other-than-myself experiences me.

A WORK IN PROGRESS

Many spiritual traditions condemn the fragmented, wounded human self and see it as the ego we need to overcome. But I don't see Tim as a spiritual burden, because I've come to love him despite his flaws. He can be difficult to live with, but I've become patient with that. I don't want to wage war with the ego that I've struggled to develop as I've become a distinct individual. I want to honour the ego as a hero on a journey of awakening to deep love.

The ecstatic Sufis encourage us to see the separate self as a work of art that we're in the process of creating. I like this idea. Tim is a work of art that I'll refine and rework until my dying day. He's imperfect of course, which is tough on everyone. But it's only to be expected. He's a work in progress. He's an attempt at a conscious, loving, human being. For as Carl Jung says:

> Every human being is an attempt at a human being…
> a throw from the depths.

LOVING BEING HUMAN

In this chapter I'm going to explore how being conscious of the deep self both changes and doesn't change my ordinary human experience. And I'm going to be critical of spiritual teachings that suggest we need to suppress our natural emotions.

I want to offer a paralogical approach to awakening that encourages us to embrace our human nature as it is, so that we can both wake up to oneness and passionately engage with the adventure of being a separate individual.

Many spiritual traditions teach that to awaken to the deep self we need to suppress our human nature. We need to eradicate our passions. Fear, anger, and desire are particularly deplorable. Lust is really bad. Our attachments are a problem too. All these human weaknesses arise because we're identified with the evil ego.

Such ideas are so ubiquitous in spiritual circles that I once took them seriously, but not any more. It seems to me that such teachings actually makes it harder to awaken, because we believe there are things about our nature that we must overcome, when actually all we need to do is notice our deeper identity *as well*.

I used to believe that if I was awake enough I'd become a spiritual *über*-being who was no longer troubled by disturbing emotions and passions. But actually I've remained as human as ever. And I'm pleased about that, because I no longer want to be superhuman. I've fallen in love with being human.

For me the wonderful thing about awakening is that it enables me to embrace my human nature just as it is. So in this chapter I want to explore a paralogical approach to our passions, which sees them as both good and bad. I want to articulate a way of awakening that embraces our humanity as well as our deep divinity. Let's start with the great bogeyman fear.

Safe Vulnerability

Being human can be pretty scary don't you think? We're so small and fragile in such a dangerous world. Suffering is a reality we can't avoid. Old age wears the body away. Death is waiting to surprise us at any moment. It seems to me that if we're not frightened by the human predicament we simply haven't been paying attention!

Some spiritual traditions teach that this fear is an obstacle to our spiritual awakening. They assure us that when we become conscious of our deeper nature we'll no longer feel vulnerable. But in my experience this isn't true. When I'm conscious of the deep self, I know that I'm essentially safe, which is a great relief. But 'Tim' remains a vulnerable human being.

Knowing that I'm essentially safe doesn't take away my human vulnerability. It does the opposite. It allows me to fully acknowledge how fragile Tim is. When I'm deep awake I can dare to be vulnerable. I can remove the psychological suit of armour I wear to protect myself from the world. And this makes me feel tender and real. It opens my heart so I can connect with others in our shared vulnerability, which is the experience of kindness.

When I'm deep awake my human fears don't magically evaporate. Rather, I can engage with the scary business of being human from the primal safety of the deep self. I'm frightened and not frightened, depending on which way I look at it. It's both/and not either/or.

When I was beginning my journey of awakening it was fashionable in spiritual circles to say that we had a choice between fear or love. But this is a false dichotomy. To love is to fear for the one we love. The more I love someone the more I'm concerned for their wellbeing. Love and fear are bedfellows not enemies.

Fear has got a bad name in spiritual circles, but fear isn't just bad. Fear can be a horribly debilitating experience, but it's also a natural part of the human condition. We're programmed by nature to be alert to predators... dangers... enemies. We could be killed at any moment and our instinctual nature is alert to this. We should be grateful for this fear.

Would I tell my children never to be fearful? Quite the opposite. As a parent I love my kids and fear they could get hurt. So I've taught them to be fearful of the cars in the road outside... of climbing too high on a tree that may not be secure... of trusting strangers who may not be as friendly as they seem.

Fear can be an appropriate response to a dangerous world, so seeing it as a spiritual enemy is absurd. I take a paralogical approach by being conscious of the essential safety of the deep self whilst also embracing my human vulnerability. Then I find that I'm able *both* to fear *and* not to fear. And this is the experience of courage.

DARING TO BE ATTACHED

Many spiritual traditions teach that to awaken we need to let go of our attachments. For years I tried to be unattached, but something in me resisted the idea. I presumed this was my ignorant ego struggling to prevent me awakening. But now it seems to me it was actually the voice of wisdom refusing to let me relinquish something so integral to my humanity.

The idea that attachments are bad is so common in spiritual circles that I used to presume it must be right. But then one day I became a father and everything changed. As I held my baby daughter in my arms for the first time I knew I was forever attached and I would refuse to let go. I wanted to be attached to this tiny bundle of life. I wanted to be *so* attached that the bonds could never be broken.

In that moment I also saw clearly why attachment could cause me terrible suffering, because with great love comes great fear. I knew that if anything were to happen to this little girl it would break me in pieces. Yet I was willing to take this risk. I had no choice. My heart demanded it.

That's when I knew I was looking for a new approach to spirituality that honoured the poignant beauty of the personal life, rather than rejecting it as some sort of spiritual obstacle to be overcome. I wanted a paralogical spirituality that was about *both* waking up to the deep self *and* celebrating our natural humanity.

It seems to me that our personal attachments are what give life its warmth and meaning. The idea that it would be more spiritual to be unattached seems utterly absurd. It's the sort of idea that could only have been thought up by celibate guys living in caves or monasteries… which is exactly what it is.

The absurdity of the teaching of non-attachment becomes clear to me when I ask myself if I'd teach my children to be unattached. When my little girl says to me 'I love you Daddy', should I reply 'That's nice but don't become attached'? I don't think so! I want her to feel attached to me and I want to feel attached to her. That's what it is to love each other.

It seems obvious to me that to be attached is both natural and desirable. It's a sign of how much I love that I'm willing to take the risk that attachment entails. I'm willing to suffer for love. And this doesn't seem foolish. It feels like a heroic response to the challenge of love.

When I'm deep awake it becomes possible to meet this challenge, because I am conscious of *both* my human attachments *and* my deep self that is never attached. I see that I don't need to become unattached, because essentially I'm always unattached. The deep self is forever free. It is because of the freedom of my essential nature that I'm able to let go of my attachments when the time is right… and move on to develop new attachments.

When I am deep awake I am *both* liberated from all the bonds of separateness *and* willingly attached because of love. I am able to bear the fear that comes with my personal attachments, because I know that I am also free. So I can dare to love.

Our attachments hurt because we try to cling onto someone or something in a world of impermanence. The great grief of life is that everything is fleeting. I will never be a young man again. I will never hold my baby daughter in my arms again. I will never argue with my deceased father again. I will never have this moment again.

The great grief of life, caused by impermanence, can't be avoided. But it's ameliorated by also knowing the great joy of life, which is that every moment is a fresh expression of the primal goodness. And then impermanence become poignantly beautiful. Each moment becomes a blessing to be cherished before it passes forever. Every meeting becomes an opportunity to fall in love that will never come again.

A PASSIONATE LIFE

Many spiritual traditions encourage us to let go of all desires and just accept things as they are, because when we want things to be different we become discontented. They encourage us to avoid the passions such as anger that disturb our calm equanimity. If we could only stop desiring and being so emotional we'd become spiritually awake. It seems to make sense, but does it really?

Powerful passions and desires can cause terrible suffering to others and ourselves. There's no denying the problem. But it seems to me that our natural emotions are only a problem when we're consumed by them. The solution is not to suppress or deny or eradicate our human nature. It's to be conscious of our deeper nature *as well*.

Desire is the fuel of life. Wanting things to be better pushes us forward to face new challenges. Passion is the spice of life. Feeling strong emotions wakes us up from the numbness of normality. Do we really need to sacrifice experiences that are integral to our humanity in order to wake up to our essential divinity? I don't believe life is that perverse.

I would never tell my children that desire is a bad thing. I might tell them to stop wanting so much and to avoid coveting what they can't have. But I would never say that desire itself is bad. I want them to desire to experience more… to see and feel more… to understand more… to *be* more. So if I wouldn't tell my kids to stop desiring, why would I demand this of myself?

Neither would I tell my children that they shouldn't experience passions such as anger. I might ask them to tame their anger if it's out of control or to find a different response if the anger is inappropriate. But I'd never say that anger itself is bad. I want them to be angry when things aren't right. I want them to be able to defend themselves if they're being abused. I want them to feel outraged at the injustice in the world. So if I wouldn't tell my kids to never be angry, why would I demand this of myself?

Spiritual awakening is about becoming more loving. But being loving doesn't mean just being *nice*. To love is sometimes to be angry because of love. I've found as a parent that I can be angry and still love. I'm angry with my kids when I need to bring their attention to the way they are unconsciously behaving, because I love them so much I want them to mature, even if it means they don't like me much.

Loving anger is a powerful emotion that propels me to compassionate action. I'm angry at all the needless suffering human beings cause each other, which fuels my desire to do something about the state of things. I'm angry that we tolerate so much unkindness in our culture, which makes me passionately insist we do something about it. Rage is sometimes the appropriate response to an outrageous world.

From a paralogical perspective there's no need to suppress our passions and desires. We simply need to be *also* conscious of the deep self. When I dive into the still depths I feel a primal peace. Then I see the paradoxity of my predicament. On the surface there may be a passing storm, but at the depths I am always in love with things just as they are.

Lust

Lust is a passion that gets an especially bad press in spiritual circles. I can understand this because when we experience raw sexual desire it's very compelling. It can cause us to see the person we desire in a purely objective way, as a physical form that is eliciting an instinctual response. Men are particularly prone to this it seems. I know that as a young man I felt terrible about my animal lust when it arose and tried to suppress it.

Now it seems to me that, as with all the passions, the problem isn't lust. The problem is *just* lust. To only see another human being as an object of our desire is to cut ourselves off from the depths of being within the other person and ourselves. But it's not an either/or situation. When lust arises along with love, our animal urges can be exhilarating fun. Then we can *both* love the essence *and* lust after the appearance. Hurray for that!

In Greek mythology Aphrodite, the great goddess of love, was honoured as Urania, who represented spiritual love, and also as Porne the 'titillator'. I adore the inclusiveness of the ancient imagination. It encourages us to make space in our lives for our animal instincts, not to repress them in our zeal to be spiritually pure. It's inherent in the paradoxity of our identity that our essential nature is pure and simple, while our human nature is earthy and complex. The deep self is always at peace, while the surface self is alive with passion.

Daring to be Passionate

Our human passions become a problem when we see *only* one pole of our paralogical identity. When we're conscious of all that we are, our human nature becomes something to celebrate not revile. What I love about artists is that they express and redeem our ambiguous humanity. What I find difficult about some spiritual teachers is that they make us feel bad about the way we naturally are.

I would hate to become a passionless person. I want to feel a fire burning in my belly. A yearning to live and express myself. A longing for a better world. I don't *just* want to feel at peace with life as it is. I *also* want to experience the tempestuous rush of new possibilities struggling within me to be born. I want to feel the heat of desire. The urgent pangs of hunger for more. The defiant will to grow.

FURTHER IN AND FURTHER OUT

When I wake up to the deep self I'm content to be human, with all of the struggles and suffering this necessarily entails. My human nature remains the same, but I'm also aware of the other paralogical pole of my identity. I'm both free from my humanity and engaged with my humanity at the same time. And this is not some spiritual feat I have to accomplish. It is simply being conscious of all that I am.

In his novel *Little, Big* John Crowley writes:

The further in you go, the bigger it gets.

I love this line because it captures how it feels to look within and become deep awake. I want to add another paradoxity that I've found to be true.

The further in you go, the more you come out.

In my experience the more I become conscious of the deep self, which is not in time, the more I can enter into the story of Tim in time. When I'm only superficially awake I hold back from life because it's so scary. I want to commit to my life and choose to *really* live, but I nervously put it off until tomorrow. But in the deep awake state of safe vulnerability I'm able to take the risk and go for my life. I can dare to passionately engage with the scary business of living. I can love being human.

DEEP LOVE MEDITATION
- WOW Experiment -

Becoming deep awake is an experience of deep love, which enables us to embrace our ambiguous humanity just as it is. In this chapter I want to invite you to embrace all the people in your life with deep love... to open your heart so big it can hold everyone within it... to expand the love you feel until it has no limits.

Here we are. You and me and everyone. All together on this astonishing journey of life. Each one of us is a unique expression of the mystery of being. Each one of us is an imperfect human being. And when we feel the deep love we can embrace ourselves and each other as we are. We can connect in love and care for one another. We can hold each other by the hand and walk each other home.

When I am deep awake it's obvious that love is what really matters in life. I recently came across a wonderful quote from Professor Jacques Decour that really captures the importance of love in a very inspiring way. He was executed by the Nazis at the age of 32 for his activity in the French Resistance in the Second World War. As he was waiting for death he wrote a beautiful letter to his family, which is extraordinarily moving. Here's what he said:

> Now each of us is preparing to die...We are preparing, thinking about what is to come, about what is going to kill us without our being able to do anything to defend ourselves... This is truly the moment for us to remember love. Did we love enough? Did we spend hours a day marvelling at other people, being happy together, feeling the value of contact, the weight and the worth of hands, eyes, bodies? Do we yet really know how to devote ourselves to tenderness? Before we pass away in the trembling of an earth without hope, it is time to become, entirely and definitely, love, tenderness, and friendship, because there is nothing else. We must swear to think of nothing any more but loving, opening our souls and our hands, looking with our best eyes, clasping what we love tightly to ourselves, walking free from anxiety, and radiant with affection.

EXPANSIVE LOVE

Our next WOW experiment offers a way of coming 'to devote ourselves to tenderness'. It involves using the imagination to expand the love we feel to include everyone and everything. It is similar to the Buddhist 'loving kindness' meditation. I call this practice 'deep love meditation'. As before, I'll describe what happens for me when I experiment with this practice, then you can try it for yourself.

Previously I've encouraged you to practise 'wondering, entering, and presencing', as a way of awakening during your everyday life. I've suggested you build a strong foundation for your journey of awakening by also regularly practising 'deep awake meditation' in which you 'dissolve' into the mystery of being. This 'deep love meditation' is a practice that you can use from time to time to root your experience of awakening in love.

Preparation

I am sitting quietly with my eyes closed and my body relaxed.

I am wondering at the miracle of life and coming into a state of profound not-knowing.

I am entering the sensual flow of my breath.

I am presencing the experience of breathing.

Breathing In Oneness and Breathing Out Love

As I breathe in I am focusing on the oneness of being.

As I breathe out I feel love expanding out from my heart into the world.

Loving Someone Close

Now I'm bringing to mind someone I find it easy to love.

Today this is my gorgeous wife Debbie.

I am becoming conscious of how much I love her.

I am remembering how it feels in my body to love deeply.

And as I do so the experience of love is arising within me.

I am enjoying bathing in the warm glow of love.

Loving a Stranger

Now I am bringing to mind someone I've never thought about *loving*.

I'm thinking of the man who came to fix our washing machine.

I don't know anything about him… but I am expanding my love to include the repairman.

I don't love him in the same way I love Debbie, because I don't have a personal relationship with the repairman.

But I'm conscious that he is a human being whose life is full of joy and suffering… just like me.

I'm conscious that at the depths of his identity lies the same mystery of being that lies at the depths of my identity.

I'm remembering the practice of connecting 'I to I' with someone I don't know and how easily strangers become lovers.

I am loving the repairman and that feels good.

Loving an 'Enemy'

Now I'm bringing to mind someone who I've exiled from my heart because they've hurt me in the past.

I don't have enemies… but there certainly have been people I've found it hard to love.

I am thinking of someone… but I'm not going to tell you who it is because that's not fair on this person.

As I allow them into my imagination I can feel the past hurt that makes me want to close my heart.

But I am staying conscious and letting these feelings pass.

I can see that this person is a wounded human being wrestling with their shadow... just like me.

I'm remembering that this person was once an innocent little child... and I can see that below the surface they still are.

I can't forget what they've done, but I can forgive.

I am opening my heart to this person as a manifestation of the mystery of being.

I am conscious that at the depths of our identity we are one.

I may not like this person or approve of how they act... but deep love is unconditional love that transcends liking and disliking.

I am loving for no reason.

I am loving because it is my deep nature to love.

Loving Myself

Now I'm bringing to mind Tim.

Like most people I find that the most difficult person to love unconditionally is myself... and that's because I know what I'm really like.

I am remembering all the things I find difficult about Tim.

I am conscious that on the surface Tim is an imperfect human being... vulnerable and wounded.

I am conscious of the deep self where there is an all-embracing love.

In my imagination I am holding Tim within my arms like a frightened child and soothing him.

I am loving Tim with all his glorious flaws… just as he is…
because he is.

Loving All

Now I am bringing to mind everyone and everything.

I am expanding my love to embrace all that is.

I love all beings as expressions of the great mystery of being.

This is a love so big it has no limits.

I am loving all… because all is one.

I am loving because I am love.

NON-DUAL PHILOSOPHY

I've been suggesting that our human experience is to be embraced not rejected. Yet some approaches to awakening teach that our separate identity is an irrelevant illusion, because oneness is the only reality.

In this chapter I want to continue my criticisms of either/or spirituality by examining this view of awakening, because it leads to a very cold way of seeing life that misses the importance of love.

I meet more and more people who intellectually understand that at the depths of life all is one. Yet many of them find it hard to actually experience the reality of oneness. This is often because they're stuck in an either/or approach to spiritual awakening. They're convinced that they will never awaken to oneness as long as they experience themselves as a separate individual. They're waiting for the separate self to disappear, but it just won't go. And it's not going to!

The big revelation of the WOW is that at the depths of our *being* all is one. And this becomes much easier to see if we stop trying to deny the reality of our individuality, and simply pay attention to the reality of oneness *as well*. If we adopt a both/and perspective it becomes much more straightforward to awaken.

When I started speaking about spiritual awakening I used to emphasize the wonder of oneness, because people seemed stuck in separateness. These days I find myself emphasizing the wonder of separateness, because I meet too many people who view their individuality as an obstacle to be overcome. This makes them dismiss the miracle of human life as a meaningless illusion, which cuts them off from the experience of deep love.

Many of these people have been influenced by 'non-dual philosophy'. There are various forms of non-dual philosophy, the most common of which is Indian advaitic philosophy. Advaita means 'not-two'. Advaitic philosophy teaches the profound perennial wisdom that essentially all is one.

I am seen by many people as a non-dual philosopher, which in one way I am. However in another way I'm saying something very different. While I certainly find that I agree with many non-dual philosophers who I respect immensely, I find myself profoundly disagreeing with certain interpretations of non-dual philosophy that are becoming popular right now.

One of those people whose understanding of non-dual philosophy troubles me is an imaginary friend I affectionately call 'Swami Blandananda'. His real name is 'Eric' but he changed that because it sounded a bit lame. He's one of my favourite philosophical sparring partners. Let's invite him in for a good chinwag.

SATSANG WITH SWAMI BLANDANANDA

Swami Blandananda: I've been listening to all you have to say and I fear you're missing the point. I'm a student of the ancient Indian wisdom of advaita, which contains the final truth on these matters.

Tim: I'm a big fan of advaitic philosophy myself. It cuts through all the superficial spiritual mumbo jumbo and gets down to the real deep stuff.

Swami Blandananda: Well all I can say is you haven't understood it very well.

Tim: I've been extremely influenced by the ancient sage Sankara. Even more so by the modern sage Sri Nisargadatta Maharaj. I love his book *I Am That*. I spent some time in Mumbai with one of his students Ramesh Balsekar, who had become a great teacher himself. This meeting changed my life, so I rate Ramesh highly. There's also Ramana Maharshi who's become very well known in the West. And now there's loads of Westerners teaching advaita, some of whom are pretty cool.

Swami Blandananda: That's all well and good, but you have not become an enlightened *gnani* yourself, so your teachings are distortions of the truth.

Tim: I certainly don't think of myself as a *gnani*… I'm a guy called 'Tim'. And I prefer to say I'm making suggestions rather than issuing teachings.

Swami Blandananda: Well your 'suggestions' certainly don't agree with the great teachings of advaita.

Tim: I feel that advaita is very good at articulating half of the paradoxity of life. It helps us recognize that 'all is one'. But it can take an either/or approach that portrays separateness as irrelevant. And I can't go with that.

Swami Blandananda: And that's why you're still unenlightened. I mean this whole book has been about some sort of temporary high you call the 'WOW'. Such peak experiences have nothing to do with awakening, which is the recognition of the permanent truth. They are irrelevant distractions. I urge my students to ignore them completely.

Tim: I agree with you in one way. Being deep awake is recognizing the permanent ground of being which is always there. But my experience of being conscious of the permanent ground changes. Sometimes it's a quiet knowing. And sometimes it's decidedly WOW.

Swami Blandananda: The discovery of truth is not a feeling. It's seeing though the illusion of separateness. That's all.

Tim: But don't you find that when you awaken to oneness a feeling of immense love arises? Didn't you at least experience this when you woke up for the first time? Wasn't it a wonderful surprise? Didn't it bring you to life?

Swami Blandananda: In the moment of enlightenment the illusion of separateness dissipated once and for all. There is no more to say.

Tim: You make awakening sound rather dull. To me it seems like an amazing adventure.

Swami Blandananda: There you go again. Always trying to make spirituality sound so fluffy and inviting. But the fact is when you awaken, no experience is any more special than any other experience. It all simply is what it is.

Tim: Yep... from one perspective I can see that. But there is also the human perspective from which some things are a bit boring and others absolutely fascinating. Don't you experience that? I bet you do.

Swami Blandananda: When you see no separation there are no differences.

Tim: But you must experience separateness as well as oneness? You're experiencing separateness right now talking to me.

Swami Blandananda: Just because you experience separateness you assume that Swami does also. This is your mistake.

Tim: But we're clearly distinct individuals having this conversation.

Swami Blandananda: To you but not to me.

Tim: Look… I'm going to think of a word… can you tell me what it is?

Swami Blandananda: Of course not.

Tim: You see… we're separate. That's the way it is.

Swami Blandananda: Separateness is an illusion. The reality is oneness.

Tim: Oneness is essentially real. Separateness is apparently real. That's the paradoxity of life.

Swami Blandananda: These are the words of someone blinded by *maya*… the veil of illusion.

Tim: The Sanskrit word *maya* can be differently translated as meaning 'magic'. *Maya* is an illusion like a wonderful magic trick that makes us go WOW!

Swami Blandananda: I see no magic trick. I see only truth.

Tim: But don't you find the appearances of life to be astonishingly beautiful?

Swami Blandananda: Beauty and ugliness are one to me.

Tim: Really? What a terrible loss that must be.

Self and No-Self

Swami Blandananda: You see, my friend, all your questions are misconceived. You ask me if I experience this or that. But this is because you cannot understand that for Swami there is no 'me'. Swami exists for you because you believe yourself to be Tim. But for Swami the separate self has ceased to exist.

Tim: Really? In my experience the separate self has *both* ceased to exist *and* continues to exist.

Swami Blandananda: You continually use this phrase… 'in my experience'. And there you display your ignorance. There is no 'me' that is the subject of experiences. This is the illusion of the 'I' which I have seen through and you obviously haven't.

Tim: *Who* has seen beyond the illusion of the 'I'?

Swami Blandananda: I have… well… there isn't actually an 'I' of course. This is just the problem that arises when you are forced to talk about deep truth in dualistic language.

Tim: I'm sure that's partly the problem. But maybe it's also a sign that you're missing something obvious.

Swami Blandananda: No… you are missing the obvious. Tim has no real existence. This is the great teaching of *anatta* or no-self.

Tim: It seems to me that self and no-self paralogically coexist. It's like in the yin/yang symbol. There's a dot of white in the middle of the black, and vice versa. In the same way when I go to the depths of the separate self I find the no-self. But when I dissolve into the no-self I see that it's Tim who is conscious of this happening.

Swami Blandananda: When the final realization comes, my

friend, there will be only no-self. You will cease to be.

Tim: To be or not to be? That is the question. Well how about this? To be *and* not to be. This is the answer.

Swami Blandananda: In your previous books you've repeatedly quoted the profound line from Nisargadatta… 'you are not a person'. That's it in a nutshell. Read your own books!

Tim: Yes.… I'm not *just* a person. Essentially we are all the oneness of being. But right now I am *also* the mystery manifesting as Tim.

Swami Blandananda: Put an end to your preoccupation with Tim and you'll become a true *gnani*.

Tim: That doesn't feel right to me. I want us to express our individuality not suppress it. In my experience, appearing to be a separate individual isn't some sort of spiritual curse. It's pretty groovy when you get into it.

Swami Blandananda: If you want to know the liberation of *moksha* you must stop being so enamoured with the story of Tim.

Tim: I don't want to be liberated *from* the story of Tim. I want to be liberated *into* the story of Tim, so I can really enjoy the ride.

Swami Blandananda: You are so consumed by passion, but the realization of advaita is not about sentiment.

Tim: It's certainly not sentimental. But ultimately awakening is all about love. Don't you feel that?

Swami Blandananda: Love is just the opposite of hate.

Tim: That's exactly what Ramesh Balsekar said when I was with him and this question came up.

Swami Blandananda: That's because he was a *gnani* who knows what he's talking about.

Tim: It all sounds very cold to me. The deep love I'm talking about is what I feel when I see we are both separate and not-separate. Don't you feel that love?

Swami Blandananda: Of course… love continually arises within Swami… I love all beings.

Tim: Does it pump away in you like an engine? Do you feel the heat of love in your body?

Swami Blandananda: I am unconcerned with such things.

Tim: I might be able to help you do something about that if you want?

Free Will and Fate

Swami Blandananda: There's your fundamental error once again. There is no separate self, so there is no 'doer' to do anything about things.

Tim: I completely agree with that from one paralogical perspective.

Swami Blandananda: There are no conscious agents with free will. That's all the illusion of separateness. Everything is just happening. When you see that you will be liberated from ignorance.

Tim: I have seen that and it did liberate me. It was amazing. I can see it now. Everything is arising spontaneously as one. From this perspective I'm not saying these words. They are happening as naturally as the Sun rises in the morning. All is the one flow of Tao.

Swami Blandananda: Very good. Now we're getting somewhere.

Tim: On a deep level it seems to me the unconscious oneness of awareness is *doing* everything, just as the unconscious dreamer is *doing* everything in a dream.

Swami Blandananda: Exactly. Tim is merely a character in the dream of life. He thinks he chooses to do this and that. Yet this is a trivial illusion.

Tim: But that's only one side of the paradoxity. From the other perspective Tim's experience of free choice is very important indeed. The primal awareness is *unconsciously* dreaming up the world. But it is *conscious* through Tim. So through Tim it can consciously choose to do this or that.

Swami Blandananda: Choice is an irrelevant chimera.

Tim: That can't be right. It's taken billions of years of evolution to get us to the place where the field of awareness can make conscious choices through us. Most of evolution has been unconscious and therefore pretty haphazard. But now the mystery of being can consciously think about what it's going to do. And it's doing that through you and me!

Swami Blandananda: For a *gnani* choice arises spontaneously in the flow of life.

Tim: I remember Ramesh selling me one of his books and telling me that all the words had simply flowed out onto the page with no editing. He seemed very impressed by this.

Swami Blandananda: There you are… no struggling with words for him. I hope you read the book and learned a thing or two.

Tim: The book was amazing and I learned a whole load. But as a writer I have to say it was in need of a good edit. And I'm not surprised by that because for me the writing process is paralogical. It involves spontaneous inspiration and painstaking editing. It's a process of create and criticize. You need both.

Swami Blandananda: Swami is not engaged with creating or criticizing. There's nothing to be done. Life is like a book that is already written. The characters in it can't alter their fate.

Tim: It seems to me that life is a paradoxical dance between possibility and actuality. It flows as it must. Yet at the depths of my being I am the creative source of all, so I can consciously shape the flow of life.

Swami Blandananda: Tim is just a puppet of God.

Tim: No. You're confusing the two paralogical perspectives. From one perspective all is one. Everything is just happening. There is no Tim. So there's no separate person to be a puppet or otherwise. Then from the other perspective everything is separate. Tim exists as a person. And he can clearly choose how he reacts to life. This is one of his defining qualities as a human being.

Swami Blandananda: You can't have it both ways.

Tim: Why not? It's a paradoxical universe. Perhaps it will help you get what I'm saying if you think about the discoveries of science.

Swami Blandananda: Don't start quoting science at me for God's sake.

Tim: Scientists see the world we live in as deterministically following the laws of nature. But they also understand that on a quantum level what exists is a collection of possibilities, so from this perspective reality isn't deterministic.

Swami Blandananda: I'm really not that interested in science.

Tim: Well it's seems to me that my experience of life is also *both* deterministic *and* not deterministic. My experience of the objective world is that it follows deterministic laws.

But my experience of the subjective psyche is that it's not deterministic, rather it's creative. It's a world of possibilities… like the quantum world. And in the same way that the Newtonian world and quantum world paradoxically exist together, my experience of a deterministic outer world and a creative inner world exist together.

Swami Blandananda: You just don't get it do you. Nothing exists together with anything else, because all is one. And this means your so-called freedom of choice is a meaningless illusion.

Tim: But surely the existence of free will is a reality it would be absurd to deny? In fact our freedom is much more extensive than we normally acknowledge. We are free in this moment to do innumerable things. Our freedom is overwhelming.

Swami Blandananda: The illusion of choice traps us in the suffering of separateness.

Tim: Really? It seems to me that if we could allow ourselves to be as free as we truly are, we'd make much better choices in our lives, and be much happier. All it takes is for us to become more conscious. Because the more conscious we are the more freedom of choice we experience.

Swami Blandananda: Look… the important thing you need to realize is this. All these 'WOW experiments' you've been suggesting people do in this book are a waste of time. They merely endorse the illusion of the 'doer'. The realization of oneness just happens when it happens. Your unenlightened attempts to help will just make things worse.

Tim: I agree you can't force awakening, like you can't make yourself fall in love. But a human being is a conscious agent who can transform their life if they choose to.

Swami Blandananda: Consciousness is a passive presence that merely witnesses the world.

Tim: Yes. That's what I see too. But in passively witnessing the world it changes the world.

Swami Blandananda: Another paradox I suppose?

Tim: When the oneness of awareness witnesses the world through Tim, this feeds back information to the primal awareness which can lead to a thought arising… 'I think I'll do this'… and this leads to action that changes the world.

Swami Blandananda: The thinking mind just gets in the way of the spontaneous flow.

Tim: You're right, but I want to add something to that. I agree that thinking slows things down, but that's its purpose. It allows awareness to consciously consider what it's doing. It can imagine acting before actually doing anything, which means it can choose to act differently.

Swami Blandananda: For the *gnani* there is no need to think. The mind is silent.

Tim: It seems to me that we need to do more thinking, not less, if human beings are going to evolve beyond the largely unconscious animal we are at the moment. Then we'll start to make better choices.

Meaning and Meaninglessness

Swami Blandananda: The truth is that none of this matters really. Life is a dream. It has no significance or meaning.

Tim: But dreams are full of meaning. And in my experience life is the same. It's so full of meaning I seem to be able to give it infinite meanings.

Swami Blandananda: I give it no meaning, which is why I am liberated from the illusion of separateness.

Tim: Don't you ever get the feeling that life is trying to tell you something... as if it's leading you somewhere... and there's a sense that life knows best?

Swami Blandananda: It's of no interest to the illuminated mind.

Tim: It feels to me as if the deep self is shaping Tim's story into a transformative narrative to help him grow into a greater expression of the deep self.

Swami Blandananda: Very imaginative I'm sure.

Tim: Sometimes the events of my life are so pregnant with symbolic meaning I find myself asking 'If this were a dream what would this be showing me about myself?'

Swami Blandananda: Ahh... yes... we should read the omens and follow signs. I'm surprised you go along with all that primitive superstition.

Tim: Carl Jung made up the word 'synchronicity' to describe the common experience of meaningful coincidence. I experience synchronicities a lot. When a synchronicity happens it's suddenly obvious there is some secret pattern underlying seemingly random events. That's why synchronicities are so interesting.

Swami Blandananda: They're a meaningless distraction.

Tim: Let me tell you about my good friend Peter Gandy, who I've co-authored many books with. He had a girlfriend called Frances Turner, who was an extremely talented artist. Sadly Fran died of a brain haemorrhage seven years ago. Last year Pete started writing a book and in one chapter he decided to describe Fran's experience of her brain haemorrhage from her point of view.

Swami Blandananda: Very courageous I'm sure, but I can't think why he'd do that.

Tim: Then on the day he started writing the chapter Pete had a brain haemorrhage himself. If I hadn't found him he'd be dead. Now he's recovered fully and he's been transformed by the experience. He's really alive and in touch with the deep love. There's much more to the story, which is full of fascinating synchronicities. But you can see why I say that sometimes what happens suggests a hidden pattern or meaning underlying life.

Swami Blandananda: It's a coincidence. They happen from time to time. It would be surprising if they didn't.

Tim: Often synchronicities can be quite insignificant, but when they happen people usually find it changes their consciousness is some significant way. Take my mum. On her wedding anniversary she was really missing my dad who'd recently died. So she opened iTunes on her computer and put it on 'shuffle' to play some music to cheer herself up. And on comes 'The Wedding March'… which she didn't even know she had on her computer.

Swami Blandananda: Very sweet. And I'm sure she felt it was a message from your father. But actually it was nothing.

Tim: This week I got a beautiful email from a lady whose husband had died recently. He was a wonderful man called Paul Appelbaum, who'd come to one of my mystery experience retreats and was a great supporter of my work. After his unexpected death she went to his favourite reading spot, looking for solace. She found that when he died he'd been reading my book *How Long Is Now?* And it was open on the chapter called 'The End of the Story', which is all about death. So she read the chapter and found the solace she needed.

Swami Blandananda: Very moving. But the fact is he could've been reading the sports section of the newspaper. Only she wouldn't have bothered to email you about that.

Tim: There's a great line in a Walt Whitman poem where he says 'I find letters from God dropped in the street, and every one is signed by God's name, and I leave them where they are, for I know that wherever I go, others will punctually come for ever and ever.' That's how I feel. Synchronicities happen so often, sometimes I take them for granted. And to me this suggests that life is full of implicit meaning. It may be impossible to say what the meaning is, but meaning is obvious everywhere.

Swami Blandananda: You're beginning to annoy me. Life is meaningless because separateness is an illusion.

Tim: It seems meaningless to you because you insist on dismissing separateness. The meaning arises when we embrace separateness as well as the oneness. The meaning is the exquisite dance between the paralogical poles.

Swami Blandananda: Please… forget the philosophical acrobatics. Just take a common-sense look at the world we live in. It's just one damn thing after another for no particular reason whatsoever.

Tim: It seems to me that life is both meaningful and meaningless. From a paralogical perspective this is what I would expect. Sometimes it seems full of meaning. Other times it doesn't. There are significant moments in the story. And then there's a lot of inconsequential development. But, as in all good stories, you can find out later that what you thought was insignificant comes to play an important role in the plot.

Swami Blandananda: How can you possibly live your life as if it's meaningful and meaningless at the same time? That's crazy!

Tim: But that's exactly what most of us already do. When we deal with the practicalities of life we expect the world to deterministically follow the laws of nature. But that doesn't stop us also having an emotional response to life as if it's a story full of meaning.

Swami Blandananda: Look... you're a fan of science... if science has shown us anything it's that life is a chance event in a meaningless universe.

Tim: Objectively, life is the meaningless unfolding of the laws of nature. Subjectively, my life is an interactive story about Tim with purpose and meaning.

Swami Blandananda: Well that's what you say... but it's not what science or advaita say.

Reductionist Spirituality

Tim: You know... come to think of it... your interpretation of advaita is not dissimilar to the reductionist interpretation of science that I criticized earlier in this book. Both approaches leave us living in a meaningless universe that operates deterministically for no reason.

Swami Blandananda: Well I'm glad that scientists have finally understood the great truth known to all *gnanis*.

Tim: Your approach to advaita is a sort of reductionist spirituality. Like reductionist science it seeks to understand life by destroying life. Reductionist science does this by cutting up existence into small meaningless pieces. Reductionist advaita does this by lumping everything together into one meaningless blob. Both approaches end up being pretty cold, because they ignore our precious humanity. They're anti-life in opposite ways.

Swami Blandananda: The way I see it, advaita isn't 'anti' anything. But it seems to me that you're 'anti' advaita.

Tim: Quite the opposite. I love advaitic philosophy. I want to articulate a way of awakening that has all the depths of advaita, but with plenty of humanity as well. That's what I'm trying to do in this book.

Swami Blandananda: I'm sure you mean well, but your efforts are misguided. It's really of no consequence what you say about awakening, because enlightenment is beyond words.

Tim: That's true. But it's also true that how we talk about awakening really matters, because it can lead us to approach life in very different ways. Take you and me for instance. I suspect that we're both actually experiencing something very similar. We're both deep awake. But we're thinking about it in very different ways. And it seems to me that you've got a one-sided way of seeing things that doesn't value our wonderful humanity, so it doesn't lead to deep love. And to me love is what really matters.

Swami Blandananda: Well I'm pleased to think about things in accordance with the perennial wisdom of advaita, rather than take your lovey-dovey approach.

Tim: Fair enough. That's your choice and I respect that.

Swami Blandananda: Look you idiot… I keep telling you… there is no free choice.

Tim: I choose not to believe that.

CHAPTER 29

CELEBRATING SEPARATENESS

We began this part of our journey by exploring the deep love that arises when we recognize we're both separate and not-separate from each other and all of life.

This has led me to articulate a paralogical approach to awakening that has its foundation in a deep knowing of the primal oneness, yet also delights in our exquisite individuality and natural humanity.

I've also been critical of an approach to awakening to oneness that doesn't value separateness, because if we reject separateness we reject love.

In this chapter I want to clearly state why I think separateness is both important and necessary. And I want to explore the paralogical relationship between oneness and separateness.

An important Buddhist text called the Dhammapada begins:

> With our thoughts we create the world.

I want to explore why I think this amazing idea is extremely insightful, because this will help us come to understand the importance of separateness. But let me start by clarifying the way I think it can also be misleading.

Clearly I'm not consciously thinking the world into existence right now. I can think intensely about there being an elephant in my office, but no elephant appears. I can imagine all sorts of things I'd like to exist, but reality resists my wishes. Tim isn't creating reality with his thoughts. However, what I'm experiencing of reality depends on how I conceptualize it.

Have a look around you and you'll see that everything you're conscious of you have a concept for. I am doing this now. I'm conscious of the computer screen… the office… the garden outside… the birdsong… the sky… my body… the table I'm working at… the time of day it is… the coffee I'm drinking. I'm conceptualizing everything I am conscious of.

My concepts divide up reality into 'this not that'. My coffee cup is 'this not that'. My computer keyboard is 'this not that'. The time of day is 'this not that'. I'm differentiating the world into comprehensible chunks, and this is defining what I'm experiencing.

Our ideas allow us to discriminate reality into a multiplicity of things. But we're also discriminating the world without using words. There are pre-linguistic concepts that babies and animals possess which enable them to negotiate the world in simple ways.

When you chew a piece of meat in your mouth you're making an instinctual discrimination between the meat that is your food and the meat that is your tongue. And if you don't, it hurts! (This is hard for me to imagine because I'm a life-long vegetarian, but it's such a good example I couldn't resist it.)

As we mature from children into adults we learn more and more concepts, which we use to divide up reality in ever more subtle ways. Through this process we steadily become more conscious of the world. As children we live in a small and simple world, but as adults we live in an enormous universe populated with an incredible diversity of separate things. And that's because we're using a huge number of concepts to discriminate reality into the world of separateness.

When we don't discriminate things we aren't conscious at all. This is the state of deep sleep. When we're awake we discriminate ourselves from the world as the subject of a flow of experience. And we understand our experience by discriminating the world into individual things with different qualities.

Consciousness Is Discrimination

So here's the big idea I want to share with you.

> Consciousness is discrimination.
>
> Consciousness arises as we discriminate the whole into separate parts.
>
> The more we discriminate the world, the more conscious we become.

The Necessity of Separateness

Now here's the realization I've been working towards.

> It's discrimination which allows us to be conscious.
>
> This means that the experience of separateness isn't a trivial illusion, because it's a prerequisite for us being conscious at all.

The Paradoxity of Awakening

This leads us to an understanding of the paradoxity of awakening.

We are only conscious because we're experiencing the world of separateness.

But now we are conscious through experiencing separateness, we can *also* become conscious of the essential oneness of being.

If we get lost in our concepts we don't experience the primal oneness, but without these concepts we wouldn't be conscious at all.

So we come to know the wordless via words… which is exactly what we've been doing in this book.

CONSCIOUS ONENESS

People often ask me 'How can I be one with everything?' I playfully advise them to go to sleep, because in the deep sleep state there is no separateness. In deep sleep we don't discriminate reality, so there is only the oneness of unconscious being.

This is an unsatisfactory answer, of course, because my questioner is interested in spiritual awakening, not going unconscious. But I like to use this question as an opportunity to point out the importance of separateness. Let me take you through it:

In deep sleep we dissolve back into the primal oneness of awareness, so we become unconsciously one with all. But this isn't the experience of spiritual awakening.

Spiritual awakening is being *consciously* one with all.

Our predicament is that consciousness arises with discrimination, so to be conscious is to experience separateness.

This means we can never *just* be conscious of oneness. We must become conscious of *both* separateness *and* oneness.

We must become conscious of the oneness of being *through* the separateness.

When this happens, we see the primal paradox at the heart of existence… all is one and one is all.

The Universe Vision

When I'm conscious that everything is essentially one, I experience the 'universe vision'. I use this new term to make it clear that this isn't *just* an experience of oneness. It's recognizing that the universe is a paradoxical 'uni-variety'. When I experience the universe vision I see that reality is an essential oneness *and* an apparent multiplicity. I see that everything is separate *and* not-separate.

Many people choose to acknowledge only one of these perspectives and dismiss the other as unreal. Those who take a common-sense approach to life dismiss oneness as a mystical fantasy. Some spiritual traditions teach that oneness is real and multiplicity is an illusion. But I see no reason to prejudice oneness over multiplicity, or vice versa. They're both wonderfully real from different paralogical perspectives.

When I experience the universe vision I see that oneness and separateness are opposites that coexist as complementaries. Reality is a fundamental 'both/and' that we discriminate into 'either/or'.

As Carl Jung put it:

No reality without polarity.

That's it in a nutshell… and it rhymes. Nice one Carl.

THE ANCIENT PHILOSOPHY OF PARADOX

I'd like to clarify the paralogical relationship between oneness and separateness by contemplating the powerfully pregnant opening lines from the 'Tao Te Ching' by Lao Tzu. Let's begin by reading the passage straight through, and then we'll examine it line by line, because it has so much in it.

Tao is not something that can be pointed to.
Tao is not an idea that can be defined.

Tao is indefinable original totality.
Ideas create the appearance of separate things.

Always hidden, it is the mysterious essence.
Always manifest, it is the outer appearances.

Essence and appearances are the same.
Only ideas make them seem separate.

Mystified?

Tao is mystery.

This is the gateway to understanding.

What-Is Before Words

Old man Lao's first two lines explore a profound realization we've
discussed a great deal in this book:

Tao is not something that can be pointed to.
Tao is not an idea that can be defined.

Tao is the mystery of being. It's the essence of everything, so we
can't point to Tao as a separate thing. It is not a concept we can
grasp with the mind. All our ideas about life are simply ideas. The
mystery is what our ideas attempt to explain. It is before our ideas.
It is the wonder we are wondering about. All we can know with
thoughts is the story we're telling about the mystery to make some
makeshift sense of life. But what-is before words cannot be said.

With Our Thoughts We Create the World

The next two lines say something very similar to the quote from the
Dhammapada we contemplated at the beginning of this chapter:

Tao is indefinable original totality.
Ideas create the appearance of separate things.

Lao Tzu is suggesting that our ideas create the appearance of separateness. Reality is an essential oneness that we experience as an apparent multiplicity, by discriminating it with concepts.

The Paradoxity of Being
In the next lines, old man Lao really nails the primal paradoxity of being:

> Always hidden, it is the mysterious essence.
> Always manifest, it is the outer appearances.

Lao Tzu doesn't say that the mysterious essence is real and the appearances are an illusion. Rather, he says that the Tao is *always* both mysterious and manifest. The paradoxity of being is that it is one essence that appears in many forms. It's both/and not either/or.

Essence and Appearances
Now Lao Tzu takes us to the depths of the paradoxity of being:

> Essence and appearances are the same.
> Only ideas make them seem separate.

From one perspective we can discriminate the essence and the appearances as opposites. But essentially they are complementary ways of understanding the paradoxity of being.

The Way of Wonder
Finally old man Lao points to the impossibility of grasping all of this with the rational either/or mind. So he invites us to follow the way of wonder we've been travelling together in this book:

> Mystified?
>
> Tao is mystery.
> This is the gateway to understanding.

The Tao is the deep mystery of life. To become conscious of the deep mystery we need to enter a profound state of not-knowing. This is the gateway to deep knowing what-is before words.

Seeing Through Your Ideas

Later in the 'Tao Te Ching', after sharing with us a whole host of great ideas, Lao Tzu impatiently declares:

> Enough ideas!
> Ideas divide up the whole.

We are conscious through discrimination, but if we want to wake up to oneness we must pay attention to the what-is before words. Let's do it now.

> Ask yourself… what is the world before you think about it?
>
> Ask yourself… who are you when you have no idea who you are?

You won't be able to say what you see in words, because these questions can only be answered by a pre-conceptual deep knowing of being. This is what makes old man Lao say:

> Those who speak do not know.
> Those who know do not speak.

And that's somewhat ironic coming from someone with so much to say for himself!

CHAPTER 30

THE WEB OF LOVE
– WOW Experiment –

I've been articulating a way of awakening to oneness that celebrates separateness... a way of coming to know the deep self that can allow us to embrace our human individuality... a way of deep-knowing the deep mystery that brings meaning to the adventure of life.

I've been suggesting that we are both separate and not separate. And that it's because we are two that we can commune as one in deep love. For me it's the deep love that really matters. So I want to end this part of the book with another WOW experiment that can help us expand our hearts to embrace everyone.

As human culture evolves we're becoming more and more connected to each other. Recent research has shown that on average there are only six degrees of separation between any of us. Through a chain of friends of friends you are connected to each of the seven billion people living on the Earth right now. Each of us loves someone... who loves someone... who loves someone... creating a web of love that enfolds the world.

In our last WOW experiment we explored the practice of 'deep love meditation', which involved using the imagination to consciously extend our compassion to other people. In this WOW experiment I invite you to play with another form of 'deep love meditation'. This practice involves using the imagination to help you become conscious of the vast web of love to which we're all connected. Let's do it together. Take it slowly and enjoy.

Take some time to come into the deep awake state by wondering, entering and presencing.

Now be conscious of your connections of love with your family and friends.

Imagine the connections like magical threads reaching out from your heart to touch the hearts of those you love.

Now imagine magical threads of love connecting those people you love with those people that they love, who you may never have met.

Then imagine magical threads of love reaching out from these people to all those people they love.

Now imagine the web of loving connections expanding further and further, so that you are connected with each person on this beautiful blue planet.

Now let love pulse from your heart out along all the connections to encompass the Earth.

We are all one in love.

Through me writing this book and you reading it we have become intimately connected in the web of love.

I am sending out my love to you.

A JOURNEY INTO
EVERYDAY LIFE

A LOVER OF LIFE

Our pilgrimage has led us to the heart of the mystery experience, which is the wonder of deep love. Now we need to turn our attention back to the challenges of our everyday lives.

In this part of the book, I want to explore how we can transform our lives into an adventure of awakening. I want to begin in this chapter by exploring the purpose of spirituality.

We are on a journey of spiritual awakening together. But where does it ultimately lead? Is there a final destination? Is there a spiritual ideal that we should aspire to fulfil in our lives? Since the influx of Indian philosophy into our culture in the last century, it's commonly assumed that we should aspire to experience the state of enlightenment. In this chapter I want to challenge this ubiquitous idea.

Enlightenment is often understood as an egoless state in which we're fully self-realized and permanently awake. We're free from the cycle of rebirth, so we don't have to reincarnate back into this troublesome human existence. Most people I meet don't really think they could ever achieve such an elevated state, but they often believe that some great master somewhere has made it to the winning post.

I no longer see the spiritual journey in this way. I don't aspire to arrive at some ultimate state. The idea of eradicating the ego seems misguided and holds no attraction. My experience of awakening makes me want to fully engage with the human adventure, not escape it. This has compelled me to conceptualize the spiritual ideal to which I aspire in a new way. I don't aspire to be an enlightened master, rather I aspire to be a humble 'lover of life'. And in this chapter I'd like to explore what that means.

WAKING UP TO ENTER IN

Becoming a 'lover of life' isn't about achieving a spiritually awakened state in which we're detached from life. It's becoming conscious of the deep self so that we can engage compassionately with the adventures of the separate self. It's discovering the love within us, so that we can express this love in the world around us.

When we become deep awake we discover the ocean of love that is our essential nature. But for me this isn't the end of the journey of awakening. Love by its very nature wants to be expressed. Love is a feeling and an activity. It's in the nature of love to give of itself... to reach out from self to other... to create goodness in the world.

One of my favourite quotes is from the 'Gospel of Philip' which explains:

> Those who are free through gnosis become slaves because of love.

This captures my experience of the paradoxity of awakening perfectly. When I deep-know my essential nature I am liberated from the confines of the story into the mystery of being. But the deep love I feel in the deep awake state impels me back into the story to compassionately engage with life... to care for others... to make the world a better place for future generations.

Becoming a lover of life means adopting a paralogical approach to awakening. It means becoming conscious of the deep self, so that we find ourselves 'loving being'. And it means expressing this love in the world by 'being loving'.

Know Yourself and Show Yourself

For me the journey of awakening isn't just about transforming my state of consciousness, it's also about what I bring to life through the way I live. The 'enlightenment' ideal pictures the purpose of spirituality as 'self-realization'. I agree with this completely, because the journey of awakening leads us to become conscious of the deep self. But there's another complementary pole to the paradoxity of awakening.

Spiritual awakening is also about 'self-expression'. This means engaging with the process through which the separate self evolves, so that we can progressively express more of the infinite potential of our essential nature. It means entering into the creative process of life as a conscious collaborator with the primal field of awareness, to bring new possibilities into the world.

Self-realization and self-expression are complementary aspects of the adventure of awakening. Aspiring to become a lover of life means becoming conscious of *what we are* and bringing forth *what we can become*. It is loving ourselves as we are, and seeking to grow into a fuller expression of our potential.

Becoming a lover of life means reaching deep within so we can come further out. It means transcending the story so we can transform the story. It means daring to be a unique expression of the mystery of being, on a journey of self-realization and self-expression. It means both *knowing* ourselves and *showing* ourselves.

CAN WE BE ALWAYS AWAKE?

Many spiritual traditions suggest that the goal of the journey of awakening is to permanently inhabit some sublime super-conscious state. But it seems to me that this is simply not possible. The nature of consciousness is to constantly change. No two moments are ever the same. Consciousness is flux.

The idea that we could be permanently awake flies in the face of our actual experience. Every day we all go through a cycle in which consciousness dissolves back into to the primal ground of deep sleep and arises again refreshed. No one is permanently awake. Surely that's obvious?!

Consciousness is like a wave that rises and falls. Sometimes we're extremely energized and more conscious, other times we're tired and less conscious. The process of awakening doesn't lead to a permanently awake state, because it's the nature of consciousness to come and go. The primal ground of being is always present, but our experience of it must change.

So what I am suggesting is this. We currently move between the sleeping, dreaming and waking states. Spirituality can help us add to this cycle the more conscious deep awake state. As we arise from sleeping into waking we can expand consciousness further to become deep awake. Then we can surf the wave of consciousness as it rises and falls from deep sleep to deep awake.

If we make it our goal to be permanently awake we will inevitably fail. If we blame that failure on our spiritual immaturity or the evil ego we will feel increasingly bad about ourselves. Rather than coming to love ourselves as we are, we'll constantly confirm our deepest fear… that we aren't good enough.

Embracing the spiritual ideal of becoming a 'lover of life'

doesn't mean aspiring to the impossible goal of being always awake. It means loving our experience of life as it actually is. It means accepting that consciousness inevitably rises and falls, because that's inherent in the paralogical nature of life. It means understanding that we must experience being *less* conscious to experience being *more* conscious.

An Evolutionary Journey

One of the revolutionary insights of science is that life is evolving. The universe is an ongoing creative process, through which the infinite potential of being is progressively actualizing. Each one of us is an evolving fragment of the cosmos.

The concept of evolution has become central to our understanding of existence. Yet many forms of spirituality are rooted in the distant past before this understanding had arisen. This means we need to update our spiritual ideas so that we conceive of awakening as a perpetual process of evolution, rather than an end-driven dash for ultimate salvation.

I want to suggest that the purpose of the spiritual journey is not to arrive anywhere, but rather to engage with the adventure of life in a new way, so that the evolutionary process unfolds powerfully within us. It's about waking up to our deeper *being* so that we can more fully engage with the evolutionary adventure of *becoming* a more conscious individual. It's about living our lives as a transformational process through which we are learning to love.

This is not a linear process in which we steadily become more awake. It's a paralogical process, which entails finding ourselves and losing ourselves… wonderful insight and deep confusion… great elation and harrowing suffering. The spiritual challenge is to willingly enter into this transformative process.

The paralogical twist we've been exploring in this book is that to make the most of the human adventure, we need to awaken to the deep self. When we feel the 'safe vulnerability' that arises in the deep awake state, we can courageously engage with the tumultuous story of life. When we're immersed in the mystery experience, we can relish the human experience and become a lover of life.

Travelling and Arriving

The spiritual journey is an evolutionary process. There are stages of realization that we can reach, but there's no final destination, because there's always further to go. My journey was initiated by the realization that it's possible to experience the deep awake state, which changed my life forever. At some point I realized that my deep self transcends Tim and essentially I am not a person in time. At a certain juncture I realized that at the depths there is no separateness and all is one.

These realizations, and many others, have been stages on my journey of awakening. But the evolutionary adventure shows no sign of running out of steam. Each new level of understanding I arrive at leads inexorably to the next challenge. Life is always a paralogical dance of *both* arriving *and* travelling.

The most important realization for me, which was there right at the start and has remained with me throughout my journey, is that what really matters is love. It's this realization that has freed me from the desire to arrive at some final spiritual destination and led me to embrace the ever-changing challenges of my life as opportunities to continually grow in love. It's this realization that has led me to adopt the spiritual ideal of becoming a 'lover of life'.

The Inconstant Lover

Many people seem to think that the journey of awakening is ultimately about achieving some sort of spiritual perfection. But I want to suggest that to be human is necessarily to be imperfect. We all have our flaws and foibles… even the best of us. Everyone who can walk, sometimes stumbles. The greatest musicians can hit bum notes.

Becoming a lover of life is accepting that it's only human to err. We are the unconscious field of being, in the process of becoming more conscious. No surprise, therefore, that we spend so much time groping around in semi-conscious darkness. When we understand this we can be patient with ourselves and our fellow travellers on the adventure of life.

To aspire to become a lover of life isn't to fantasize about becoming a spiritual superman. Quite the opposite. It's acknowledging that there can be no evolution unless there is always something missing and more to discover. It's embracing the glorious imperfection of personal existence. It is creatively engaging with the ambiguity of being human.

To aspire to become a lover of life is to aspire to become wise by accepting we'll sometimes be foolish. It's recognizing that we'll always make mistakes because of our lack of consciousness. This is the process of evolution. If we didn't err we'd never learn. And if we didn't learn we'd never grow. Indeed, it seems to me, if we're not continually making mistakes we're getting too comfortable and should be taking more risks.

To become a lover of life we must be willing to be a foolish lover… a lost lover… a vulnerable lover… a lonely lover… a broken lover… a frightened lover… a flawed lover… a wounded lover… an inconstant lover. We must be willing to love being human, with all that this entails.

A NEW SPIRITUAL IDEAL

What it means to become a lover of life is so paralogical it must be said in many ways to capture the fullness of the idea. Here's some of what it means.

Being a lover of life means waking up to oneness and passionately engaging with your individual journey through life.

Being a lover of life means 'loving being and being loving'. It means waking up to your deeper nature, which is love, and learning to express that love more expansively and inclusively in the world.

Being a lover of life means knowing yourself and showing yourself. It means expressing your secret potential so that the

world is richer for you being here. It means being on a journey of self-realization and self-expression.

Being a lover of life means embracing your flawed humanity.
It means accepting that you will stumble on the journey of
life… that you become wise by being foolish… that you can't
always be awake and at your best.

Being a lover of life means welcoming the challenges of life
through which you grow as a person. It means seeing life as
a mysterious adventure, in which each summit you ascend
reveals a whole new range of possibilities to master.

Being a lover of life means being open to the present moment
as a precious opportunity to experience the richness of life
and feel its transformational power. It means loving your life
as it is and working for a better future.

THE DEEP PURPOSE OF LIFE

In this book we've been exploring a story about the mystery of
existence that brings meaning and purpose to life. Of course trying
to definitively state the purpose of life is as futile as trying to tame
the wind. Life is always more than words can say. Yet we need a
compass with which to travel through life. And this story can give
us a guiding principle to help us navigate the journey.

According to this story, the primal field of unconscious awareness is 'dreaming' itself to be many conscious individuals, through
which it is coming to know itself and love itself. So, from this perspective, by becoming a lover of life on a journey of self-realization
and self-expression we are playing our part in fulfilling the great
purpose of life itself.

The scientific story points to this deep purpose of life. It tells
how the evolutionary process has filled the world with ever more
conscious forms of life, until it has created human beings. What
makes us so special is that we're not just conscious, *we're conscious
that we're conscious*. We know that we exist. We are conscious of *being*.

And if we focus our attention on our deepest being we become deep awake. And then we can live as a lover of life.

Life is an evolutionary process, so the purpose of life is not to arrive but to make the journey. The only arriving is death and that is a destination we'd prefer to remain in the future. And even this destination, I suspect, is a transition into a new way of travelling. The purpose of life is never fulfilled, because the purpose is the process.

LOVING BEING
BEING LOVING
– WOW Experiments –

*In this chapter I want to share with you a powerful
practice that you can use to transform your everyday
existence into a love affair with life.*

The WOW experiment I want to explore with you now, brings together all the experiments we've explored previously in this book. It offers a simple way to become a lover of life, by 'loving being and being loving'. You can use this practice whenever you want to awaken to the deep self and compassionately engage with the adventure of life.

The paralogical practice of 'loving being and being loving' is the beating heart of the new way of awakening I've been exploring with you. The form that I've given this practice is original, but in essence it's nothing new. It's also found at the heart of many spiritual traditions.

The great Tibetan sage Milarepa teaches that the essence of Buddhism is:

> Know emptiness.
> Be compassionate.

We need to become conscious of our essential nature as the spacious presence of awareness, so we deep-know that all is one, and find ourselves in love with all. Then we need to express that love by living compassionately.

The same essential message is also at the heart of the Christian tradition. When Jesus is asked 'what is the greatest commandment?' he replies:

> Love God with all your heart and with all your soul and with all your mind. This is the first and greatest commandment. And the second is like it: Love others as yourself.

The first commandment is to love God... to immerse yourself in the mystery of being... to be conscious of the primal oneness of awareness. The second commandment is to love others as yourself, because when you wake up to oneness you see that others *are* your self. These two commandments are like each other, because they are paralogically complementary perspectives on the spiritual journey, which involves 'loving being and being loving'.

LOVING BEING

Let's start our exploration of this practice by looking at 'loving being'. We've been exploring how to practise 'loving being' throughout this book; I've described it as a process of 'wondering, entering, and presencing'. These are all ways of deepening your love of being. To begin with, it can be helpful to follow this process step by step, but as you practise these techniques they will start to happen simultaneously as one movement in consciousness. Here are the basic steps involved in 'loving being', which we've explored in detail already.

Wondering

When you're only superficially awake, the simplest way to start becoming deep awake is to wonder... to look at the world with amazement... to be conscious of the breathtaking mystery of existence... to recognize that you really don't know what life is. If you wonder deeply you'll come out of your story and into the mystery of the moment. And when you realise how wonderful the world really is, you'll love *being* in the world.

Entering

You can intensify the experience of wonder by entering the immediacy of your sensual experience and becoming intensely conscious of looking... listening... touching. The simplest way to do this is to focus your attention on the delicious feeling of breathing. As you enter your sensual experience the mind will become still, and you'll feel sensually alive. And when you realise how amazing it is to sense this present moment, your love of *being* will deepen.

Presencing

Now you can presence the present moment. You do this by focusing your attention on your essential nature, which is witnessing all you are experiencing, yet can't be seen or heard or touched. Then you'll become conscious of being the spacious presence of awareness within which your experience is arising like a dream.

You'll come to deep-know that you are one with the primal field of awareness. And when you deep-know that you are one with the mystery of being, a primal, unconditional, limitless love of *being* naturally arises.

BEING LOVING

Having briefly revisited how to practise 'loving being', let's explore how we can practise 'being loving'. This simply involves expressing love in your life, so it's something you can do at any time. It's something you can do all of the time! I'm going to suggest four basic ways you can experiment with practising 'being loving'. I'm confident you'll find these practices will transform both your state of consciousness and your life story.

I've approached the paradoxity of awakening by talking first about 'loving being' and then about 'being loving', because when we're conscious of the deep self it becomes natural to love. But we could equally approach awakening from the other direction, because when we practise 'being loving' we find ourselves 'loving being'.

My greatest teacher has not been a spiritual master but my own mum. This isn't because she's a wise philosopher who's studied the wisdom of the world. She'd never have time for that. She's simply someone who unconditionally gives of herself to everyone around her. She loves everybody, so everybody loves her, and she loves life.

My mother is 85 years old and, despite a stroke and three bouts of cancer, she's still bouncing with energy. This is because she's energized by love. She naturally practises 'being loving' and then finds herself 'loving being'. She loves to love and this means she loves living.

My mum's secret is simple. She doesn't dwell on her own problems, rather she surrenders to the flow of her life and looks for ways she can help others. She's not perfect, of course, but she loves in such a natural, unassuming, everyday way that she spreads goodness wherever she goes. One day I aspire to be like my mum. She's my role model for becoming a lover of life.

Loving The World

How can we practise 'being loving'? A good place to begin is to simply love the world around us, by entering into our immediate experience with love. The Hindu sage Ramana Maharshi explains:

> The experience of Self is only love – which is seeing only love, hearing only love, feeling only love, tasting only love and smelling only love, which is bliss.

WOW Experiment

Here are some ways of experimenting with 'being loving' in your everyday life by 'loving the world'.

> As you are walking *enter* the sensation of your feet meeting the earth below you. Walk on the earth whilst feeling one with the earth. Walk on the earth with love. If you do I think you'll find there is an experiential difference between *just* walking and *walking with love*.

> In the same way you can look at the world with love, conscious that you are separate and not separate from life. If you do you'll find there's an experiential difference between *just* looking and *looking with love*.

> In the same way you can listen to the world around you with love, conscious that you are separate and not separate from life. If you do you'll find there's an experiential difference between *just* listening and *listening with love*.

Acting from Love

'Being loving' is acting from love. It's responding to the challenges of life with compassion. It is being generous with your time and energy. As it says in *The Cloud of Unknowing*:

> Love is not love without giving away of itself.

'Being loving' is being self-sacrificing. It's offering yourself up for the benefit of others. It's being of service to the world. As Mohandas Gandhi puts it:

> When a person loses himself into God, he immediately finds himself in the service of all that lives. It becomes his delight and recreation. He is a new person never weary in the service of God's creation.

'Being loving' is bringing your deepest wisdom to life so that you can make the world a better place. The Tibetan Buddhist master Chagdud Tulku Rinpoche tells us:

> If you discover your true nature, you will discover resources of kindness and compassion you didn't know you had. It is from this mind of intrinsic wisdom and compassion that you can truly benefit others.

'Being loving' is having faith in love to carry us through the challenges of life. One of the little mantras I repeat to myself when I face difficult situations is 'love always works'. In my experience this is true. Whatever the dilemma, if I bring love to the problem it eventually melts away. I don't have faith that I won't experience the difficult side of life, but I have faith that love will sustain me when I do. Love will hold me and heal me. Love will dissolve the barriers that divide me from others. Love will be with me through the journey of learning to love.

WOW Experiment

Here's a way of practising 'loving being' in your everyday life by 'acting from love'. Whatever the situation confronting you ask yourself these questions:

> What is the loving thing to do right now?

> How can I bring love to this situation?

How can I offer my best in this predicament?

How can I express my deepest wisdom?

Don't look for the comfortable response or the way of acting that will get you liked. Find the authentic way to act compassionately.

Loving Others

Practising 'being loving' means loving others. It means opening your heart to everyone you meet. It's understanding that it's only your judgements about who is and isn't loveable that block the natural flow of love. It's immersing yourself in the mystery, so that these judgements melt away. And there is only love.

When we embrace someone with deep love, we don't do so because we like that person… or because we hope to get something back from them… or because it's the morally right thing to do. We love for no reason. We're unconditionally compassionate. We love for love's sake. We love because that's the natural way to express our deepest nature. We love because we can't help but love.

Practising 'being loving' is expressing kindness to others, regardless of how kind they are to us, because we want there to be more kindness in the world. As Lao Tzu puts it:

> Be good to the good and good to the bad, because it's
> good to be good.

Practising 'being loving' is humbly acknowledging our own flawed humanity, so we can be forgiving of others. Then we find ourselves wanting the best for everyone, because we recognize our shared essential being and have compassion for our shared human vulnerability.

We are constantly surrounded by other people who're struggling with difficult challenges in their lives, and wrestling within themselves with countless contradictions. So I agree with the ancient philosopher Philo Judaeus who counsels:

Be kind to all for everyone you meet is involved in fighting a hard battle.

My dear friend Peter Gandy often muses 'I feel sorry for everyone'. I resonate deeply with this sentiment. How could you not? We're all thrown into this messed-up world as helpless babes who've got no idea what's going on. We're brought up by parents who've no idea what's going on. We're taught in school by teachers who've no idea what's going on. We work for employers who've no idea what's going on. No wonder we're all a bit crazy! The least we can do is be kind to one another.

WOW Experiment

Here's a powerful way of 'being loving' in your everyday life by 'loving others', using the practice of 'I to I' connecting that we explored in detail previously in this book.

> When you are interacting with someone make sure you connect 'I to I'… even if they seem only superficially awake.
>
> This doesn't mean staring into their eyes. You can connect 'I to I' without looking. Simply be conscious of the depths of being in yourself and the other person.
>
> If they seem lost in separateness, then be a silent reminder of the deep self. Give them a loving space to wake up within should they want to.
>
> Be conscious that you are both separate and not separate from others. Authentically share your vulnerable humanity and deep divinity.
>
> Try it out and you'll see how easily we can be transformed from strangers to lovers.

Loving Yourself

Being kind to everyone means being kind to yourself. Most of us find it easier to forgive others their flaws than we do ourselves. I know I do. And this doesn't surprise me, because I only get to see other people in certain situations. But I get to be with myself 24/7. I see what I'm like in every situation. So it's no surprise I don't always see myself in a very flattering light.

Like everyone, I want to be loved as I am. But actually I'm the only person who can love me as I am, because I'm the only person who really knows what I'm like. The love I crave I must give to myself. What a beautiful irony!

I find it interesting that spiritual people often find loving themselves to be particularly difficult. Those who have yet to really engage with the process of awakening often unconsciously love themselves and blame others for their own failings. But the more we become conscious of our ambiguous human nature, and bring the shadow self into the light, the more we can form a very dim view of ourselves.

Yet 'being loving' is living patiently with ourselves. It's seeking dialogue between all the conflicting personas we find within, and listening to their diverse points of view. It's coaxing the unloved self out of the shadows and holding it tenderly until it heals. It's appreciating our qualities and forgiving our foibles, so that we can progressively evolve into a more loving embodiment of the deep self.

WOW Experiment

Here's a way of practising 'being loving' in your everyday life by 'loving yourself'.

When you feel down on yourself, back off and see your separate self from the perspective of the deep self.

See yourself like a wise parent with a troubled child.

Embrace your separate self with the same compassion you would a little child who's struggling with life.

Try it out and you'll find that you're lovable just as you are.

PRACTICE AND POETRY

You can practise 'loving being and being loving' at any moment, while you're going about your everyday life. It's a continual practice you can return to whenever you want to awaken. It becomes much easier to awaken in your daily life if you build your practice on a strong foundation. This means focusing on 'loving being' in 'deep awake meditation'. And using your imagination to open your heart by practising 'deep love meditation'.

I've also shared with you the 'web of love' meditation, which you can explore from time to time. And I'm going to add a 'loving your life' meditation to your repertoire at the end of this book. If you have the opportunity, I also encourage you to keep exploring the 'I to I' practices with your spiritual friends, because they're incredibly powerful ways of awakening.

If we want to become good at anything in life we need to practise... and this is true of awakening. But it's important to remember that awakening is a not a spiritual achievement, it's a natural state that is available to all of us in every moment. The practice of 'loving being and being loving' allows the deep awake state to spontaneously arise. And, in my experience, when this happens I feel like Rumi who writes:

> All practice is gone.
> I am filled with poetry.

THE HEROIC LOVER

*In this chapter I'm going to suggest that to become
a lover of life we need to courageously engage with
the challenges of living.*

Some approaches to spirituality make it sounds as if life is a breeze. If we could just be more spiritual we'd sail through life, borne forward by the winds of grace towards an ever more wonderful horizon. But we all know that life isn't like that. Life can be tough. We all suffer. We all face obstacles that we feel we'll never be able to surmount. We feel despair as well as elation. We feel defeated as well as empowered.

Aspiring to be a 'lover of life' doesn't mean hoping that the Sun will always shine. Quite the opposite. Becoming a lover of life means finding the courage to meet life with love, even when all seems lost. Especially when all seems lost!

Being a lover of life means becoming a human hero on the adventure of a lifetime. The fact that life can be so bitter and cruel demands a heroic response. The experience of impermanence and loss demands a heroic response. The unkindness and callousness of others demands a heroic response. The knowledge that we will die demands a heroic response.

To be a lover of life is to be a heroic lover on a sacred quest to become an embodiment of love. This means facing the dilemmas that confront us with bold determination to love. But the hero doesn't start triumphant, win every war, and return victorious. The hero struggles and fails, yet finds the inner strength, which wells up from the deep self, to come back from defeat and love again.

The word 'quest' comes from the same root as 'question'. To be a heroic lover is to ask a deep question of life: 'what are you?' And in return to be asked: 'who are you?' Through undertaking the adventure of life the heroic lover discovers who they are. And they find they're stronger than they imagined. Their inner resources are deeper than they thought.

The heroic lover understands that the challenges they face are mighty. They humbly acknowledge that life can lift them up and cast them down. They know that if they aren't humble they will be humbled. And with that knowledge they step valiantly forth on the adventure of love.

In the ancient world the word 'hero' referred to someone who was devoted to the goddess Hera, who set the hero their challenges. To be a heroic lover is to be devoted to the Goddess of life. It is welcoming the trials she sets us, through which we can become worthy lovers... the heroic feats she demands of us through which we can prove our love... the storms we must endure to chisel beautiful lines of wisdom into our unformed features.

GOOD AND BAD

To become a lover of life we need to accept that our experience of life is *both* good *and* bad. Some traditional approaches to spirituality offer the dream of overcoming suffering. Some modern approaches to spirituality promise a perfect life if we use the power of positive thinking. I feel there is something to be learned from both ideas. Yet I feel they can also be extremely misleading.

Existence is predicated on paradoxity, so our experience must flow between good and bad, joy and suffering, yum and yuk. We hope for yum without yuk. We fear there will be yuk without yum. But there will always be both. We can focus on the good, but we can't exile the bad. We can make our lives better, but we can't make our lives perfect.

Buying into the fantasy that we could have yum without yuk leads to profound disappointment and confusion. We're attempting the impossible, so we inevitably fail. Then we blame ourselves for not being spiritually awake enough to create the perfect life we long for. But actually we're not at fault. It's the unrealistic idea that we can have good without bad that is at fault.

Enjoying and Enduring

Life is to be enjoyed *and* endured. That's one of the great paradoxities the heroic lover must understand. When we enjoy life it feels good to be alive. When we endure life it deepens our wisdom and compassion. To 'endure' is to become 'durable'... to become strong. When we endure it strengthens the soul. And life wants us to become strong, so we can withstand the storms as well as delight in the sunshine. So we can love, whatever the weather.

Often we attempt to endure the trials of life by becoming hard and defended, or numb and withdrawn. The spiritual challenge is to bear the suffering without closing our hearts. More than this. It's letting the suffering open us up.

Suffering is awful, but it can awaken us just as much as joy and wonder. The heroic lover is ready to be shook up so that they can be shaken free. They understand the lover's heart must break open at some time... maybe many times... for love to flow.

The heroic lover endures the suffering of life, because they know that dark periods transform into golden days. They hold on to hope when life seems meaningless, because they know that it will become meaningful later. When the night comes they don't despair, because they know the dawn will follow.

Enduring the trials of life isn't easy. Yet as Joseph Campbell, the great champion of the heroic life, says:

> If you are lifeworthy, you can take it. What we are really living for is the experience of life, both the pain and the pleasure.

The heroic lover accepts the pain of life and relishes the pleasure. They endure tenderly and enjoy passionately. They're prepared to suffer the grind that polishes away their rough edges. And they're hungry for every sweet moment that comes their way. They feast on the bittersweet banquet of life.

Diving and Surfing

If you put a yin/yang sign on its side it becomes an image of an undulating wave. This is a wonderful image, because our experience of life is like a wave rising and falling between joy and suffering... ease and struggle... consciousness and unconsciousness.

The spiritual challenge is to surf the wave. To do this we must first dive into the depths of the ocean of being. When our point of balance is rooted in the depths, we can surf the wave on the surface of life. When we're conscious of the primal goodness of being, we can live with our ups and downs.

To surf the wave as it rises and falls we need to pay attention to *both* the perpetual now *and* where we're travelling in time. If we only pay attention to where we hope or fear the story is going, we'll misjudge the wave as it crashes through the present and lose our balance.

When this happens we find ourselves drowning not surfing. But the heroic lover understands that learning to surf means frequently falling off the wave. They know that real success is constantly coming back from failure.

The heroic lover accepts that life is characterized by paradoxity, which means that their experience always flows between good and bad. They don't dream of one without the other. They surf the wave up and down through despair and hope... failure and success... grief and ecstasy.

THE WOUNDED LOVER

The lover of life is a heroic lover, because life demands a heroic response. But the lover of life is also a wounded lover. No one makes it through the maelstrom of life without being wounded on the way. Everyone carries the scars of the hurt they've felt and the pain they've endured. We're all damaged goods.

If our flesh is wounded it will hopefully heal, but this may still leave a scar that can easily be aggravated into an open wound. I want to suggest that, in a similar way, the psychological wounds we've suffered leave scars on the soul which can be easily opened.

We all have soul wounds left by painful experiences. Often we suffer soul wounds when we're at our most vulnerable as children. For some of us the wounds heal, but leave a scar that is tender when touched. For others, these wounds are so deep they never really heal.

The Cycle of Suffering

When our physical wounds are irritated we instinctively react to protect our broken body from further harm. In the same way, when our soul wounds are irritated it can hurt so much that we lash out in protective anger. We may behave in brutish ways that arise from an animal instinct to avoid pain.

This can lead to terrible conflict in our relationships, because it often creates a cycle of suffering, which leaves everyone sore. I know there've been countless times in my life when I've irritated someone's soul wound and they've reacted with psychological violence to protect themselves. And this has aggravated one of my own soul wounds, which has made me react aggressively to protect myself. This reaction has opened up the other person's wound deeper, so they've reacted… so then I've reacted. And so the cycle of suffering turns.

Understanding that soul wounds are similar to physical wounds helps me break the cycle of suffering. It enables me to bring understanding to the conflicts I experience. I stop being angry with others because they are sore. I stop blaming myself for being wounded.

Healing our Soul Wounds

When our soul wounds don't heal, they can fester in the shadows to become the unloved self… that part of our inner world we don't want to visit, which overwhelms us when we aren't looking. And this is why the heroic lover doesn't turn away from the dark places within, but willingly enters the forbidding forest to bring the healing power of love to our deepest hurt.

Just as deep sleep heals the body, so being deep awake heals the soul. When we bring deep love to our psychological wounds, miracles can happen. But just as no amount of sleep can heal every physical wound, deep awake healing can't mend every fracture of the heart. So we need to learn to be gentle with those parts of the psyche that are most inflamed.

One of the greatest challenges we face is to live tenderly with our soul wounds and the soul wounds of others, so that we ameliorate rather than aggravate our suffering. We've all been hurt by life and carry the scars. So we need to be kind and take care of each other.

SAYING YES TO YOUR LIFE

In this chapter I've suggested that becoming a lover of life means engaging heroically with the challenges we face. It means daring to enter into the evolutionary turbulence of life, as a vulnerable, tender, wounded human being on an adventure of awakening to love. It means welcoming the moment, whether it brings transcendent bliss or gritty transformation. Joseph Campbell says:

> The warrior's approach is to say 'yes' to life:
> 'Yea' to it all.

CHAPTER 34

THE TRANSFORMATIONAL DRAMA

In this chapter I'm going to explore how we're transformed by the adventure of life. I want to show how a paralogical understanding of life can help us change our lives for the better. And I want to celebrate the magical state of 'enlivenment' that arises when we live in the WOW of life.

How many successful films have there been that start with all going well, progress with everything working out, and end happily ever after? We don't want to watch a story like that. We want tension and drama... misfortune and humour... catharsis and transformation... chaos and resolution. We want a story that moves us to feel something. We want a story that leaves us richer for the telling.

Comedy relieves us from the burden of being too serious, so that we can play in the moment. Yet a romantic comedy with no bite becomes sentimental and sickly. Tragedy reminds us of the gravitas of life, so that we can feel compassion and empathy. Yet a harrowing tragedy with no redemption becomes dark and bitter. We want the paralogical play of opposites in our stories. And that's what we've got with the great tragicomedy of life.

The story of life is a dramatic narrative through which the hero is transformed. Much of the time our lives may feel ordinary and orderly, but soon or later the chaos of life explodes us out of our comfort zone. Then life ceases to be a safe routine and becomes a grand adventure.

To be a lover of life is to welcome this call to take up a new quest for deeper wisdom and greater love. It is facing the challenges we confront, even when we fear we'll fail, because we know that within us lie the limitless resources of the deep self. It's having faith in love to sustain us through our trials, knowing that we'll be richer for the ordeal.

To be a lover of life is not to turn away from the reality of suffering... failure... breakdown... horror... illness... old age... death. It's embracing those aspects of life we don't like and don't want to acknowledge. If we can take love into those places that seem unlovable, we'll truly come to be a lover of life... all of life... life as it is.

To be a lover of life is to heroically enter the darkness we would prefer to avoid, because we know that this is where the holy grail is hidden. As Joseph Campbell says:

> The agony of breaking through personal limitations is
> the agony of spiritual growth. Art, literature, myth and

cult, philosophy, and ascetic disciplines are instruments to help the individual past his limiting horizons into spheres of ever-expanding realization. As he crosses threshold after threshold, conquering dragon after dragon, the stature of the divinity that he summons to his highest wish increases, until it subsumes the cosmos. Finally, the mind breaks the bounding sphere of the cosmos to a realization transcending all experiences of form – all symbolizations, all divinities: a realization of the ineluctable void.

CHANGING THE STORY

To be a lover of life is to willingly endure the transformative drama of life. But this doesn't mean being a passive victim of circumstance. Quite the opposite. Being a lover of life means engaging with the story of life, so we can transform it for the better. It's *both* accepting the moment as it is *and* working to create a better future. It's drawing on the power of our free will, which arises from the deep self, to guide the narrative in a new direction.

To transform the story we need to transcend the story. When we're only superficially awake we respond to life habitually, so it's hard to live creatively. But when we become deep awake we recognize that we really don't know what's going on. And this sets us free to see our predicament in new ways.

Then we can act creatively and turn things around when we feel that life is going in the wrong direction. We can avoid habitual patterns of thought, so that we approach each moment as a new moment. We can untangle the knots in our relationships, so they flow and grow. We can transform the world we inhabit, so that it becomes a kinder place.

Our freedom to think and act in new and creative ways is the greatest freedom we possess. And it's more powerful than we imagine. The more we become conscious of the deep self, the freer we become to act in new ways. We can bring creativity to bear on the rigid nature of life. We can change the story.

A PROBLEM OF PERSPECTIVE

It's not easy to live with the chaos and conflict of this ambiguous world. It's not easy to live with the chaos and conflict that can rage within. Sometimes the challenges we face seem so big they can overwhelm us. But every problem is big or small depending on how we look at it. If you'd like to get a visceral understanding of what I am suggesting try this.

> Take this book right up close to your eyes so that it fills your field of vision.
>
> Then reach it out as far away from you as you can, so that it's a small object in a bigger picture.

When we get too close to something it becomes all that we can see, but if we back off we see things in perspective. It seems to me that it's the same with our problems in life. If they dominate our attention, life seems pretty bleak. But if we back off and become deep awake, we create some space around our problems. Then we can see our problems in perspective, so they no longer dominate us.

Just as when you held the book too close you couldn't read the words, when we focus too closely on our problems it becomes harder to make sense of our predicament. Just as when you held the book away from you it didn't vanish, so our problems don't magically disappear when we become deep awake. The problem is still a problem, but we see it from a new perspective.

I remember when I was in my 20s hearing the American teacher Ram Dass confess that, after a lifetime exploring consciousness and spirituality, he still had all of the same personal hang-ups he'd been wrestling with throughout his life. The difference was that they no longer took possession of him in the way they once did, because he saw them from a new perspective.

As a young man I felt disappointed to hear this, because if someone as wise as Ram Dass couldn't overcome his personal problems... what hope was there for me?! Now I'm about the same age that Ram Dass must have been when I first met him and I feel very differently. I understand what he was saying, because it's been the same for me. As I've made the journey of awakening, my personal problems haven't changed, because they are part of what it is to be Tim, but they don't dominate me in the same way.

Ram Dass puts it beautifully when he says:

> I haven't gotten rid of one neurosis. Not one. The only thing that has changed is that while before these neuroses were huge monsters that possessed me, now they're like little Shmoos that I invite over for tea. I say, 'Oh, sexual perversity! Haven't seen you in weeks!' They're sort of my style now. When your neuroses become your style, then you've got it made.

LIFE IS ALWAYS GOOD

When we face challenges in our lives we think of them as problems. But they are also opportunities to learn and grow, so that we become more awake and loving. Nothing that happens is *just* bad and nothing is *just* good. Life is always *both* good *and* bad, depending on how we look at it.

Even at the best of times there are things we wish were different. Even at the worst of times there are things we wouldn't change. If we look at life paralogically with both eyes open, we can see every moment as *both* good *and* bad. Good and bad exist within each other. Like yin and yang on the *taijitu* symbol, within the light is a dot of dark and within the dark is a dot of light.

> So the bad news is that there's always something bad about life we can choose to focus on.

> And the good news is that there's always something good about life we can choose to focus on.

Life may be yuk, but it's never *just* yuk. The world remains a marvel to be wondered at. There's always the delicious feeling of breathing. There's always the joy of simply being. There's always hope for a better tomorrow.

Life may be bad, but it's always good! This means that when times are bad we can seek out the good that is also present. We can appreciate that what seems bad can lead to positive transformation, so contains good hidden within it. Then, as Walt Whitman writes, we see that:

> What is called good is perfect
> and what is called bad is just as perfect.

In my experience, when I see it's all perfect I can embrace my life as it is. It's also imperfect of course. I could give you a long list of things that could be better. But the imperfections of my life are also perfect. It's the grit that creates the pearl.

What are We Missing?

To transform our situation we need to understand that the problem is not the problem. The problem is that we're missing something significant about our predicament. So we need to use paralogical wisdom to help us see things from another perspective.

When we see our situation as bad, we need to see how it is also good. When we feel trapped, we need to see how we are also free. When it all gets too serious, we need to find some humour.

Life is complex on the surface and simple at the depths. On the surface each problem is unique. But when we look deeper we see there's really only one problem. The problem is that we're not deep awake. And this means we're not really seeing things as they are.

When we realize this, we know that the first step in transforming what's happening in our story is to change our state of consciousness and become deep awake. Then we can treat our challenges as precious opportunities to learn and grow. Then we can find creative solutions to our problems. Then we can bring love to life.

ENLIVENMENT

Engaging with the transformational drama of life can be difficult. Yet it's not all struggle. Far from it. Sometimes life is effortless and magical. It's easy to feel the wonder of the WOW, and we delight in our love affair with life.

In any love affair there are special times when we're deeply in love and life becomes a seamless flow of miraculous moments. We're dancing together as separate and not-separate. We intuitively feel what our lover needs from us, and give unconditionally. We spontaneously know what to do without thinking. It's simply natural to be together. We're completely at ease being ourselves.

In my experience it's the same with my love affair with life. When I'm deep awake and engaged with my life, I can enter a state of 'enlivenment' in which there's a spontaneous flow to the story. I'm in love with the moment and intuitively know what it's asking from me.

When I'm enlivened I find myself living lucidly, conscious of the dreamlike nature of life, so that the events and my response to them unfold as effortlessly as a dream. My life seems replete with meaning, like a dream. I feel one with my life, like a dreamer is one with a dream.

With the Flow

In the enlivened state it feels as if I'm being carried by a river flowing to the sea, and all I need to do is navigate around the rocks. Insights about what to do next float up into consciousness, like messages emerging from the depths. I'm responsive to the changing currents, not caught up in eddies of endless repetition.

The Chinese sages call this going with the Tao... the flow of life... the way things naturally come into being. But it's not like being a dead fish floating down a river. When I'm enlivened I see that everything is happening as a natural flow of events, but I'm not just a passive witness. I'm also an engaged actor in the drama, spontaneously playing my part in the present moment, whatever that needs to be. I'm in and out of time. Both an active participant and a passive appreciator.

When I *unconsciously* go with the flow of life, I'm habitual and repetitive. But when I *consciously* go with the flow of life I'm creative and resourceful. I'm more conscious of what is happening, so I can respond more consciously. I'm entering and presencing the flow of experience, then responding to what happens from the deep self.

In the Zone

Enlivenment is a high-performance state of spacious engagement. When I'm enlivened I am in the zone and at my best. I allow appropriate action to naturally emerge, without the internal monologue of thoughts slowing things down. I go with the creative inspiration that naturally swells up into consciousness from the depths.

This state can arise at any time, but I regularly experience it when I'm leading my mystery experience retreats. When I talk I have no idea what I will say next, but the right words come. If no words arise, I'm silent until I spontaneously start to speak. I'm intensely conscious of what I'm doing, but I'm not thinking about what I'm doing. Talking happens of itself. It feels as if life is talking through me.

Unconscious Competence

Learning is a process whereby we bring conscious attention to something we've previously not been conscious of. But this is the beginning, not the end of the learning process. Once we've become conscious of how to do something we can allow it to happen without conscious volition. Conscious learning leads to unconscious competence.

We learn to play a musical instrument by painstakingly becoming conscious of the technique involved. But once we have mastered the technique we can express ourselves freely without thinking about it. We consciously practise so we can spontaneously flow.

In my experience it's the same with awakening. My spiritual practice can bring me to an enlivened state in which I'm awake without consciously practising being awake. Then I find my actions are spontaneously happening in harmony with the flow of events. I'm extremely conscious of what I am doing, but I'm not thinking about it. I can improvise, with unconscious ease, to the music of life.

Life is Living You

Normally I feel that I'm living my life. But when I'm enlivened I also see things from the other paralogical perspective, so I feel that life is living me. I'm conscious that the separate self is animated by the deep self. I see that the mystery of being is 'doing' everything, because everything is one.

A lovely lady called Colleen wrote to me to say what a joy it was to experience this change of perspective. She'd seen herself as trying to wake up to 'God', which felt like an impossible challenge. Now she felt that 'God' was trying to wake up through her. So there really was nothing to worry about! She explained:

> I love this magnificent flip-flop: Consciousness or presence or love is trying to come up through the vehicle of this body/mind/spirit to know itself more fully and directly. It may feel like this little 'Colleen' is trying to reach God, but really it is God wanting to know itself through all life forms, including the life form called 'Colleen'. This flip-flop is a burden lifted off. 'Colleen' doesn't have some humongous task to accomplish; rather, consciousness is an enormous up-welling that is moving through these human forms. What joy! What a gift to be alive.

SHOWING UP FOR LIFE

The state of enlivenment naturally arises when we really commit to our love affair with life. Most of us hold back from life because it's so challenging. If we keep our heads down we hope we won't get hurt. Yet we pay a high price for this reticence to really live, because we only feel partly alive. We get on with our lives, like we get on with a lover in a stale relationship.

To make our love affair with life vibrant and exciting we need to give ourselves to life… to show up for life… to bring ourselves to life. The Goddess of life is reluctant to be wooed by a reticent lover. She wants to be WOWED. And each one of us can WOW her in our own unique way by bringing her our own special gifts. And this means daring to be ourselves. It means courageously following our dreams.

The Sufi poet Rumi writes:

> Don't be a glass full of water with a dry brim.
> Start a huge crazy project like Noah!
> Live a life you believe in.

The deep self has a huge crazy project for all of us. It may be grand or it may be humble, that makes no difference. What's important is that we hear the call and dare to respond, so that we bring out the potential within us and make it an offering at the altar of life.

Joseph Campbell famously advised 'follow your bliss'. To become a lover of life you need to find that which moves you deeply, and become dedicated to it. Not in the naïve hope that this will be easy, but with the heroic recognition that this will be intensely demanding. Campbell once quipped that he should have said 'follow your blisters'!

To become a lover of life means contributing to life. It means expressing the deep love within us in our own unique way. It means finding ourselves, so we can give ourselves away. Wise old Joe tells us:

> The ultimate aim of the quest must be neither release nor ecstasy for oneself, but the wisdom and the power to serve others.

LOVING YOUR LIFE
– WOW Experiment –

In our final WOW experiment I want to invite you to look back over your life from the deep awake state, so that you appreciate what an amazing adventure it has been, and fall in love with the story of being you.

Whoever you are and whatever your story, your life is amazing, precisely because it is *your* life. You are the hero of the story, who has had to face the trials and tribulations every hero must endure. You have been exulted and humbled. You've been admired and condemned. You've been happy and disconsolate. You've felt numb and enlivened. But through it all... you have been *you*. Joseph Campbell reminds us:

> The privilege of a lifetime is being who you are.

The meditation we're going to explore in this chapter is a way of coming to love your life story, with all the joy and suffering it has brought you. It was inspired by listening to reports of near-death experiences, from people who'd been declared clinically deceased, yet had been revived to tell extraordinary tales of what happened while they were 'dead'.

There are many recurring themes to descriptions of NDEs. People report entering a wonderful light and being immersed in love. And then they often experience what has become known as the 'life review'.

During the life review, people describe witnessing the whole of their life passing before them, but they're able to see all that has happened from a more conscious perspective. They're able to appreciate what a gift their life has been and to see the conse-quences of their choices from a deeply compassionate state.

In this 'loving your life' meditation I'm going to invite you to come into the deep awake state and review your life, so you can experience this profound appreciation for the journey you have been on, and return to your life story with new commitment and passion.

A BITTERSWEET FEAST

Whilst preparing to go through this meditation with you, I've been thinking about my own life journey. What a paradoxical adven-ture it has been... at times so beautiful... and yet so cruel. So exhilarating yet so suffocating. So intoxicating yet so sobering. So *everything!* I feel flooded with poignant memories.

I've held my newborn baby girl for the first time and been engulfed by an ocean of love. I've watched my father struggle to move his paralysed body and listened to his guttural groans of 'help, help, help'.

I've gazed across a dancing circle at a young woman dressed in wedding white and known I would love her forever. I've felt my heart crack open and been flooded with despair hearing the words 'I'm leaving'.

I've walked in grace and every accidental encounter has seemed charged with significance. I've stood alone in the night and felt the meaningless chill of the endless void.

I've laid side by side with my lover and known a peace beyond understanding. I've awoken in the dark, sweating with fear and utterly alone.

What about you? Is that how it's been for you?

I've sat in meditation with no financial security and few possessions, and had more than enough. I've become so stressed about making money I've made myself ill.

I've indulged myself with luxury in a 5-star spa, like a king who deserves only the best. I've stared from a hotel window in Delhi at a family living in a waste pipe and wept with shame.

I've strolled through verdant woods and felt one with nature's beauty. I've watched a dog tear a weasel to pieces and been horrified at nature's casual brutality.

I've been numb with the relentless repetition of mundane life… the eating and excreting… the wearing and the washing. I've been shocked to feel blissfully happy for no reason at all, whilst clearing the dishes and making the bed.

I've seen astonishing miracles that have filled me with faith and marvelled at the perfection of all that occurs. I've seen a horrible fate befall honourable people and railed against the blows of capricious chance.

You too I am guessing?

I've run naked in the rain through the city night in reckless ecstasy. I've crouched in the corner of a disused bandstand, tired and lost, drinking whisky with a friend.

I've desired a woman's beautiful body because it was the most exquisite thing I'd ever seen. I've been conscious of myself as a mortal meat-bag and become nauseated by my raw physicality.

I've known someone so well I could feel what they were thinking. Then I've discovered I didn't know them at all.

I've known who I am with confident certainty. Then found dark things within me that I cannot confess.

I've been elated by triumph and belligerent with hope. I have cuddled down with my broken dreams and wished for unbroken sleep.

Have you felt the same? Have you heard the soaring highs and rumbling lows of the symphony of life?

I've been with a friend, eaten away by cancer, who's smiled whilst he confided he was enjoying dying. I've seen a friend become a millionaire and lose the joy of living.

I've known passionate purpose turn to disappointed ennui. I've known the black dog of depression transform into rebirth and liberation.

I've laughed so hard it's become agonizing pleasure. I've cried so tenderly my tears have dissolved my despair.

I've been open-heartedly optimistic about human creativity

and our collective awakening to oneness and love. I've been hard-headedly pessimistic about human depravity and an impending collapse into chaos and division.

I have surfed the waves of hope and despair as they have risen and fallen.

But looking back on it all I can say this. It's been a marvellous trip.

REVIEWING YOUR LIFE

In this WOW experiment I want you to recall your own life journey. I'll guide you through what I do when I experiment with this meditation, so you can explore it with me now. But I suggest you then put the book down and go deeper into your memories.

I'm going to touch upon some of our soul wounds, so be tender with yourself. If there are places where you are deeply scarred, only go there when you feel strong enough. Make sure you are with friends who love you.

When I lead this meditation I play music in the background to open the heart. I often use a poignant piece for electric piano and blues horn called 'Le Singe Bleu' by Vangelis.

Preparation

I am sitting quietly and relaxing.

I am filled with wonder and immersing myself in the deep mystery.

I am sinking into the sensuality of breathing.

I am entering and presencing the moment.

I am resting in the deep awake state.

Life Review

Now I am imagining my life like a river of time that I've been navigating as it flows to the ocean.

I'm imagining that I'm soaring upwards, high above the flow of time, so that I can see the whole river of my life... from source to sea.

I feel free from being at any particular place on the journey. I am appreciating the sweep of my life as it has unfolded.

I'm reviewing my life as if I was about to leave it behind and this was my parting moment to take in all that has happened.

Childhood

I am bringing to mind my childhood.

I'm remembering how it felt to be an unformed presence in the world... fresh and innocent.

I'm remembering the joy of playing and learning.

I'm remembering the pain I experienced when the world around me didn't treat me with kindness.

Now I'm tenderly embracing my childhood, as if it were a delicate flower, with deep love and poignant appreciation.

Adolescence

I am bringing to mind my adolescence.

I'm remembering how it felt to be a young person struggling to become a distinct individual.

I'm remembering the pleasure of new discovery and the special bond I felt with my friends.

I'm remembering the suffering, alienation and fear I experienced as I came to understand the profound challenges that a human life entails.

Now I am tenderly embracing my adolescence, in all its splendid tumult, with deep love and poignant appreciation.

Adult Life

I am bringing to mind my adult life.

I'm remembering how it has felt to be a grown-up person in the world, striving to sustain myself and those in my care.

I'm remembering my affection for my loved ones.

I'm remembering my struggles to live well and become wiser.

I'm remembering times when I failed and let myself down.

I'm remembering the unexpected twists and turns of my adventure.

I'm remembering wonderful surprises and bitter disappointments.

I'm remembering the mundane drudgery of ordinary life and my tiredness with living.

I'm remembering feeling passionate and empowered.

Now I am tenderly embracing my adult life, in all its glorious ambiguity, with deep love and poignant appreciation.

Beautiful Moments

I am bringing to mind some of the most beautiful moments of my life.

Moments of deep connection with others.

Moments of revelation and elation.

Moments of triumph and achievement.

Moments of wonder and awakening.

And I'm embracing all these marvellous moments with deep love and poignant appreciation.

Painful Moments

I am bringing to mind some of the most difficult moments of my life.

Moments of heartbreak and loss.

Moments of division from others.

Moments of failure and despondency.

Moments when I've acted badly and hurt those around me.

I'm seeing how I've been shaped by these painful moments, which have demanded that I become deeper and stronger.

I'm gathering into my arms all my broken dreams and mourning their loss.

I'm forgiving my life for all it has demanded I endure.

I'm forgiving myself for those times when I couldn't be my best.

And I'm embracing all these painful moments with deep love and poignant appreciation.

Missed Moments

I am bringing to mind all the ordinary moments of my life that I barely noticed and can hardly remember.

Moments in which I missed the opportunity to feel truly alive.

Moments in which I took life for granted as if it was nothing at all.

Moments in which I forgot to show my loved ones how much they meant to me.

Moments in which I felt numb and hardly present.

And I'm embracing all these missed moments with deep love and poignant appreciation.

Those Who Have Shared the Journey

I am bringing to mind those people who have shared my journey through life with me.

People with whom I enjoyed magical moments.

People I loved so much I gave myself to them.

People I loved who are no longer alive, but will always be in my heart.

People who have taught me great lessons.

People who have caused me great hurt.

People who I hardly noticed and failed to truly recognize.

And I'm embracing all these people who have touched my life with deep love and poignant appreciation.

Loving it All

Now I am once again seeing my life as if it were one flowing river of time and taking in the expanse of my life.

I am accepting that there have been times when the river has flowed peacefully and times when it has crashed chaotically over the rocks.

I'm appreciating the wonderful, tragic, exquisite story that has been my life.

I'm feeling profoundly grateful for all I have experienced.

I am loving my life.

The Story Continues

Finally I am bringing my attention back into the present moment... here and now.

My story isn't over and there's still time for more adventures.

I'm thankful for the chance to experience more… to learn more… to give more.

I'm asking myself where I would like the story to go next.

How can I live more fully?

How can I be more loving?

How can I give of myself to others?

How can I create more moments I can look back on in amazement?

THE END AND THE BEGINNING

In this final chapter I want to look back over the journey we've made together, reflect upon the future of spirituality, and enjoy a last moment in the mystery with you, delighting in the wonder of life.

This is where our journey ends and, like all endings, it's also a new beginning. We've walked the way of wonder into the depths of the mystery experience. We've found the secret treasure that lies waiting there for those daring enough to seek it. We've discovered an unconditional love of being. And we've brought this precious love back with us into our everyday lives.

I've written this book to share the mystery experience with you, because it's been so important to me throughout my life. I've attempted to create a new approach to awakening that offers a simple way of engaging with the vast complexities of life, through 'loving being and being loving'.

I've attempted to articulate a story that can help us both understand life in a deeper way and make our lives richer. A way of thinking that has its foundations in profound not-knowing. A way of living that has the mystery experience at its heart. A spiritual philosophy based on an understanding of paradoxity, which avoids the dead ends I've been down on my own journey.

I've aspired to be authentic with you, because so much of modern spirituality seems inauthentic to me. I've aspired to be real about life as we actually experience it, so that we can live with our suffering and broken dreams, as well as appreciate the wonder of existence. I've aspired to help you become conscious of the primal oneness of being, and to leave you feeling personally empowered in your individual life.

As we come to the end of our journey together, my greatest hope is that you feel inspired to become a lover of life... to be the hero of your story... to passionately enter into the bittersweet drama. I want you to be confident that you can make a difference to the world, because you feel the awesome power of love within you.

THE FUTURE OF SPIRITUALITY

I've written this book for *you* and for *us*, because I feel that something exciting is happening right now on our collective evolutionary journey. We're being propelled to awaken to a new level of consciousness, which only a deep understanding of spirituality can help us achieve. Yet something stands in the way. And that is the state of spirituality today. It's simply not up to the job. It urgently needs to evolve and mature.

At the moment spirituality is largely consigned to the fringes of mainstream culture. The hard truth is that it's often seen by thinking people as irrelevant and irrational, which is unfortunately often the case. If we're going to make the next evolutionary leap, spirituality needs to shape up. The task today is to evolve a new approach to awakening for the 21st century, and this book is my contribution to that exciting project.

In our eclectic age this means synthesizing the essential insights of traditional wisdom into a newly alive form. In our rational age this means clearly discriminating the art of awakening from dogmatic religion and groundless superstition. In our scientific age this means ensuring that spirituality can be harmonized with the awesome discoveries of science, so that there's no longer a divisive split between our understanding of awakening and our understanding of objective reality.

Our Collective Awakening

I travel the world and meet a lot of amazing people, which has made me realize that a major transformation is happening in our collective consciousness. But it's not happening as quickly or as extensively as many people want to believe. We are awakening at an exponential rate, but there's still a long way to go before things really start to change.

When I examine the state of spirituality today I see that more people than ever are awakening. Many people are doing extraordinary work to bring a new consciousness into the world. I'm constantly coming across new initiatives that I find immensely inspiring. That's the good news. But here's the bad news.

Many people are still immersed in out-dated religion. Others have rejected the religions they grew up with, but uncritically embraced foreign religions imported from the East. Others have retreated from the soulless mainstream into childish forms of spirituality. Others have discovered the deep wisdom of non-duality, but found themselves marooned in a colourless, loveless, lifeless vacuum.

In this book I've questioned these forms of spirituality. And I've offered an alternative paralogical approach to awakening, which encourages us to wake up to oneness and love the experience of separateness… to be conscious of the deep self and embrace our flawed humanity… to transcend the mind and appreciate the mind… to know deep peace and feel intense passions… to play in the moment and evolve through time.

If this paralogical approach to spirituality resonates with you, I invite you to join me in the adventure of bringing it into the world. It doesn't belong to me, it belongs to everyone who embraces it. And working together is the only way to take forward our collective awakening. The future is calling and I can hear it… can you? If enough of us hear the call we can create a new world in which human beings are awake and loving. If we wake up to the magic of life, we can work miracles.

FURTHER TO GO

I hope you've enjoyed our journey together. I know that for me, writing this book has been an experience I'll never forget. There have been times of ecstatic inspiration in which the words have written themselves. But there have been times when I've had to labour to find ways to make the ideas come to life. I've felt I was creating the book I was born to write. But I've also felt inadequate to the challenge I'd undertaken. And through this paralogical process I've been transformed in ways I didn't expect, so that I'm not the same person who set out on the adventure.

It feels good to complete this book, but there's so much more I want to say about this wonderful life. There's so much left that needs to be done to truly create a form of spirituality adequate to the needs of our times.

I want to explore the scientific story of evolution from a new perspective.

I want to explore the spiritual story of survival of death... and show how it paralogically complements the story of evolution.

I want to explore the stages of life we go through from birth to death as a natural process of awakening.

I want to explore what it is to find life meaningful.

I want to explore the relationship between the inner world of the soul and the outer world of the body, so we can understand how our choices and intentions affect our lives.

I want to explore our cultural evolution and how we can bring the creative power of love to the dilemmas we face in the world today.

As I end this book I see that another journey lies before me. I've called this book *The Mystery Experience*, because it has been first and foremost about how to wake up to the WOW. Now I can feel its paralogical twin emerging into my mind. I'll call the next book *The Mystery Story*, because it will focus on the story with which we understand the mystery. But that will have to wait. I'm tired now and I need to rest.

A MOMENT TOGETHER

So here's where we say 'goodbye'. Our journey is over. Yet we're still where we started in the mystery of the moment. T S Eliot writes:

> We shall not cease from exploration
> And the end of all our exploring
> Will be to arrive where we started
> And know the place for the first time.

In my imagination we're together relaxing in the mystery, taking a last opportunity to delight in the wonder of life, before we go our separate ways. And I feel like Walt Whitman who enthuses:

> I lie abstracted and hear beautiful tales of things and the
> reasons of things,
> They are so beautiful I nudge myself to listen.
> I cannot say to any person what I hear – I cannot say it to
> myself – it is very wonderful.

Life is so amazing, I'm overcome with wonder. I'm humbled and speechless. What is life? I don't know… but I know I love it.

Let's decide together now to continually wonder, so we don't sleepwalk through life and miss the show. Let's inspire each other to awaken to the depths of our being, so we know that we're truly one. Let's encourage each other to become vulnerable heroes on the human adventure, so we can dare to be real and authentically connect. And, most important of all, let's always remember to love.

In our final hours, when we look back at all that has happened, it'll be the love that we've given and received that will really matter. I remember the breathless words of my father on the night he died, reaching out from his depths with such determination: 'Tell everyone how much I love them.' It's impossible to capture the sincerity of a dying man.

Our lives are so precious. Each one of us is a particular expression of the oneness of being. You and I are unique individuals, who've never existed before and will never exist again. We are living lives that have never been lived before and will never be lived again. So let's play our parts in the great drama with style and panache.

Amongst all the drudgery and broken dreams, what makes life worth all the fuss? The great lover of life, Uncle Walt, answers:

> That you are here – that life exists, and identity;
> That the powerful play goes on, and you will contribute
> a verse.

So let's sing that verse with passionate intensity. Let's hold our own note and create new harmonies with the symphony of life. Let's think our own thoughts and find our own way.

Life is such an amazing show, how could we not want to be a part of it? It's all so miraculous. Indeed, science has shown that if the fundamental nature of the universe were infinitesimally different, then life would've been impossible. I really don't know what's going on, but *something* significant is happening, of that I'm convinced!

Do you know what the chances are of the universe being set up in precisely the right way, so that you and I can be here contemplating this question? The eminent physicist Sir Roger Penrose has worked it out as 1 in 100, 000, 000, 000, 000, 000, 000, 000, 000, 000, 000, 000, 000, 000, 000, 000, 000, 000, 000, 000, 000, 000, 000, 000, 000, 000, 000, 000, 000, 000, 000, 000, 000, 000, 000, 000, 000, 000, 000, 000, 000, 000, 000, 000, 000, 000, 000, 000, 000, 000, 000, 000, 000, 000, 000, 000, 000, 000, 000, 000, 000, 000, 000, 000, 000, 000, 000, 000, 000, 000, 000, 000, 000, 000, 000, 000, 000, 000, 000, 000, 000!!!

Doesn't that make you feel lucky? Doesn't it fill you with awe and gratitude? Doesn't it make you appreciate the wonder of life? As the poet E E Cummings writes:

> i thank You God for most this amazing
> day: for the leaping greenly spirits of trees
> and a blue true dream of sky; and for everything
> which is natural which is infinite which is yes

The Buddha once said:

> If you could see the miracle of a single flower clearly, your whole life would change.

During one of his sermons he fell silent and held out a flower before him. His student Mahakasyapa began to laugh. He awoke in that moment and his life was never the same.

I hold up this moment before you to wonder.

If you see what a miracle this moment is your life will change.

It will be WOW!

Because the mystery experience is happening now.

THE MYSTERY EXPERIENCE RETREAT

If you want to continue our journey together beyond this book, and deepen your experience of awakening, I invite you to join me on a mystery experience retreat. There's a magic that happens when we're present in the same place, so come and dive into the deep love.

During my retreats we use the philosophy and practices we've been exploring to take us progressively deeper into the mystery experience, building towards what I call the 'deep love initiation'. I haven't shared what happens during this 'initiation' because we need to be together to experience its transformational power.

I like the word 'initiation' because it reminds me of the ancient 'mystery schools' that initiated aspirants into the mystical gnosis. I feel that I am continuing this tradition with my retreats, by offering a new way to experience the natural initiation of awakening to the WOW.

THE ALLIANCE FOR LUCID LIVING

If you'd like to connect with others who have been drawn to this way of awakening, I invite you to join the Alliance for Lucid Living. The ALL is a nascent community of free-thinking individuals who want to explore the mystery experience together. It is an organically evolving experiment in spiritual community that we're creating together.

Many members of the ALL regularly attend retreats to meet up with old friends and dive deeper into the WOW, because it keeps their personal journey alive and energized. Members also connect online to support each other on the journey of awakening… to share their insights and challenges… to inspire each other to live lucidly as lovers of life.

You can find out more about the mystery experience retreats and the ALL on my website www.timothyfreke.com.

TIM FREKE